Turning Points
in
Pastoral Care

Psychology and Christianity

Edited by David G. Benner

Turning Points in Pastoral Care

The Legacy of Anton Boisen and Seward Hiltner

Edited by LEROY ADEN and
J. HAROLD ELLENS

BAKER BOOK HOUSE
Grand Rapids, Michigan 49516

Printed in the United States of America

The editors acknowledge permission to reprint the chapter by Liston O. Mills, "Seward Hiltner's Contribution to Pastoral Care and Counseling," which first appeared in *Pastoral Psychology* 29, 1 (Fall 1980): 8–12.

Library of Congress Cataloging-in-Publication Data

Turning points in pastoral care: the legacy of Anton Boisen and
   Seward Hiltner / edited by LeRoy Aden and J. Harold Ellens.
      p.   cm.—(Psychology and Christianity)
   Includes bibliographical references.
   ISBN 0-8010-0222-2
   1. Pastoral psychology—History of doctrines. 2. Pastoral
counseling—History of doctrines. 3. Boisen, Anton T. (Anton
Theophilus), 1876–1965. 4. Hiltner, Seward, 1909– . I. Aden,
eRoy. II. Ellens, J. Harold, 1932– . III. Series.
4012.T82 1989
'.092'2—dc20   89-28922
                                                     CIP

Contents

Introduction to the Series

This volume is the fourth in the Psychology and Christianity Series, a collection of books published cooperatively by Baker Book House and the Christian Association for Psychological Studies (CAPS). Founded in 1952 in Grand Rapids, Michigan, by a group of psychologists, psychiatrists, and pastoral counselors, CAPS is an international society of Christian helping professionals committed to the exploration of the relationship between psychology and Christian faith.

Books in this series draw on previous CAPS publications and supplement them with original articles written for each volume. The purpose of the series is to present psychological and theological reflection on the most important issues encountered in human relationships, particularly relationships of counseling, education, parenting, and ministry.

Further information about the Christian Association for Psychological Studies may be obtained by contacting the head office:

Christian Association for Psychological Studies
P.O. Box 628
Blue Jay, CA 92317
(714) 337-5117

David G. Benner
Series Editor

Contributors

Herbert Anderson is a pastor of the Lutheran church and professor of pastoral care at the Catholic Theological Union, Chicago, Illinois.

Glenn H. Asquith, Jr., is associate professor of pastoral theology at Moravian Theological Seminary, Bethlehem, Pennsylvania.

Donald Capps is professor of pastoral theology at Princeton Theological Seminary, Princeton, New Jersey.

James E. Dittes is professor of pastoral theology and psychology at Yale University, New Haven, Connecticut.

Gene T. Fowler, Jr., is assistant professor of pastoral care at Memphis Theological Seminary, Memphis, Tennessee.

G. A. Elmer Griffin is a graduate student at the Graduate School of Psychology at Fuller Theological Seminary, Pasadena, California.

Rodney J. Hunter is professor of pastoral theology at Candler School of Theology, Emory University, Atlanta, Georgia.

K. Brynolf Lyon is assistant professor of pastoral care at the Christian Theological Seminary, Indianapolis, Indiana.

H. Newton Malony is professor of psychology at the Graduate School of Psychology at Fuller Theological Seminary, Pasadena, California.

Liston O. Mills is Oberlin Alumni Professor of Pastoral Theology and Counseling at Vanderbilt Divinity School, Nashville, Tennessee.

Kenneth R. Mitchell is director of consultation services at the Presbyterian Counseling Service, Seattle, Washington.

John Patton is professor of pastoral theology at Columbia Theological
Seminary, Decatur, Georgia.

Ralph L. Underwood is professor of pastoral care at Austin Presbyterian Theological Seminary, Austin, Texas.

The editors wish to express their appreciation to Nancy Regan for her
copyediting.

Introduction

LeRoy Aden

Anton T. Boisen (1876–1965) had five psychotic episodes in his lifetime, three of them severe enough to require hospitalization. The first disturbance was the most intense, and it started
Boisen on a journey—we might even say an obsession—that lasted the
rest of his life. It began unpretentiously. Boisen, then forty-four, was
unemployed, and because he had time on his hands he decided to
rework his personal statement of belief which had been required of
him by the Presbyterian church. This process of religious reflection
triggered a flood of ideas, ideas of grandeur and world destruction, of
life and love sacrificed for the strong.

Three weeks after hospitalization, Boisen emerged from the acute
phase of the psychosis as quickly as he had sunk into it. The agenda
for his life was set—to study acute mental disturbances of the functional type in order to increase both our understanding of them and
our ability to minister to those experiencing them.

Gradually, Boisen developed a core of ideas that became the hall-
mark of his work. He believed that certain forms of mental illness,
especially those marked by anxiety, were not bad in themselves but
instead were problem-solving attempts to unify the personality around
more enduring values. He found that disturbances are usually precipitated by immediate situations, but under the surface lingers a deeper,
more important problem, specifically a sense of failure for not living

11

up to introjected standards and, therefore, a sense of isolation from "the fellowship of the best."

Raised to its highest level, the fellowship of the best is represented in the idea of God. Thus some forms of mental illness can be a profound and productive experience, equivalent in some respects to a religious experience, an experience of radical upheaval and spiritual healing. What is interesting is that unlike Sigmund Freud and others, Boisen did not focus on psychotherapy but on mental illness itself as a means of healing. He did not dismiss other forms of healing (in fact, some of the following chapters show that he contributed substantially to them), but he explored the means—an extraordinary means—that he himself had experienced. In the process, he calls us back to the paradoxical truth that we are healed by being broken, that by being shaken to our bootstraps we are made whole.

Though preoccupied with a few basic themes, Boisen's thought has contributed to many different aspects of contemporary pastoral ministry. It has been a turning point in our understanding of mental illness and religious experience, in our understanding of our inner world and our communal existence, and in our understanding of theological education, ministry, and the church. Although our understanding has gone far beyond Boisen, this is not to imply that his contributions to the present scene are minimal or unidentifiable. For this reason alone we should turn back to Boisen, recognize our debt to him, and reconsider how his thought is relevant to our day, especially since he can serve as a corrective lens to our own myopia.

Seward Hiltner (1909–1984) represents another turning point in our pastoral history, even though in some sense he was a prophet without honor in his own country. He was a pivotal leader in pastoral care and pastoral theology, but the extent of his profound and pervasive influence in the field was never fully recognized. He belonged to the era of Carl R. Rogers and, in fact, reshaped Rogers's thought for the church's use in ways that have had enduring value. During those years it was said that Rogers "exerted an almost normative influence upon pastoral counseling in American Protestant circles," but it was never fully recognized that Hiltner was the man behind the man, the one who actually gave birth to our contemporary form of pastoral counseling. Hiltner was a prolific writer, a brilliant teacher, and a perceptive and creative innovator who shaped pastoral care and counseling for at least thirty-five years.

Hiltner was restless with his own formulations. Like Freud, he constantly pressed forward, retaining those elements of his system that were basic but changing and exploring new elements as he went along. In this sense, present-day pastoral care and counseling is a true child of the master, even though new names and different approaches have transformed the field since the days of Hiltner's demanding leadership.

It may be too early to assess Hiltner's impact on pastoral ministry, and yet there is a need to evaluate where we have been and where we are going. We need to assess the thought and influence of both Hiltner and Boisen. The authors in this book are eminently qualified to do that. In one way or another, each of them has been influenced by the Boisen/Hiltner legacy. Several of them knew Boisen personally and even worked with him. Many of them took graduate study with Hiltner at either Chicago or Princeton, and a few of them became colleagues with him in teaching. In every case the author knows Boisen's and Hiltner's thought well, and collectively they give us a treasury of refined ore.

Looking back, all of us might agree that the era of Boisen and Hiltner was a great and exciting time in the field of pastoral care and pastoral theology. On occasion we have been tempted to freeze, even to glorify, these times. We hope that in this volume we have resisted this temptation as we go back now and assess our legacy from the pioneers.

Each author was asked to reflect on a specific dimension of Boisen's or Hiltner's multifaceted work, bringing the author's own particular perspective to the discussion. The result, we think, is itself a turning point. The reader is presented not only with an insightful summary of Boisen's or Hiltner's thought on a particular topic but also with an incisive critique of their relevance and importance for our day.

Glenn H. Asquith, Jr., opens the discussion by focusing on Boisen as pastoral theologian. Boisen defines pastoral theology in a way that is congruent with his emphasis on mental illness and religious experience. He is not concerned with traditional formulations of such theological concepts as God, sin, and salvation. Instead he focuses on the individual's experience of these realities and on their value and validity in his or her life. For Boisen, this is pastoral theology. Specifically, it refers to the empirical study of particular persons, especially of their mental illness or religious experience, in order to determine the origin and meaning of their beliefs, and the function that those beliefs have in their lives. Boisen also considers what the beliefs imply for a "general system of values," but the heart of his pastoral theology—and its continuing contribution to our scene—is that it represents an idiographic study of the concrete richness of religion in crisis and custom.

In chapter 2 Donald Capps, though never a student of Hiltner's, expresses great appreciation for his dynamic approach to theology, especially for his emphasis on theological themes. Capps offers an

incisive look at three of the eight themes and then steps back to offer
a helpful critique. He contends that Hiltner failed to give dynamic
psychology a secure place in his overall approach to theology. In a
final section, Capps spells out what this might mean by reviewing the
work of other individuals who have incorporated psychological
themes into their dynamic approaches to theology.

Rodney J. Hunter focuses on what has been called Hiltner's most
creative and important contribution—his perspectival approach to
pastoral theology. Hunter divides his discussion into two parts: the
first part is a fine exposition of Hiltner's theory, including a detailed
consideration of the shepherding perspective; the second part is a critical review of two major aspects of Hiltner's theory, namely, his empirical method and his pragmatism. Hunter's discussion is clear and
insightful all the way, laying down guidelines for further work in the
area of pastoral theology.

In a thoughtful and carefully reasoned chapter, K. Brynolf Lyon
examines not only Boisen's ethical thought and his understanding of
the dynamics of the moral life but also how he related the two. Lyon
appreciates Boisen's sensitivity to the relation between psychology and
ethics, even though he is explicit about some of the dangers and shortcomings of Boisen's way of conceptualizing the relation. Instead of
summarizing his argument here it is better to highlight two points
that follow from his discussion. First, though Boisen posits a concept
of Christian perfectionism, he does not fall into moralism. For Boisen,
"being perfect" does not mean being holy or righteous but rather
"being whole." More specifically, it means being in harmony with one's
social world, and ultimately, with one's idea of God. Second, Boisen's
understanding of the healing process tends to reverse psychotherapy's
implication that one must be healthy (that is, free of destructive defenses and resistances) before one can believe and give oneself to ultimate loyalties. Boisen's ethical and theological stance maintains that
one must believe and give oneself to ultimate loyalties before one is
truly healthy.

In chapter 5, Lyon turns his perceptive eye to Hiltner's position on
ethics and pastoral care in order to clarify where he stood on the issue.
He finds that while Hiltner may have contributed to the present situation inadvertently, Hiltner himself was interested in an ethics that
was sensitive to, and honest about, the ambiguities of human existence
("the sincerity of ethics") instead of an ethic that was merely attentive
to one's feelings ("the ethic of sincerity"). Lyon's thesis is intriguing;
his elaboration of it is informed and first-rate.

Boisen found in William James a kindred spirit but went beyond
him to revitalize the study of the psychology of religion. With words

similar to these, G. A. Elmer Griffin and H. Newton Malony consider Boisen's contribution to a stagnant psychology of religion. Boisen brought a new orientation to it, as well as his own impelling conviction that a study of certain types of mental illness is a study of religious experience. From George Albert Coe he came to appreciate the social nature of religion, from Macfie Campbell he learned about the role of values in personality integration, and from William McDougall he came to see that the mind is dynamic and purposive. Boisen combined these various elements into a "new force" in the psychology of religion. In terms of method, he developed "full-fledged case studies with a longitudinal perspective," and in terms of content he showed that mental disturbances of a functional kind may be religious struggles in which the individual is dealing with ultimate issues and loyalties. In any case, he took a step beyond James, studying abnormal people in order to illuminate the truly healthy minded.

Chapter 7, written by Herbert Anderson, deals with Hiltner's sensitivity to human ambiguity, especially as it is manifested in Hiltner's theory of personality or, as Anderson puts it, in his constructive anthropology. Anderson maintains that Hiltner's psychological understanding of persons was influenced by three major schools of thought: psychoanalysis, Kurt Lewin's field theory, and Rogers's self theory. He goes on to show that Hiltner transformed these influences to construct a theological understanding of persons that was paradoxical in order to take into account the double-sidedness of human life. Anderson, as usual, is suggestive and on target.

What can a person who devotes his whole life to people who are mentally ill contribute to our understanding of ministry with "normal" people? Ralph L. Underwood does not pose the question in this way, but he certainly is helpful in answering it. He lifts out four factors that gave shape to Boisen's understanding of ministry, and in each case he uses the discussion to illuminate aspects of his central thesis, namely, that for Boisen the central task of ministry is to provide understanding guidance in the midst of crises in order to effect reconciliation with the fellowship of the best. If this task is a reflection of Boisen's own needs (and we know that it is), we know the depth to which he felt rejected by and shut out from significant others and from God. Boisen was a sensitive soul, and as Underwood's rich and informed discussion shows, he continues to contribute to our understanding of Christian ministry today because of it.

John Patton turns our attention to Boisen's contribution to pastoral care and counseling. Boisen, as Patton implies, was much more interested in the study of persons in intense crisis than he was in the theory and practice of pastoral counseling. In fact, he objected strongly to

the tendency of clinical pastoral education to focus on techniques and
skills rather than on "the forces involved in the spiritual life and the
laws by which they operate." Given this fact, Patton's article is all the
more remarkable, because he is able to show that Boisen made a direct
or indirect contribution to pastoral care and counseling in four decisive areas: in the pastor's role with the mentally ill, in the relationship
between illness and health, in our understanding of suffering and crisis, and in the content and method of pastoral theology. Patton's fine
discussion of these areas establishes Boisen as a carer of souls, not
necessarily as we might imagine but in the way that his own experience taught him. With cane hooked over one leg, he would sit with a
disturbed but mute patient for thirty to forty minutes without saying
a word. The silence was comfortable; his presence was healing. He
had been where the patient is, and he could communicate interest and
concern without using words.

In chapter 10, Kenneth R. Mitchell deals with the aspect of Hiltner's
thought that is probably most well-known to and appreciated by pastors—Hiltner's theory of pastoral counseling. Mitchell notes the parallels between Hiltner's eductive approach and Rogers's client-
centered approach, but he also maintains that Hiltner's theological
perspective colored his theory of counseling with a distinctively pastoral hue. Mitchell's fine chapter is enriched by references to his personal interactions with Hiltner.

Gene T. Fowler, Jr., considers the wider context of Hiltner's
thought, the way in which he saw pastoral care in the context of the
church and its ministry. He finds in Hiltner's concept of precounseling
a particular form of pastoral care in which the church's relation to
caregiving is especially illuminated. His discussion proceeds along
four dimensions—the four ways in which Hiltner described the
church: as a body, as a doctrine, as a community, and as a context.
Fowler makes a real contribution to the overall object of the book by
dealing skillfully with what is often unexplored territory in Hiltner's
thought.

Fowler brings the same skill to his examination of Boisen's system
in the next chapter. He focuses on Boisen's understanding of the
church and its interaction with society. In the process, he gives us a
new understanding of the nature and concern of pastoral care. He
highlights Boisen's idea that the church, starting as a sect, is often a
spontaneous response to a social crisis and that, in turn, it is to serve
as an agent of societal change. Fowler lays out the details of Boisen's
position in a helpful way and ends his provocative discussion by drawing out the implications of Boisen's thought for pastoral care. Pastoral
care is given a healing function, not just in terms of individuals but

in terms of society itself. It is to care in the prophetic sense of critiquing and correcting values and standards of conduct that make community less than the best.

Boisen was a serious student of psychodynamics, a penetrating explorer of our inner world. It is appropriate, therefore, to end our study of Boisen's thought by reflecting on and critiquing his own study of himself. James E. Dittes uses the image of Boisen's monocular vision to characterize his autobiographical *Out of the Depths*. While Boisen himself found the writing of his "case record" difficult, like "a day of judgment," Dittes finds little depth in it, at least in any Freudian sense. He compares it to Carl Gustav Jung's autobiographical *Memories, Dreams, Reflections* and shows that Boisen, unlike Jung, strove to control unconscious impulses, leaving them uninterpreted and unintegrated. Dittes has a point: Boisen's study does not dig deeply into the unconscious. But what if Boisen knows something that we do not, namely, that Freud's or even Jung's unconscious does not exhaust the hidden recesses of the mind? What if Boisen's experience—that earthshaking ideas came surging into his head and overpowered him—points to a divine/human encounter that comes from beyond anything we can will and that when it comes, it does something to us rather than we doing something to it.

With Boisen, we have always known that healing of the human spirit entails upheaval of old patterns. It is, after all, the old patterns that are part of our brokenness and bondage. But Boisen jars our expectations. When he talks about upheaval, he is talking about profound disturbance, a world turned upside down, ideas of global destruction and rebirth, a sense of failure and isolation that renders one mute. We do not want to hear about that kind of upheaval, and yet Boisen reminds us that sometimes the upheaval must be that radical for healing to occur.

Hiltner did not have the same passion for profound disturbance that Boisen had, but he shared with Boisen a passion for the theological and psychological value of the living human document. In chapter 14, Liston O. Mills helps us to appreciate the nature and scope of that passion. He reminds us that Hiltner's basic identity was as a minister of the church and that, as a minister of the church, his basic concern was with troubled people. It was out of this orientation that he reshaped every aspect of pastoral ministry, from the content and instrumentation of human healing to the church's critical reflection on acts of care. At every step he was demanding and unrelenting, but that is why he joins Boisen in being a crucial turning point in contemporary pastoral care and counseling. He was demanding at precisely the right points, maintaining, as Mills puts it, that pastoral care and counseling be both "practical and theoretical, scientific and existential, psychological and theological, religious and secular, for clergy and for laypersons." We live in the light of that legacy. We cannot afford to ignore it or fail to examine it critically, because it has become a part of who we are as pastoral carers.

1

An Experiential Theology

GLENN H. ASQUITH, JR.,

$\mathbf{A}$nton T. Boisen has been identified as the father of clinical pastoral education. It can also be argued that he is the father of modern pastoral theology. His assertion that theological students should read "living human documents" in addition to the classical texts of theology gave rise to important definitions of the field by other people such as Seward Hiltner.[1] Rodney J. Hunter has noted that "Hiltner's concept of an operation-centered discipline was . . . his attempt to conceptualize Boisen's thesis in formal disciplinary terms."[2] In this way, Hiltner took Boisen's clinical approach and refined it to make it the "gateway to a pastoral theology."[3]

Boisen and his method also had a profound effect upon the work of Wayne E. Oates. In addition to his many literary contributions to the field of pastoral theology, Oates was given the difficult task of incorporating clinical training into the curriculum of the School of Theology of Southern Baptist Theological Seminary, including gradu-

1. See Seward Hiltner, *Preface to Pastoral Theology* (Nashville: Abingdon, 1958); Seward Hiltner, *Theological Dynamics* (Nashville: Abingdon, 1972).
2. Rodney J. Hunter, "A Perspectival View of Theology: A Critique of Hiltner's Theory," *Journal of Psychology and Christianity* 4, no. 4 (Winter 1985): 20.
3. Liston O. Mills, "Seward Hiltner's Contribution to Pastoral Care and Counseling," *Pastoral Psychology* 29 (1980): 9.

ate degree programs in the psychology of religion.[4] This achievement added to the academic respectability of pastoral theology as a discipline.

Boisen's basic method is also seen in writings such as Edward E. Thornton's *Theology and Pastoral Counseling*. Thornton uses human experience, for example, the case of "Mr. Mills," to approach the subjects of repentance, salvation, and faith. In close similarity to Boisen's theory, Thornton notes that pastoral counseling is not just an *application* of theology but that it also contributes to the *apprehension* of theology.[5]

Boisen's fundamental influence on these and other pioneers in the discipline of pastoral theology is evidence of his own seminal work as a pastoral theologian. In order to examine this aspect of Boisen's thought, we will view Boisen's theological history, his definition of theology, his clinical method of theological inquiry, and his continuing relevance to the field.

Theological History

At the beginning of the twentieth century, science and technology began to have a significant impact upon American society. For religion, the threat of science was symbolized by Charles Darwin's theory of evolution, while at the same time traditional rural values were giving way to the values of big business and urban life. The sharp contrast between these two sets of values was emphasized in American religious life by the fundamentalist-modernist controversy. As Allan H. Sager says, this controversy was due in part to the fact that, in this period, "a method of inquiry and of judgement arose that discredited reliance upon authority and tradition."[6]

Boisen was a product of this modernist tradition. Ironically, his first clinical training program at Worcester State Hospital in Massachusetts began in 1925 while the Scopes trial was being held in Dayton, Tennessee. In an article published that year, he took a position critical of both sides of the issue and called for a moderating view.[7] On the one hand, he felt that the fundamentalist churches were giving treatment

4. See Edward E. Thornton, *Professional Education for Ministry: A History of Clinical Pastoral Education* (Nashville: Abingdon, 1970), 155.

5. Edward E. Thornton, *Theology and Pastoral Counseling* (Philadelphia: Fortress, 1964), 15.

6. Allan H. Sager, "The Fundamentalist-Modernist Controversy, 1918–1930," in *Preaching in American History*, ed. D. Holland (Nashville: Abingdon, 1969), 263.

7. Anton T. Boisen, "In Defense of Mr. Bryan: A Personal Confession by a Liberal Clergyman," *American Review* 3 (1925): 323–28.

without diagnosis, but at least it was treatment. On the other hand, he felt that the liberal churches were giving neither treatment nor diagnosis with their apologetic message but were turning the sick of soul over to the doctor. He concluded that "what was needed was to bring the two groups together by building up a new authority on the basis of careful studies of persons in difficulty." Boisen sought to "bring the two groups together,"[8] but his attempt was based solely on the methods embodied in the modern tradition.

Clinical pastoral education was also formed within the historical context of social reform. The Social Gospel movement, led by Walter Rauschenbusch, called attention to humanity's responsibility to move institutions, as well as individuals, toward the kingdom of God. This outlook joined with the Progressive movement to fight the economic injustices of the time. Continuing in this tradition, the clinical training movement sought to reform both religion and theology to make them more relevant to the needs of modern society.[9] While the concerns of clinical training were generally more individual than societal, Boisen never lost sight of the social focus. He was "convinced that personality is social and that mental illness can only be understood as we take the social factors into account."[10]

The specific theological tradition forming the context of Boisen's views needs to be examined more carefully. Some of Boisen's theological thinking found its genesis under the guidance of William Adams Brown, his professor of systematic theology at Union Theological Seminary in New York. Influenced by Ritschl and William James's pragmatism, Brown has been classed as one of the early "evangelical liberals." He saw himself as the mediator between traditional theology and those who wanted to relate it to contemporary thought. His important work, *Christian Theology in Outline*,[11] was largely a revision of William Newton Clarke's *Outline of Christian Theology*. Both works were the most widely used textbooks of liberal theology at the time that Boisen studied at Union.[12] In a later publication, Brown discusses

---

8. Anton T. Boisen, *Out of the Depths: An Autobiographical Study of Mental Disorder and Religious Experience* (New York: Harper and Row, 1960), 151. See also Anton T. Boisen, letter to Chester A. Raber, March 25, 1960 (Boisen Files, Chicago Theological Seminary).

9. Hugh B. Hammett, "The Historical Context of the Origin of C.P.E.," *The Journal of Pastoral Care* 29, no. 2 (1975): 84–85.

10. Boisen, letter to Chester A. Raber, March 25, 1960.

11. William Adams Brown, *Christian Theology in Outline* (New York: Charles Scribner's Sons, 1906).

12. Kenneth Cauthen, *The Impact of American Religious Liberalism* (New York: Harper, 1962), 41–43.

the contribution of modern theology to preaching. He invites the reader to look with him "at the old view from a new view-point. What is the place of our Christian religion in the new world? What has science taught us about God and man, Christ and the Bible, sin and salvation?"[13] These statements are a precursor to Boisen's desire to apply scientific method to theology as the "queen of the sciences."

In light of the fact that the roots of Boisen's thought are found in the principles of liberalism, Edward E. Thornton has placed Kenneth Cauthen's classification of "evangelical liberal" upon Boisen, putting him in the company of Brown, Harry Emerson Fosdick, Rauschenbusch, and others.[14] However, certain basic disagreements between Boisen's thought and the thought of these other men call this classification into question. A significant disagreement with Brown is found in an unpublished statement by Boisen concerning the sovereignty of God:

> According to William Adams Brown the subject matter of theology is not religious experience itself but the God whom that experience reveals. While I can by no means agree with this proposition, I do hold that the idea of God symbolizes something which is operative in the lives of all men whether they call themselves religious or not.[15]

This statement was in the first draft of the manuscript for chapter 12 of Boisen's *Religion in Crisis and Custom*. It is not known whether Boisen or his editors were responsible for its removal, but nevertheless a disagreement on something as basic as the subject matter of theology makes it difficult to add "evangelical" to Boisen's brand of liberalism.

Boisen once classified himself as a disciple of Fosdick, but Fosdick did not share the same perception. The original title of Boisen's article on the Scopes trial was "In Defense of Mr. Bryan by a Disciple of Dr. Fosdick." Boisen wished to exempt Fosdick from his criticism of liberalism, because he felt that Fosdick did have a message for the sick of soul. However, when Boisen sent the original manuscript of this article to Fosdick, Fosdick retorted that Boisen could publish it under this title only over his dead body! Apparently, the only point of agreement which Fosdick found was that much of his message was based on his own experience in a mental hospital during his adolescence.[16]

Another part of Boisen's theological history can be seen in the milieu

---

13. William Adams Brown, *Modern Theology and the Preaching of the Gospel* (New York: Charles Scribner's Sons, 1914), 10.

14. Thornton, *Professional Education for Ministry*, 65–66.

15. Boisen, n.d.a.

16. Boisen, *Out of the Depths*, 152.

of Chicago Theological Seminary (CTS), where he began teaching part-time in 1926 and then full-time from 1938 to 1942. Founded in 1855 as a result of an ecclesiastical rebellion led by Philo Carpenter, CTS was organized by a group of ethically concerned Christian leaders from New England who cherished the tradition of a learned ministry. However, they were convinced that the classical forms of education that were employed in the east were inadequate for the frontier, and they sought teachers who would communicate the Christian heritage to a new type of person facing new kinds of demands.

The first curriculum at CTS provided that, during several months each year, students would be scattered throughout the midwest to learn about community life and church needs in the experimental culture. Pioneer thinking about theological education continued until 1923, when CTS was established at its present site on the University of Chicago campus. At that time, innovative thinking was seen in the subject matter being taught. Graham Taylor established the first distinct department of Christian sociology in the American theological school. Arthur Holt pioneered in the church's role in the rural-urban conflict. Fred Eastman introduced the study of the arts and literature and promoted the use of drama in the church. Finally, Anton Boisen was recognized alongside these other pioneers as the founder of clinical training. Thus he took his place in a seminary noted for its innovative approach to theological education as well as its desire to apply traditional theology to contemporary problems.

Alongside the innovative CTS, the Divinity School of the University of Chicago built and promoted an alternative to orthodox theology. The "Chicago School" became noted for its tradition in empirical theology.[17] In fact, it was there that the empirical method in theology found its strong adherents between 1900 and 1940.[18] Several faculty members had a significant influence on Boisen: Douglas Clyde Macintosh, John Dewey, Edwin E. Aubrey, Henry Nelson Weiman, and Ernest Hocking.

The usual definitions given for empirical theology seem close to what Boisen was trying to achieve, but we can still raise the question, "Was Boisen an empirical theologian?" *Empiricism* itself is commonly defined as that method of inquiry that presumes to find knowledge and its verification by appealing to experience. Friedrich Schleiermacher is usually referred to as the father of empirical the-

17. Bernard E. Meland, "Introduction: The Empirical Tradition in Theology at Chicago," in *The Future of Empirical Theology*, ed. Bernard E. Meland (Chicago: University of Chicago Press, 1969), 1–62.
18. Randolph Crump Miller, *The American Spirit in Theology* (Philadelphia: Pilgrim, 1974), 19.

ology because his appeal was ultimately to religious experience. He maintained that in the religious consciousness there is a relation between the reality which is called God and one's own sense of absolute dependence. As Miller points out, Schleiermacher's method and the methods of many in the Chicago School who followed him did not follow the empirical method in a purist sense. That is also true of Boisen. With Brown and Fosdick, he had some basic disagreements with those of the Chicago School whose works he cited in his writings. Nevertheless, his theological history is firmly rooted in Brown's liberalism, in the milieu of the Chicago Theological Seminary, and in the thinking of the Chicago School.

Definition of Theology

It has already been seen that Boisen differed from the traditional view of theology as the study of God and related doctrines. In fact, the goal of theology for Boisen was not to *construct* any kind of system of belief, whether liberal or fundamentalist. Rather he believed that the task and method of theology is to organize and test the validity of religious views in light of human experience. Thus, while Boisen's method may be in the context of empirical theology, his subject is different. Instead of appealing to human experience as a way to God, he uses experience as a way of testing the validity and meaning of beliefs about God, sin, and salvation. In *The Exploration of the Inner World*, Boisen gives this definition of theology:

> THEOLOGY. The attempt, either individually or collectively, to organize and scrutinize the beliefs regarding the end and meaning of life, the spiritual forces which operate within us and the relationships which exist between their various manifestations, all in the light of the belief in a supreme reality to which men generally give the name of "God."
> . . . As currently used in our schools the term "theology" is limited to the consideration of the fundamental tenets of the Christian religion as represented in the authoritative sources. In this inquiry we have been concerned with the religious beliefs of a number of individuals, most of whom have been reared in the Christian faith. We have sought to determine the origin and meaning of these beliefs, their function in the individual's life, and their implications for a general system of values.[19]

From this definition it can be seen that for Boisen theology is the *study* of religious belief—the "spiritual forces"—rather than a *state-*

---

19. Anton T. Boisen, *The Exploration of the Inner World: A Study of Mental Disorder and Religious Experience* (Philadelphia: University of Pennsylvania Press, 1971), 306.

ment of belief itself. In this sense, although theology is the queen of the sciences, it is still a social science that is concerned with religious experience as a biological fact. It is at this point that Boisen's differences with the empirical theologians can be seen. For example, Boisen is critical of Macintosh for being concerned primarily with the problem of religious knowledge without drawing upon empirical studies of actual human experience, even in his discussion of conversion. Boisen is also critical of Aubrey's discussion of mysticism for being merely a reflection on the subject without any attempt to examine the experiences of particular mystics. Likewise, he is critical of the dialectic method which, while "precise and discriminating," still does not begin with specific human experiences.[20]

Clinical Method

Having an understanding of Boisen's view of the nature and task of theology, we can now examine the clinical method which Boisen, as pastoral theologian, used to study human experience. To gather data on a patient's experience, Boisen employed lengthy case analysis forms designed to research all aspects of the patient's life. It appears that the basis for one of these forms was an unpublished "Syllabus for the Examination of Psychiatric Patients" by Adolf Meyer. Another form was designed in cooperation with Helen Flanders Dunbar, who worked with Boisen at Worcester State Hospital and had a particular interest in studying the symbolism used by acutely disturbed patients.[21]

In gathering data on a patient's experience, Boisen and his students asked several detailed questions about social and religious background, developmental history (including social, sexual, and vocational adjustment), physical health, history of present illness, characteristics of the disorder, and diagnostic impressions. There were also lengthy sets of questions regarding religious attitudes and concerns, philosophy of life, and questions related to Dunbar's interest in the patient's symbolic understanding of various aspects of the universe.[22]

20. Anton T. Boisen, "Cooperative Inquiry in Religion," *Religious Education* 40 (1945): 292–93.

21. See Boisen, *Exploration of the Inner World*, 17; *Out of the Depths*, 160. Cf. Allison Stokes, *Ministry after Freud* (New York: Pilgrim, 1985), 71–72, who notes that Dunbar's doctoral dissertation was on the thought of Dante, who believed that in symbolism science and religion are not antagonistic but complementary.

22. See Glenn H. Asquith, Jr., "The Case Study Method of Anton T. Boisen," *The Journal of Pastoral Care* 34 (1980): 84–94, for a complete review of the content of Boisen's case study questions.

A Case Example

Once Boisen had gathered the necessary data on a given case, he presented it in a form conducive to discussion and interpretation. In order to illustrate Boisen's clinical method as a pastoral theologian, one of the cases which he edited for teaching purposes will be used as an example. We will focus on the case of Oscar O.—"A Devoted Husband"—because of the frequency with which it appears in Boisen's work. It was one of the 173 cases studied at Worcester State Hospital which formed the basis for *The Exploration of the Inner World*. He published this case in two separate articles[23] and used it as a basis for discussion in a lecture on "The Significance of the Idea of God in Periods of Personal Crisis." In the form discussed here, it was used in his "Types of Mental Illness" manual, an unpublished collection of cases and interpretations which he distributed to various centers of the Council for Clinical Training following his retirement.[24]

Boisen probably favored this case because of its similarity with his own situation. He classifies it as a "Reaction of Panic and Upheaval," which is the same classification he gave to his own experience. He contrasts this reaction to other types of mental illness, believing that it is not negative in itself but that such reactions are "attempts at cure and reorganization which are closely related to certain recognized types of religious experience."[25] In his lecture, he presented this case alongside those of George Fox and Paul of Tarsus, which is to say that the case of Oscar O. describes the type of religious experience that Boisen believed should be the object of his clinical method of theological inquiry. It is a case that is of interest to the pastoral theologian.

Boisen followed the general format of his clinical analysis form in gathering information for this case. However, he devotes much of the presentation to Oscar's religious ideation, which was the central problem in the case. Oscar had been committed to the hospital because of a suicide attempt, which he saw as a "self-sacrifice in order to relieve the world of its sins." Following this introductory comment, Boisen gives the standard information regarding family and developmental history. Oscar's sexual development seemed normal, but under "social adjustments" Boisen noted that Oscar "demand[ed] proof" when it

23. See Anton T. Boisen, "Schizophrenia and Religious Experience," in *Collected and Contributed Papers*, vol. 1 (Elgin, Ill.: Elgin State Hospital, 1932); Anton T. Boisen, "Theology in the Light of Psychiatric Experience," *Crozer Quarterly* 18, no. 1 (1941): 47–61.

24. Anton T. Boisen, "Types of Mental Illness: A Beginning Course for Use in the Training Centers of the Council for the Clinical Training of the Theological Students," vols. 1 and 2. Unpublished mimeographed booklets, 1946.

25. Boisen, *Exploration of the Inner World*, 29–30.

comes to religion and that he hated being forced to go to church by his grandmother. In his adult life he was not much of a churchgoer.

Oscar's wife ascribed the illness to an extended period of unemployment combined with his increasing feelings of uselessness. Oscar himself attributes it to a night thirteen years prior to the illness when he felt challenged by a speaker at a socialist meeting who asked if there were many men who would be willing to give up their lives for others as Jesus did. That night he made a bet with God that he would be willing to give up his life for his family. Later, he reported being awakened from sleep with an overpowering sense of messianic identification. About a week later he reported having the "feeling that there were two sides and that I had to go to one side or the other in order to get salvation." He then became violent and was hospitalized. He recovered quickly and returned home in three weeks, putting his Bible in the attic because the hospital staff had said that it was the source of his trouble.

In a second attack, Oscar felt that he had not paid off his bet with God. He got his Bible and began to pray, feeling very lonesome. Then he attempted suicide in a symbolic way, turning on the gas in honor of his wife and slashing a wrist for each of his two daughters. He was hospitalized shortly afterward. The rest of the case account describes Oscar's religious ideation at the time of the interview. In response to one of Dunbar's questions about the symbolism of the sun, he said it made him think of God.

Theological Implications

In Boisen's manual on "Types of Mental Illness," he has a set of questions for consideration in studying each case. In Oscar's case, he asks the following questions:

What do you consider the major factor in Oscar O's disturbance? Why should the socialist speaker's question start him thinking so hard? Why should this steady, fairly intelligent, rather free-speaking mechanic suddenly become so much concerned about religion? Where did he get his idea of God and what did it mean to him? Why the profound disturbance? What was the significance of his putting the Bible in the attic after he recovered from the first disturbed period? Or getting it again at the beginning of the second disturbed period? What was the significance of his attempt at suicide? How are we to explain his identification of himself with Christ? What was the outlook for his "not having any more of them fits"?[26]

26. Boisen, "Types of Mental Illness," vol. 1.

These questions are, for Boisen, theological questions. They attempt to help the student determine the origin and meaning of Oscar's beliefs as well as their function in his life and their implications for a general system of values. They are questions about the "living human document," designed to point to "The Significance of the Idea of God in Periods of Personal Crisis."

In his case presentation, Boisen usually wrote a lengthy narrative pointing out what he felt were the theologically significant factors in the case. Often, he gave his own answers to the questions in order to ensure that the student understood the issues from his point of view. In Boisen's narrative on Oscar O., he classifies it with his own case. He notes that it was "an acute disturbance of the more constructive type" which "may be regarded as a problem solving experience." It was therefore worthy of the theological student's attention because of its potentially religious significance.

In discussing the socialist speaker's question, Boisen notes that one must be careful not to place too much emphasis on the precipitating factor of a disturbance. Acute disorders have to do with the *accumulation* of inner stresses through a person's developmental history. Hence Boisen stressed careful gathering of personal history data in his case study method. The religious significance of the reactions of panic and upheaval lie in the way in which they attempt to reorganize and solve the gathered problems of one's life.

It is at this point that Boisen makes a careful analysis of the nature of this reorganization process for Oscar O. The dynamics appear to be very similar to those in Boisen's frustrated relationship with Alice Batchelder. Oscar was a devoted husband; his wife had become supreme in his system of loyalties and his entire life was built around her. His love for her was "the equivalent of a religion," but this was not sufficient for Oscar. He had to find an object of ultimate loyalty beyond this finite love object and this "pressed heavily upon him." Boisen "hazards the guess" that the source of strain in Oscar's case was not so much a sense of guilt as "the need of achieving a higher level of adjustment, the level represented by the psychoanalytic doctrine of autonomy and the Christian doctrine of the sovereignty of God." Boisen maintains that modern psychiatric experience supports the idea that "true autonomy is achieved through finding one's role as a child of God and taking one's place in the larger universe." Oscar, a rugged, self-reliant male in search of autonomy and meaning in the face of extended unemployment, experienced panic and upheaval in transferring his supreme loyalty from the finite to the infinite. Such dependence upon God, Boisen said, is "entirely consonant with self-reliance in that it makes the individual independent of the trials and

vicissitudes of his temporal existence by providing a sense of fellowship which is deepened and strengthened through suffering and
danger."[27]

This is the mystical dimension of Boisen's understanding of mental
illness as a problem-solving experience. The crisis of panic and
upheaval brings one in touch with the "fellowship of the best"—the
fellowship represented by the idea of God. Citing Mead's concept of
the social basis of the personality, Boisen goes on to say that the
confrontation with the mystical reality of this fellowship does indeed
bring disturbance. In addition to the individual's system of loyalties,
the disturbance is related to the concept of the self. Boisen affirms
that "the enlarged concept of the self is one of the eternally valid
insights of religion." He feels that Oscar's distorted identification with
Christ is disturbing in the same way as Paul's concept of the indwell-
ing Christ and Jesus' teaching regarding the fatherhood of God. When
an individual comes into this mystical communion, while at the same
time recognizing his or her individual insignificance in relation to the
universe, "such an idea born in upon him (or her) with any sense of
reality could hardly fail to be upsetting." This understanding of the
acute disturbance that comes when one confronts the reality of God
is in line with traditional concepts of mysticism and religious
conversion.[28]

Boisen concludes his analysis with summary comments about the
role of religion in mental illness. He sees the Bible not as the cause of
the problem, but as the symbol of the problem which could not be
shelved but had to be dealt with. He asserts that "religion is not a
cause of mental illness" but rather "an attempt at orientation and
adjustment in the face of the great realities of life." He points out that
religious concern often appears spontaneously in persons who are not
normally religious when they are faced with a major crisis. This is the
thesis of Boisen's *Religion in Crisis and Custom*, which examines both
the individual and the social dimensions of this experience.[29]

Boisen's closing statement about Oscar's call to preach reflects his
interpretation of his own illness. He admits that, while the prophetic
messages received by such persons may be "crazy," they represent at
the same time the principle that it is "of the very essence of religion
that it must express itself socially." Emotions and insights are translated into institutions and social structures and as such they become

---

27. Boisen, "Types of Mental Illness," vol. 2.
28. See Wayne E. Oates, *The Psychology of Religion* (Waco: Word, 1973), 114–18.
29. Anton T. Boisen, *Religion in Crisis and Custom: A Sociological and Psychological Study* (New York: Harper, 1955).

socially significant. Boisen viewed his work in clinical training as the socially significant result of his "idea of prophetic mission." Oscar O. did not end up having a similar impact on society, but at the same time his illness helped him find his proper role in relation to others. Thus Boisen gives him a good prognosis.

Following a case discussion and interpretation, Boisen often concluded his seminars with questions regarding the general implications of the case study. Of course, as his students report, it was important to him that they agree with his interpretation! Nevertheless, such questions also reflect the pastoral theology which Boisen brought to mental illness. A set of questions, related to the case of Oscar O. and entitled "Theology in the Light of Psychiatric Experience," was found in his files. Here are a few excerpts:

> To what extent do you agree with the presuppositions on which this interpretation is based? Consider specifically the view that . . .
> 5) the primary evil in the functional mental disorders is the sense of estrangement;
> 6) psychotherapeutic procedure is based upon the principle of forgiveness;
> 7) the curative power of acute disturbances such as that of Oscar O. lies in the sense of being directly forgiven by God;
> 8) the study of such experiences offers a fruitful approach to the problems with which theology is concerned.
> What is the present-day position of psychiatrists with reference to these presuppositions? To what extent are our theologians disposed to accept them?[30]

Continuing Relevance

The last two questions reflect the fact that Boisen's views were indeed out of step with the psychiatric and theological perspectives of his time. His unique idea that a reading of the living human documents would complete one's understanding of theology gave rise to clinical pastoral education and became the cornerstone of modern pastoral theological method. But it was fifty years after Boisen became chaplain at Worcester State Hospital that theologians began articulating the importance of narrative, or story, as a necessary element in constructing theology. In 1974, James W. McClendon, Jr., asserted that biographical material can give meaning to theological doctrine. Without this "living contact," McClendon believes, theology becomes "remote from actual Christian life, a set of empty propositions more

30. Boisen, "Theology in the Light of Psychiatric Experience."

suited to attacking rival theologians than to informing the church of God. With this living contact, theology may develop its propositions in the confidence that their meaning is exemplified in contemporary Christian experience."[31]

Theologian Harvey Cox also reflects this "new" trend by fusing theology with his own autobiography. In *The Seduction of the Spirit*, he sees the compelling impulse to listen to the stories that come from human experience (of which most Scripture is a good example) and to add one's own story to this collective legend.[32] Cox's story, like those of Boisen and his patients, is an urgent search for personal identity and integrity in the midst of the forces which threaten to strip that identity away. A full sense of salvation comes in the affirmation of one's own heritage and finding meaning in it. In this age when many people, ethnic groups, and nations are striving for a place and for a heritage, Boisen's work takes on new and important theological significance.

The recent work of Charles V. Gerkin is a further important development of Boisen's pastoral theology. He asserts that Boisen's image of the person as a document to be read means that that person's experience demands "the same respect as do the historic texts from which the foundations of our Judeo-Christian faith tradition are drawn." Using modern hermeneutical methods, the pastoral counselor brings a "horizon of understanding" to the counselee's experience which enables them together to interpret and to understand that experience in the light of the Christian story and experience. Boisen's image of the person as sacred document holds the possibility for restoring pastoral counseling to its theologically defined mission and purpose.[33]

Indeed, Boisen's vision of the theological meaning of human experience stands as both a cornerstone and a continuing challenge to all who engage in the activities related to pastoral theology. At the same time that the field of theology is turning to the importance of narrative, the fields of pastoral care and counseling are seeking new ways to understand and apply Boisen's seminal idea. As this continues to happen, all fields that are involved will benefit. The interdisciplinary dialogue that Boisen sought to create will further establish pastoral theology as a discipline with its own unique identity, method, and relevance to the ministry of the church.

31. James W. McClendon, Jr., *Biography as Theology* (Nashville: Abingdon, 1974), 178.

32. Harvey Cox, *The Seduction of the Spirit: The Use and Misuse of People's Religion* (New York: Simon and Schuster, 1973).

33. Charles V. Gerkin, *The Living Human Document: Re-Visioning Pastoral Counseling in a Hermeneutical Mode* (Nashville: Abingdon, 1984), 38–39.

2

A Dynamic Approach to Theology

DONALD CAPPS

During Seward Hiltner's lifetime, his personal presence loomed so large that it was not always easy for others to make careful and objective assessments of his written work. Now that he is gone, it should be possible for these assessments to proceed. If Hiltner's legacy is to survive, it is vital that such assessments occur. For, as memories fade and personal reminiscences grow faint, his written work will be virtually all that survives of his legacy. I agreed to contribute to this volume, not because I am personally indebted to Seward Hiltner (I was never a student or colleague of his) but because I believe this assessment of his written work can now proceed. By doing so, we will be better able to chart the course that pastoral theology has taken during the years that he was at the helm and also be better able to determine where we want it to go in the years ahead.

I will focus on one of Hiltner's major books, *Theological Dynamics*.[1] His earlier book, *Preface to Pastoral Theology*,[2] is generally considered to be his most important contribution to pastoral theology since it deals directly with the theory and methods of pastoral theology. But, as its title indicates, *Theological Dynamics* develops his dynamic

1. Seward Hiltner, *Theological Dynamics* (Nashville: Abingdon, 1972).
2. Seward Hiltner, *Preface to Pastoral Theology* (Nashville: Abingdon, 1958).

33

approach to theology and makes the case for a particular way of doing theology. Thus, even though it gives little direct attention to pastoral theology, it serves as an important companion to *Preface to Pastoral Theology* because it offers a way of doing theology that is congenial to the theory and methods of pastoral theology developed in the *Preface.*

In my discussion of Hiltner's *Theological Dynamics,* I will give particular attention to his emphasis on theological themes, the central feature of his dynamic approach to theology. Later in this chapter I will consider the work of others who have also used the theological themes approach. As my discussion of Hiltner's dynamic approach to theology via theological themes will clearly reveal, I am extremely sympathetic with this approach. I believe that the future of Hiltner's legacy depends, to a very significant degree, on our ability to capitalize on this feature of his work. But I also have some criticisms to make of his treatment of this approach in *Theological Dynamics.* I hope that these criticisms will be helpful to Hiltner's students and to others, like myself, who want to further his work.

Hiltner's Dynamic Approach to Theology

Theological Dynamics developed out of a series of lectures that Hiltner presented to the psychiatric community at The Menninger Foundation. Karl Menninger wrote a foreword to the book commending it to psychiatrists and related professionals. The book itself consists of a preface and nine chapters. Chapters 1–8 address selected theological concepts or themes, approaching these themes in terms of their inherent dynamic tensions and equilibriums. These themes include freedom and destiny, grace and gratitude, providence and trust, sin and sinfulness, church and community, sexuality and love, death and courage, and word and sacraments. Chapter 9 is a more general discussion of theological dynamics, focusing primarily on different ways of understanding the theological task, that is, theology as expression of faith, theology as critical inquiry, and theology as life guidance.

In the preface, Hiltner briefly explains what he means by "dynamics." He points out that "dynamics comes from the Greek word for power, force, or energy. Dynamics, then, is a study of energy components: the conflicts among energy dimensions, the tensions and counterbalances among forces, and the variety of equilibriums" (p. 14). Later, in chapter 9, he points out that his use of dynamics differs from Paul Tillich's in *Dynamics of Faith,* for Tillich's use of the word *dynamic* simply means movement (as opposed to structure or form), whereas Hiltner's use is more specific. Deriving his view of dynamics from dynamic psychology, he has in mind energy forces, especially forces that conflict with one another and therefore create dynamic tensions. Given his Freudian orientation, he is primarily concerned with intrapsychic and interpersonal dynamics, but he notes that he has also been influenced by dynamic social theories, so dynamics may also apply to intergroup conflicts and tensions. The scope of his use of the term *dynamics* is indicated in the following observation: "An intuitive grasp of the dynamic forces at work within persons, families, small groups, and even societies and nations, is not an invention of our own day. But the systematic study of such dynamics is comparatively recent, and it has brought rich fruit" (p. 14).

How does this view of dynamics apply to theology? Hiltner answers this question in the preface to *Theological Dynamics* when he points out that members of his original audience at The Menninger Foundation "were thoroughly familiar with the dynamics of human personality and of interpersonal relationships. I could therefore concentrate on the dynamics within theological doctrines, hoping that the similarity between theological dynamics and psychiatric dynamics would be sufficiently clear to interest my hearers whether or not they shared my religious views" (p. 13). Here, Hiltner asserts that theological doctrines are inherently dynamic, and dynamic in the same sense as persons and groups. That is, theological concepts or themes are like any human energy system. They have their internal conflicts among energy dimensions; there are tensions and counterbalances among the energy forces, and there are a variety of equilibriums. A dynamic approach to theology, then, involves the study of theological concepts or themes in terms of their energy components. As we will see, this entails identifying the energy *dimensions* in a given concept or theme, and then exploring the tensions within and between these dimensions.

As indicated, Hiltner deals with eight different theological themes or concepts. He offers no explanation for why these themes and not others were chosen, but he explicitly acknowledges that many important theological themes were left out. For example, "this book provides no systematic treatment of the incarnation and the atonement, of creation and redemption and sanctification, of suffering, of faith, of hope, and even of God" (pp. 14–15). While he suggests that these other topics might be treated in a sequel to this book (a sequel which was, in fact, never written), the clear implication is that, in contrast to the systematic theologian, who is obliged to offer some principle or rationale for including certain themes and not others, and for beginning with one and not another, the pastoral theologian may exercise more freedom in selecting certain themes and omitting (or postponing treatment of) others.

While this gives the book a rather eclectic appearance, this approach can be justified, at least up to a point, on the grounds that the book seeks to exhibit dynamic theologizing at work; and, for this, virtually any theological themes will do. But it would have been helpful if Hiltner had explained his principle of selection at the outset, or had made some attempt to draw some general conclusions from his analyses of these eight themes at the end. After the brief preface in which he defines dynamics and makes his claim that theological themes are inherently dynamic, he immediately launches into a discussion of the themes themselves.

In some chapters (the chapters on freedom and destiny, church and community, and death and courage), he addresses not only the dynamics within the themes of freedom, church, and death but also the dynamic tensions between these themes and their counterparts. In other chapters (such as those on grace and gratitude, and providence and trust), he focuses on the dynamic interaction involved in divine initiative and human response. Thus, these chapters note that acts of *grace* from the divine side entail *gratitude* from the human side of things, and that divine *providence* entails human *trust*. In these two chapters, Hiltner contends that the matter must be viewed from the human, as well as divine, side, and specifically in terms of the dynamic tensions between ourselves and God. Insights into these tensions are provided by human interpersonal relationships, where similar tensions in matters involving gratitude and trust often occur.

Other chapters (those on sin and sickness and sexuality and love), directly link traditional Christian themes—that is, sin and love—to contemporary psychiatric discussions of pathology, and thus draw on modern psychiatric understandings of intrapsychic dynamics to illumine the meanings of these traditional Christian themes. In the chapter on sin and sickness, Hiltner cautions against attributing sickness to sin, since this leads to inappropriate and pernicious moral indictments of the sick, but he recognizes that sin is itself pathological and that certain types of sin are more pathological than others. In the chapter on sexuality and love, he explores the possible masochistic element in self-denying love, and thus raises questions concerning Christianity's tendency to place a high value on disinterested love.

Certain chapters in the book provide particularly good illustrations of how one goes about a dynamic exploration of a theological theme. In my view, the best chapters for this are those about freedom and destiny, sin and sickness, and church and community. In these three chapters, he clearly identifies the major dimensions of the theme in question. Thus, in the chapter on freedom and destiny, he identifies three Christian views of freedom: self-fulfillment, self-direction, and self-transcendence. In the chapter on sin and sickness, he identifies three Christian views of sin: rebellion, missing the mark, and isolation. In the chapter on church and community, he identifies three major understandings of the church: body of Christ, covenant, and household of God.

While other theologians might view these terms as alternative understandings of freedom, sin, and the church, Hiltner considers them *dimensions* of an energy system (theme). Thus, these three dimensions within each theme need to be explored, first, for their inherent dynamics, and second, for the dynamic interaction between them. (In point of fact, however, Hiltner does not devote much attention to the dynamic interactions *between* these dimensions.) While it may seem odd to view *themes* as energy systems, there is a longstanding tradition in psychology that so regards them.[3] Perhaps the most well-known example is the Thematic Apperception Test developed by Henry Murray and his associates at Harvard Psychological Clinic. In this test, subjects' intrapsychic and interpersonal dynamics are studied via personality themes. So Hiltner's association of themes and dynamics is not as unusual or idiosyncratic as readers uninformed of this tradition might assume.

To illustrate Hiltner's method of identifying dimensions of a theme and exploring its inner dynamics, we will take a brief look at each of these chapters. In the chapter on freedom and destiny, he begins with the dimension of freedom as self-fulfillment. The dynamic inherent in freedom as self-fulfillment is the tension between bondage and release from bondage. The dynamic inherent in freedom as self-direction is the conflict between self- and other-direction. The dynamic inherent in freedom as self-transcendence has to do with detachment and engagement. In this chapter, Hiltner focuses mainly on the individual dimensions and their dynamics and does not give a great deal of attention to the dynamic interaction among the three dimensions. However, on the basis of his analyses of their individual dynamics, he does conclude that "self-transcendence is a more comprehensive way of understanding man's freedom than is self-fulfillment or self-direction" (p. 35). Indeed, this dimension of freedom tends to absorb the dimension of freedom as self-direction. What especially impresses Hiltner with the dimension of freedom as self-transcendence is that, like dynamic theory itself, it takes account of the ambiguities of life, emphasizing the importance of engaging life with courage, in full awareness of its ambiguities, contradictions, and uncertainties.

In the chapter on sin and sickness, Hiltner identifies the three

---

3. See Donald Capps, *Pastoral Care: A Thematic Approach* (Philadelphia: Westminster, 1979).

dimensions of sin as rebellion, missing the mark, and isolation. Here, again, he begins by exploring the dynamics inherent in each dimension. In sin as rebellion, the dynamic is one of aggression. In sin as missing the mark, the dynamic is bondage. In sin as isolation, the dynamic is the experience of being cut off, both from other persons and from dimensions of oneself. In each case, Hiltner also identifies the characteristic way in which the Christian theme of sin is misused or misapplied. In the case of sin as rebellion, the charge that others are in rebellion, and thus engaged in sinful attitudes and behavior, may be an illegitimate defense of the status quo. In the case of sin as missing the mark, there is the danger of moralistic indictment of the conduct of others. In the case of isolation, there is danger of attributing personal isolation to the alienating forces of society and refusing to take any personal responsibility at all for one's isolation. Hiltner diagnoses this denial of personal complicity in one's alienation as possibly due to unresolved narcissism.

As in the previous chapter, Hiltner does not discuss the dynamic interaction between these three dimensions of sin. But he does note that they share the assumption of Western theology that the purpose for having a concept of sin is not to supply "a special term for either dire or naughty deeds," but to "attempt to link the means of change and reparation with the nature of the trouble" (p. 86). Also, later in the chapter, he discusses traditional classifications of sins (the "deadly sins"), contending that a case can be made, on dynamic grounds, for such classifications, because each of these sins can be shown to be rooted in personal dynamics, with each sin reflecting a unique dynamic configuration. He argues that, because of the dynamic value of such classifications, the decision of Protestantism to eliminate such classification in favor of a general category of sin—Sin with a capital S—needs to be reversed. What he does not do, and what I have myself tried to do in my *Deadly Sins and Saving Virtues*, is to relate the three major dimensions of sin to the traditional classification of deadly sins, showing how the deadly sins are dynamically rooted in one or more of these major dimensions.[4] I have also given some attention to the dynamic interplay between individual deadly sins, and thus to the interplay between the major dimensions of sin in which they are rooted.

In concluding his analysis of the three dimensions of sin, Hiltner makes a clear statement of what he had tried to accomplish. This statement is applicable to his efforts in the chapters on freedom and the church as well. He writes: "This discussion of the three leading

---

4. See Donald Capps, *Deadly Sins and Saving Virtues* (Philadelphia: Fortress, 1987).

metaphors to convey the meaning of sin has tried to show the dynamics involved in each conception, the basic meaning of each and how it may be distorted, and the continuing utility of each if brought up to date" (pp. 91–92). A major purpose of the dynamic approach to theology, then, is to bring its traditional concepts or themes up to date, which means viewing them not as static truths but as efforts to understand the divine-human relationship and to provide life guidance.

In his chapter on the church and community, Hiltner again identifies three major dimensions of the church's self-understanding: the body of Christ, the covenant, and the household of God. The basic dynamic involved in the body of Christ image is interrelatedness. For the covenant image, it is human responsibility coupled with divine sovereignty. For the household of God image, it is belongingness. As in his chapter on sin and sickness, he explores the distortions to which these dimensions are subject. For the body of Christ, typical distortions are inappropriate conceptions and exercise of leadership, and the tendency of the church to turn in upon itself, to be a closed body. For the covenant community, a major distortion is its tendency to allow the promises made by the community to one another and to God to place inappropriate limits on the future. Here Hiltner argues that, unlike ironclad contracts, covenants may be reformulated in light of changing circumstances, many of which are owing to the salutary effects of the covenant itself. For the household of God, there is the same tendency toward ingrownness to which the body of Christ is prone, and the limited usefulness of this image for Christian groups that are much larger than a "household."

In this chapter, as in the chapters previously cited, Hiltner's major objective was to demonstrate "some of the dynamic factors involved in the way the church is and can be understood" (p. 124). Here, as in the chapters on freedom and sin, he does not give much attention to the dynamic interplay between the three images of the church, so work that is yet to be done is a dynamic analysis of the tensions that exist between these conceptions of the church. Also useful might be some rethinking of what, in fact, the major metaphors of the church might be. While Hiltner's claim that these three metaphors "have been of major importance in the two thousand years of history" is certainly true, there might be some argument as to whether there are other metaphors of equal importance. In *Images of the Church in the New Testament*,[5] Paul Minear suggests that there are four major metaphors of the church in the New Testament, including the people of God, the

5. Paul Minear, *Images of the Church in the New Testament* (Philadelphia: Westminster, 1960).

new creation, the fellowship in faith, and the body of Christ. The two schemas, Hiltner's and Minear's, might be reconciled by viewing the new creation and covenant as concerned with similar dynamics (i.e., both oriented to the future, and the people of God and fellowship in faith as related to the household of God). In any event, there will always be questions about a dynamic theologian's decisions concerning which dimensions to talk about with any given theological theme. The dynamic theologian is likely to be amenable to suggestions for expanding the number of dimensions, for the validity of his project does not depend on the exhaustiveness of his treatment of dimensions, but on his argument that theological themes are inherently dynamic. At least to a point, the addition of dimensions to the original formulation enhances our understanding of the dynamic complexity of a theological theme.

The Need for a Dynamic Psychology

More could be said about how Hiltner approaches specific theological themes in his book. We have only touched the surface of his dynamic analyses of freedom, sin, and the church, and we have not considered the other five themes at all. But we need to move on to some more general issues that his book, as a whole, raises. As we move into this discussion, it will become clear that I have some criticisms to make of Hiltner's treatment of his subject, the dynamic approach to theology. But I hasten to emphasize that these are criticisms of certain features of his dynamic approach, and not a criticism of the approach itself. I would hope that these critical comments will not in any way obscure my great appreciation for this approach and for what Hiltner has to say about it in *Theological Dynamics*. For the most part, my criticisms are not of what he has said in the book, but of what he has failed to say.

My criticisms all stem from the same root, that is, the fact that Hiltner does not provide a secure place for dynamic psychology in his dynamic approach to theology. Aside from a brief description of what dynamics mean for dynamic psychologists, he has virtually nothing to say about how dynamic psychology fits into his project. The reasons for this have partly to do with the fact that his original audience were psychiatrists and members of related mental-health disciplines. This meant that he could "concentrate on the dynamics within theological doctrines," knowing that his audience brought an understanding of dynamic psychology with them. But it also means that he never had to address directly the question of the place of dynamic psychology in a dynamic approach to theology.

The insights of dynamic psychology are frequently used throughout the book, but they are used as circumstances require or warrant, and not because dynamic psychology was deemed to be essential or integral to his theological method. As Hiltner points out in the preface, "The content of the book is clearly focused on understanding selected theological teachings, or doctrines, dynamically. Very often the dynamic insights are drawn from theology itself. But I have no apology for the fact that, on occasion, they come from psychiatry and psychology and the related disciplines" (p. 13). This statement clearly indicates that dynamic psychology has an "occasional" role to play in his dynamic approach to theology. Its use is largely ad hoc. Moreover, because these "dynamic insights" come from a number of disciplines, including psychiatry, psychology, and disciplines that are "related" to psychology, the role that psychological disciplines play in his project is highly eclectic.

Because Hiltner does not make a secure place for psychology in his project, he never offers a clear statement of the *psychological theory of dynamics* being employed or assumed in the discussion. What we are given is a brief definition of what dynamics will be taken to mean, that is, the study of such energy components as conflicts within and among the dimensions of an energy system, the tensions and counterbalances among forces, and the variety of equilibriums. This tells us what he includes in the study of dynamics but does not say anything about what he excludes. Nor does it tell us very much about what he understands the source or sources of these energy forces to be, how we would identify an equilibrium between two or more such forces, and whether the optimal goal of the energy system is to achieve equilibrium. What is most strikingly missing in Hiltner's whole discussion of dynamics is a theory or concept of dynamic change. We are not informed as to what constitutes dynamic change, what makes dynamic change possible, or even whether significant dynamic change is possible. And what would be the focus of a concern for dynamic change in a dynamic approach to theology: dynamic change with theology itself, or the role of theology in effecting dynamic change in persons and groups?

Certainly, Hiltner has written on this topic in other writings. So the reader who is informed of his views on this subject will know the answer to these questions. Also, there are "occasional" references to change in the course of his discussion of specific theological themes (such as the passage I quoted earlier from his chapter on sin and sickness, and a number of illustrations involving counselees whose personalities underwent significant change). But my point here is that there is no clearly stated psychological dynamic theory in the book, and therefore dynamic psychology has no secure place in his dynamic approach to theology.

The Ambiguities of Life

My major criticisms of Hiltner's dynamic approach to theology are directly related to this failure to make his psychological theory of dynamics explicit. The first has to do with the tone of irresolution that pervades *Theological Dynamics*. Persons who knew Hiltner have given those of us who did not know him a portrait of Seward Hiltner as resolute, decisive, and very difficult to push around. But, in *Theological Dynamics*, we are given a very different theological picture of what human life is all about. A major motif that runs through the book, informing virtually all the themes it treats, is that life is an ambiguous affair. Hiltner prefers the dimension of freedom of self-transcendence to self-fulfillment and self-direction precisely because it takes seriously the profound ambiguities of life.

Similarly, in the chapter on sin, he appears to take most seriously the sin of isolation because it recognizes the ambiguities of responsibility for sin (i.e., such responsibility cannot simply be assigned to society, but neither is it simply the fault of the individual). He returns to this emphasis on moral ambiguity in the final chapter of the book, where he discusses theology as life guidance (pp. 193–94). In this discussion, he says that there are two basic approaches to life guidance. One is the *legalistic* approach, where the individual does not "admit the ambiguity that is present in all human situations," but instead settles the issue on the basis of external rule or law, and thus does not creatively use the inner tensions that are clearly present. The other is the *responsible freedom* approach, where the individual does recognize the ambiguities that are present in the situation, but does not resort to the simple option of conformity or rebellion. Instead, this person analyzes the situation with the conscious intention not to distort, and then acts on the basis of principles, such as freedom and love. This person knows that, given the ambiguities of the situation, the eventual decision may be wrong. But this person is willing to live with the consequences of this fact, and "accepts the anxiety of never being sure he is right or wrong until later. In terms of anxiety, things are never wholly rounded off for him" (p. 194).

Hiltner clearly favors the second type, for "a theology of life guidance mainly concerned with teaching people to obey rules, rather than to become responsible, is faulty" (p. 195). His argument for preferring the one over the other is based, to a large extent, on the fact that the one accepts the ambiguities of life while the other seeks to avoid them. Given these two options, few of us would disagree with Hiltner that the one is much preferable to the other. But there is a third type of person who falls somewhere between the legalist and the person for whom all moral decisions are anxiety-producing. These are persons who rely on accrued wisdom about themselves and the world, and who "know" what to do because they have met similar situations in the past.

If we generalize this point from moral decision-making to life in general, we can see that there is a serious gap in Hiltner's discussion of the ambiguities of life. He has virtually nothing to say about the possibility that at least some of life's ambiguities get resolved or simply no longer cause us anxiety. Possibly, such resolutions are implicit in this recognition of *equilibriums* as one of the energy components in a dynamic system. But, if so, he never suggests that certain equilibriums may become highly stable and relatively permanent.

Again, it may well be the case that he has somewhere written about this issue and has, in fact, indicated that he believes such resolutions of ambiguity are possible. But the fact that he does not address this issue in *Theological Dynamics* points up, again, the fact that the book lacks a clearly articulated theory of dynamics. A psychological theory of dynamics, especially one that took developmental process seriously, would almost certainly have something to say about the resolution of at least some of life's ambiguities. For example, Erik H. Erikson's life cycle theory[6] with its series of stages has a great deal to say about relatively permanent resolutions of at least some of the ambiguities of life. While life is an adventure in which we are often at risk, Erikson does indicate that there can be relatively stable and enduring solutions to the ambiguities of life as we move from stage to stage. Thus, in addition to the "peak experiences" in which we temporarily experience the surcease of all ambiguity and experience perfect clarity and peace, there are the more modest but enduring resolutions that we achieve by confronting life's inevitable crises and learning from them. Many of life's ambiguities remain intractable and will always be anxiety-producing. But many can be resolved. Indeed, a developmental theory like Erikson's assumes that, with maturation, certain ambiguities are simply left behind.

With this illustration, I do not mean to minimize life's ambiguities, or to question their enormous significance for theology. My point is simply that this is an issue that a dynamic psychology, especially one that takes a developmental view of the matter, will normally address. Hiltner is profoundly sensitive to the dynamic tensions of life, but, in *Theological Dynamics*, he exhibits scant appreciation for their developmental trajectories.

6. Erik H. Erikson, *Childhood and Society*, 2d rev. ed. (New York: Norton, 1964).

Hiltner's Perspectivism

A second major criticism of Hiltner's dynamic approach to theology concerns his emphasis on the *perspective* of the theologian. This is a core element of his thought, and it figures prominently in his statements of theological method in *Theological Dynamics*. As we will see, my criticism of his perspectivism is also directly related to his failure to make his psychological theory of dynamics explicit.

In pointing out that he approaches theological dynamics from the perspective of one who has a profound appreciation of psychology and related disciplines, Hiltner observes:

> In the rethinking and re-articulation of theology that must be done in every age, it is my conviction that each theologian may contribute more to general understanding by open acknowledgment of his perspective and its limitations than by writing as if his were "theology in general." The details of the position he holds may in fact be far less significant than the perspective, or background slant, that he brings to the investigation.[7]

Thus when *he* approaches theology, he does so as one who thinks about theological issues and concepts in a psychodynamic way. And this accounts for the distinctive approach of the book:

> The argument of this book has been that the understanding of dynamics, while by no means the sole perspective that can illuminate the meaning of theological teachings, is nevertheless of great importance. And I have had no hesitation in showing that my original grasp of psychodynamics and sociodynamics was made possible by the psychological and sociological disciplines.[8]

He concludes that, once one grasps this perspective (i.e., "that theological doctrines themselves always exist in a dynamic relationship, containing tensions and equilibriums and the temptation to distort"), "then we can proceed to deal with these dimensions whenever theological teachings are discussed."

This perspectival approach to theology has become so ingrained in pastoral theology that it is now virtually taken for granted. Other features of Hiltner's thought have been questioned or challenged, but his emphasis on the perspective of the theologian, and the influence of this perspective on the resulting theological contribution, has not been seriously questioned. Indeed, the point he is making here seems so

7. Hiltner, *Theological Dynamics*, 183.
8. Ibid., 201.

self-evidently true that no one has really thought to question it. Nor do I want to question its truth or importance. The issue, however, is not its truth or importance, but its adequacy as a theological method.

In *Pastoral Care and Hermeneutics*, I summarized E. D. Hirsch's discussion of four general methods employed in the task of understanding a written text.[9] These four approaches include *intuitionism, positivism, perspectivism,* and *schematism.* While Hirsch is concerned with understanding written texts, I believe that his discussion of these four interpretive approaches may also be applied to theology, including the theology that Hiltner advocates, that is, dynamic theology. I will not take time to discuss all four of these approaches. Instead, I want to center on what Hirsch has to say about *perspectivism,* since this is the method that Hiltner has advocated.

Hirsch notes that this approach grows out of a modern scepticism regarding the possibility of a correct interpretation of a text. Its psychological version says that a given text cannot mean the same for me as it does for you because we look at it from different subjective standpoints. Its historical version makes the same argument for interpreters who stand at different points in cultural space and time. Both stress that interpretation is relative to the interpreter. Hirsch agrees with the perspectivist view that any given text may yield different interpretations. But he takes issue with perspectivism when it presents its views dogmatically, claiming that there can be no general agreement among interpreters regarding the meaning of a given text. He contends that perspectivism places so much emphasis on the interpreters and their differences that it fails to take seriously enough the "self-identity" of the text. Using visual perception as an analogy, he argues that two observers can see the very same thing—for example, a large building— even though their perspective on it may differ (i.e., looking at the building from two very different angles). Thus, for Hirsch, it is possible for persons coming at the text from differing perspectives to arrive at a common understanding of it. He does not base this argument on the claim that interpreters might reach a consensus through social process, but on the fact that a text is the same however we approach it, and this self-identity of the text can be recognized whatever our angle of vision may be.

To illustrate what Hirsch means by the *self-identity* of the object of study, and to show why he believes we need to take it seriously, we might compare two conflicting views of the predatory behavior of

9. See Donald Capps, *Pastoral Care and Hermeneutics* (Philadelphia: Fortress, 1984); E. D. Hirsch, Jr., "Old and New in Hermeneutics," in *The Aims of Interpretation* (Chicago: University of Chicago Press, 1976), 17–35.

wolves. Farley Mowat, in *Never Cry Wolf,* claims that wolves will stalk
and kill only the weak and sick animals in a herd, those that are not
likely to have survived. In contrast, Ed Gelbins, quoted in John
McPhee's *Coming Into the Country,* claims that wolves do not limit
their attack to the weak and sick, but attack indiscriminately.[10] We
might say that these two views reflect the perspective of a naturalist
(Mowat) and the perspective of a hunter (Gelbins). These differing
perspectives may help us to understand why they take the positions
they do regarding the wolf's predatory habits. But, eventually, we will
come to the point where explaining why Mowat and Gelbins take these
positions is not the issue. We want to know the answer to the question
they raise: Do wolves attack and kill indiscriminately or do they follow
a principle (i.e., kill those that were not likely to survive anyway)?
This, I believe, is what Hirsch is asserting when he argues that we
need to go beyond perspectivism because it is insufficiently concerned
with the "self-identity" of the object being studied. Perspectivism is
more interested in explaining why Mowat and Gelbins say what they
say, and less interested in settling the question of what wolves actually
do.

Hirsch does not deny that everyone comes to a text from a particular
perspective. So Hiltner has every right to make the point that he comes
to theology from a certain perspective, and that this influences the
way he looks at theology. But the effect of perspectivism is that it
places so much emphasis on the particular stance of the interpreter,
and on the fact that there may be many different perspectives being
brought to bear on the same object of inquiry, that the "self-identity"
of its object is virtually neglected.

The result in the case of Hiltner's *Theological Dynamics* is an over-
emphasis on the subjective character of his theological interpretation,
and the invitation to an extreme relativism. If theological work is so
heavily influenced by the perspectives of those who engage in it, can
there ever be any consensus as to the object of inquiry and its meanings? Moreover, perspectivism appears to allow any interpretation of
a theological concept or theme, as long as the interpreter acknowledges his perspective and its limitations. The obvious problem with
this is that a theme may not allow the interpretation we have given it.
Even as we do violence to a text when we ascribe meanings to it that
are simply not there, we do violence to a theological theme when we
ascribe meanings to it that it does not or cannot have. (The same, of
course, goes for wolves' predatory acts.)

10. See Farley Mowat, *Never Cry Wolf* (New York: Bantam, 1979) and John
McPhee, *Coming Into the Country* (New York: Bantam, 1979).

Hiltner's dynamic approach to theological themes works because the dynamics he observes in these themes are, in fact, inherent in them. So I have no quarrel with his dynamic approach to theology. Nor do I have any fundamental quarrel with the interpretations he actually offers of these theological themes. The problem arises when he makes such a point of his personal perspective that he appears to justify his dynamic interpretations of theological themes not on the fact that these themes are inherently dynamic, but on the claim that everyone views theology from a particular perspective, and his happens to be informed by dynamic psychology.

The way out of this dilemma is Hirsch's fourth approach to interpretation of a text, which he calls *schematism*. This model says that we approach texts in much the same way as any other object we want to come to know and understand. We begin with some predispositions or preconceptions of what the text is about and what it is likely to mean. These predispositions may be informed by our unique perspective, but they are more than this. For they become more than the angle of vision from which we view the text. In addition, they provide "schemas" by which we engage the text and seek to understand it. These schemas may be completely confirmed as we engage the text, or they may be thoroughly mistaken and misguided and thus subject to complete rejection. Usually, they are accurate in some respects but subject to correction or revision in others. Thus, when the schema engages the text, there is a "making-matching, constructive-corrective process." Understanding occurs when we take the schema that we have formulated and test it against the text itself.

It may well be the case that, when Hiltner talks about the perspective of the theologian, he actually has in mind something closer to schematism than perspectivism. Indeed, it would appear that his own interests in psychological dynamics are more than perspective-setting, that dynamic psychology actually contributes to the working schema by which he engages a theological theme and seeks to understand it. But we cannot know this for certain, because he does not set forth in any explicit and systematic fashion the psychological theory that is to inform his investigation. The most that he claims is that "insights" from dynamic psychology are "occasionally" employed in his interpretation of a theological theme. Thus, we must conclude that dynamic psychology informs the angle of vision from which Hiltner initiates his work, and occasionally provides insights, but does not achieve the status of a "schema," or aspect of a schema, that is actually employed in the "making-matching, constructive-corrective" interpretive process itself.

In short, Hiltner's perspectivism allows him to make occasional use of dynamic psychology in his dynamic approach to theology, but it does not require him to formulate any coherent theory or conception of dynamic psychology to be used in engaging theological themes. Had he given dynamic psychology the status of schema rather than simply perspective, we would have seen what psychology can contribute to a dynamic approach to theology when incorporated, in a systematic way, into the interpretive process. I would not predict how this would have changed or influenced Hiltner's interpretations of given theological themes. But I have suggested that it would have at least required him to give sustained attention to two important features of theology as life guidance: its contribution to dynamic change and to the resolution of at least some of life's ambiguities.[11]

As I conclude this section of my discussion of Hiltner's *Theological Dynamics*, I want to emphasize that I raise these concerns not for the purpose of criticizing Hiltner, but in order to further the work that he began. Obviously, *Theological Dynamics* is a significant book, a major contribution to pastoral theology. The problems that I have raised are certainly not intended to challenge this basic fact, for the book's significance and importance are self-evident. But I do think that his students, and others who want to further his work, need to address the question of the status of dynamic psychology in the dynamic approach to theology. Hiltner left its status ambiguous, linking it too closely to his personal perspective. Unless we give it a more objective status, it may come to have no place at all.

Dynamic Theology: Later Developments

Hiltner indicates that he envisioned writing a sequel to *Theological Dynamics*. He did not do so, but others have taken up the work that he began and have contributed to the furtherance of his dynamic approach to theology. Space does not permit me to discuss these developments in any detail. But they should at least be mentioned, for they demonstrate that Hiltner's dynamic approach to theology is one aspect of his legacy that promises to endure.

11. It is true that Hiltner, in *Preface to Pastoral Theology* and other writings, advocated a pastoral theology method involving the correlation of theology and psychology. But, in my judgment, it would be inappropriate to view this correlational method as comparable to schematism's "making-matching, constructive-corrective" process. As Don S. Browning's discussion of Hiltner's correlational methods indicates, this was conceived as a "correlation of perspectives," with theology and psychology informing the perspective taken, for example, on an act of ministry. This conception of the correlation of theology and psychology simply underscores the fact that Hiltner's theological method does not go significantly beyond perspectivism.

Most of the focus in these continuing efforts to develop the dynamic approach to theology has centered on theological themes. In his influential book, *The Minister as Diagnostician,* Paul W. Pruyser (clinical psychologist at The Menninger Foundation) used many of Hiltner's themes in proposing that theology be employed diagnostically in pastoral counseling.[12] Among his seven diagnostic themes, four are directly parallel to Hiltner's themes. These are *providence* (corresponding to Hiltner's theme of providence and trust), *grace or gratefulness* (Hiltner's theme of grace and gratitude), *repentance* (Hiltner's theme of sin and sickness), and *communion* (Hiltner's themes of sexuality and love, and church and communion). Two others, *faith* and *vocation,* relate directly or indirectly to themes that Hiltner mentions but deferred to a sequel to *Theological Dynamics.* The seventh theme, *awareness of the holy,* has no discernible parallels with Hiltner's themes, reflecting Pruyser's own deep appreciation for Rudolf Otto's emphasis on the experience of the holy, though it may be noted that Hiltner actually uses the phrase *awareness of the holy* in *Theological Dynamics,* when he suggests that "theologizing begins, as does religion, from an awareness of the 'holy' in the sense of Rudolf Otto. . . ."[13]

Hiltner's emphasis on theological themes also appears to have had some influence, direct or indirect, on William B. Oglesby, Jr.'s, *Biblical Themes for Pastoral Care.*[14] Oglesby's five themes, derived from the Bible, are less closely linked to Hiltner's than Pruyser's themes, but there are some parallels, including his themes of *initiative and freedom* (Hiltner's freedom and destiny), *death and rebirth* (Hiltner's death and courage), and *conformity and rebellion* (Hiltner's sin and sickness). The two other themes, *fear and faith* and *risk and redemption,* are related to themes that Hiltner deferred to a sequel to *Theological Dynamics.*

There have also been efforts to link theological themes more closely with psychological themes. These efforts have made particular use of Erikson's life cycle theory, viewing the labels he assigns to each of the eight stages as *psychosocial themes* having their own dynamic tensions and equilibriums. An important contribution along these lines is LeRoy Aden's linkage of dimensions of faith with Erikson's life stages. Based on the view that "faith as a human response is a dynamic and multidimensional reality rather than a static and monolithic one,"[15]

12. Paul W. Pruyser, *The Minister as Diagnostician: Personal Problems in Pastoral Perspective.* (Philadelphia: Westminster, 1976).

13. Hiltner, *Theological Dynamics,* 185.

14. William B. Oglesby, Jr., *Biblical Themes for Pastoral Care* (Nashville: Abingdon, 1980).

15. LeRoy Aden, "Faith and the Developmental Cycle," *Pastoral Psychology* 24 (Spring 1976): 215.

Aden's model makes these connections between faith dimensions and psychosocial stages: faith as *trust* (infancy), *courage* (early childhood), *obedience* (play age), *assent* (school age), *identity* (adolescence), *self-surrender* (young adulthood), *unconditional caring* (middle adulthood), and *unconditional acceptance* (mature age).

I, too, have made various contributions to the effort to link Erikson's psychosocial themes and theological themes. The first, in *Pastoral Care: A Thematic Approach*, linked Pruyser's theological themes and Erikson's psychosocial themes.[16] Using the theme of *vocation* twice, the model is this: *providence* (basic trust versus basic mistrust), *grace or gratefulness* (autonomy versus shame and doubt), *repentance* (initiative versus guilt), *vocation* (industry versus inferiority), *faith* (identity versus identity diffusion), *communion* (intimacy versus isolation), *vocation* (generativity versus stagnation), and *awareness of the holy* (integrity versus despair). The underlying assumption of these linkages is that the theological theme and the psychosocial theme have similar internal dynamics.

In more recent writings, I have linked Erikson's psychosocial themes to the traditional deadly sins and to Jesus' beatitudes. The linkages for the deadly sins are these: *gluttony* (basic trust versus basic mistrust), *anger* (autonomy versus shame and doubt), *greed* (initiative versus guilt), *envy* (industry versus inferiority), *pride* (identity versus identity diffusion), *lust* (intimacy versus isolation), *apathy* (generativity versus stagnation) and *melancholy* (integrity versus despair).[17] (There are eight, not seven deadly sins in this schema; this is based on the rationale that *sloth* is an amalgam of two more traditional deadly sins, *apathy* and *melancholy*.)

The linkages for the beatitudes are these: *pure in heart* (basic trust versus basic mistrust), *meek* (autonomy versus shame and doubt), *hunger and thirst for righteousness* (initiative versus guilt), *poor in spirit* (industry versus inferiority), *persecuted for righteousness' sake* (identity versus identity diffusion), *peacemakers* (intimacy versus isolation), *merciful* (generativity versus stagnation) and *those who mourn* (integrity versus despair).[18] These two sets of linkages, the deadly sins and the beatitudes, go together, for the one concerns life lived under a curse, and the other concerns life that is blessed. (The beatitudes are "blessed assurances.")

Needless to say, Erikson's life cycle theory is only one of many

16. Capps, *Pastoral Care*.
17. Donald Capps, *Life Cycle Theory and Pastoral Care* (Philadelphia: Fortress, 1983).
18. Donald Capps, "The Beatitudes and Erikson's Life Cycle Theory," *Pastoral Psychology* 33 (1985): 226–44.

psychological theories that may prove useful to us as we attempt to augment the role of dynamic psychology in the dynamic approach to theology. But Erikson's theory has particular promise because it stands in that tradition of dynamic psychology which is oriented toward thematics.[19] Moreover, Erikson's life cycle theory is compatible, religiously speaking, with some of the fundamental assertions of the Christian faith.[20] For these reasons, together with the fact that the most useful dynamic psychologies for a dynamic approach to theology will undoubtedly have a developmental thrust, I suggest that Erikson's life cycle theory may provide the dynamic psychology that Hiltner's dynamic approach to theology so urgently requires.

In the meantime, Hiltner's *Theological Dynamics* has brought us a considerable distance toward our ultimate destination. Menninger said that it gave him great pride to be asked to write the foreword to *Theological Dynamics*. I take similar pride in being asked to write this chapter on what I consider to be Seward Hiltner's most important book.

19. See Capps, *Pastoral Care*, 19–30.
20. See Donald Capps, "Erikson's Life Cycle Theory: Religious Dimensions," *Religious Studies Review* 10 (1984): 120–27.

3

A Perspectival Pastoral Theology

RODNEY J. HUNTER

For more than a quarter century, Seward Hiltner was one of the principal advocates and theoreticians of the rapidly expanding field of pastoral care and counseling in America. His writings, including nearly a dozen books and scores of articles and editorials, were widely appreciated by the clergy for their perceptive insights into human nature, their shrewd and sensitive practical help in the work of care and counseling, and for their insightful integrations of theological understanding with the emerging new discoveries in dynamic psychiatry, psychology, and the social sciences.

Yet it is a curious fact that Hiltner's most creative and important work, *Preface to Pastoral Theology*,[1] which advanced a new method by which theology might be related to the practical work of ministry and offered a challenging new vision of the field of pastoral theology, has stimulated so little serious interest among pastors, counselors, and theologians. At least this seems to be the case if one is to judge from the limited critical discussion that it has received in the professional literature[2] and the equally limited amount of empirical research in

1. Seward Hiltner, *Preface to Pastoral Theology* (Nashville: Abingdon, 1958).
2. Principally Alastair V. Campbell, "Is Practical Theology Possible?" *Scottish Journal of Theology* 25 (1972): 217–27; Thomas C. Oden, *Contemporary Theology and*

pastoral theology that it has inspired.[3] Hiltner's theory has had considerable influence in the teaching of pastoral care and counseling in a number of seminaries where his students are located, but generally it has had little impact on theological curricula, has been ignored or grossly misunderstood by theologians,[4] and has been overlooked or forgotten by parish clergy and pastoral counselors.

Several factors may have contributed to this situation. Some of Hiltner's key ideas were derived implicitly from the often unfamiliar thought world of process philosophy, thereby giving the impression of ambiguity or obscurity to readers who are unacquainted with that conceptuality. In any case it requires basic changes in previous thought patterns. Also, Hiltner may have erred in terms of the level at which he chose to pitch the book: It is too complex and removed from practical concerns for many pastors and counselors, and yet it is not sufficiently developed intellectually for professional theologians and educators. Thus Hiltner must share some responsibility for the neglect and misunderstanding of his *Preface*.

At a deeper level, however, I think the book meets resistance precisely at the point of its central thesis. The idea that anything truly fundamental can be learned about the Christian faith by examining the concrete work of pastors or other Christian "practitioners" with hurting people presents a double challenge. It challenges theology to consider the possibility that something of truly theological (and not merely psychological) significance can be learned by studying care-

---

Psychotherapy (Philadelphia: Westminster, 1967); William B. Oglesby, Jr., ed., *The New Shape of Pastoral Theology: Essays in Honor of Seward Hiltner* (Nashville: Abingdon, 1969); Don S. Browning, ed., *Practical Theology: The Emerging Field in Theology, Church, and World* (San Francisco: Harper and Row, 1982).

3. Primarily James G. Emerson, *Divorce, The Church, and Remarriage* (Philadelphia: Westminster, 1961); James G. Emerson, *The Dynamics of Forgiveness* (Philadelphia: Westminster, 1964); Kenneth R. Mitchell, *Psychological and Theological Relationships in the Multiple Staff Ministry* (Philadelphia: Westminster, 1966); James N. Lapsley, "Reconciliation, Forgiveness, Lost Contracts," *Theology Today* 23 (1966): 44–59; Ian F. McIntosh, *Pastoral Care and Pastoral Theology* (Philadelphia: Westminster, 1972); Rodney J. Hunter, "Moltmann's Theology of the Cross and the Dilemma of Contemporary Pastoral Care," in Jurgen Moltmann, *Hope for the Church*, ed. and trans. Theodore Runyon (Nashville: Abingdon, 1979); cf. Murray Stewart Thompson, *Grace and Forgiveness in Ministry* (Nashville: Abingdon, 1981) and various doctoral dissertations at the University of Chicago and Princeton Theological Seminary; cf. also Seward Hiltner and Lowell G. Colston, *The Context of Pastoral Counseling* (Nashville: Abingdon, 1961).

4. See M. Douglas Meeks, "Moltmann's Contribution to Practical Theology," in Jurgen Moltmann, *Hope for the Church*, ed. and trans. Theodore Runyon (Nashville: Abingdon, 1979), 59.

fully the experiences of ordinary people caught up in various forms of suffering, confusion, sinfulness, and despair. Hiltner got the idea from his great teacher, Anton T. Boisen, who had done pioneering work in the psychology of religion and mental illness and had been one of the founding fathers of the clinical pastoral education movement.[5]

At the same time Hiltner challenges theology to reflect on the potential importance of practical skills and knowledge as a source of theological understanding. That practical arts of any sort might constitute occasions for gaining fundamental knowledge, and not merely for applying knowledge learned elsewhere, runs counter to the Western academic and theological tradition since Aristotle in which theory and practice have been sharply distinguished in the pursuit and organization of knowledge. Hiltner challenged this tradition, and though he may not have made his case clearly or persuasively, the strangeness of his basic notion of practical or "operation-centered" knowledge is probably another reason why the *Preface* has not produced sustained discussion or serious research. Moreover, as I shall indicate in the development of this chapter, there is also a conceptual tension and, perhaps, confusion between the two components of his basic thesis (the study of human experience and the study of pastoral operations). This confusion may contribute to the poor reception that the book has received, though some would probably regard its dual focus as potentially its greatest asset.[6]

In any case, the subsequent neglect and misunderstanding of Hiltner's pastoral theology is unfortunate. Whatever its limitation, *Preface* is an original and important book for the church and its ministry. In fact, it is important to anyone who is interested in relating theology to the practical task of caring for needy human beings. Therefore, in the first part of this essay I will attempt to sketch Hiltner's position in such a way as to highlight its originality and importance, even while I try to interpret and clarify certain particular points that have been commonly overlooked or misunderstood. The remaining part examines, at a more technical level, two of the basic critical problems entailed in Hiltner's proposals: the problem of empiricism and the problem of pragmatism.

5. E. Brooks Holifield, *A History of Pastoral Care in America: From Salvation to Self-Realization*. (Nashville: Abingdon, 1983), 231–49; Edward E. Thornton, *Professional Education for Ministry: A History of Clinical Pastoral Education* (Nashville: Abingdon, 1970), 55–71.

6. James N. Lapsley, "Practical Theology and Pastoral Care: An Essay in Practical Theology." In *Practical Theology: The Emerging Field in Theology, Church, and World*, edited by Don S. Browning (San Francisco: Harper and Row, 1982).

Exposition of Hiltner's Views on Pastoral Theology

Hiltner did not define his subject in the *Preface* as the relation between theology and pastoral care and counseling, or between theology and psychology. As its title suggests, the book is rather an attempt to construct the basic methodological principles of the discipline of pastoral theology. This endeavor may strike readers who are interested mainly in the contemporary theology-psychology dialogue as too churchy, clerical, or academic. Besides, the historical discipline of pastoral theology, which flourished mainly in the nineteenth century, left an undistinguished intellectual record consisting mostly of practical manuals that instructed clergy in their sacred duties and exhorted them to live lives worthy of their calling. If this background seems to be an unpromising point of departure, it is at least important to grasp the larger significance of Hiltner's effort to transform this quaint tradition of ministerial wisdom into a modern theological discipline.

Pastoral Theology as Operation-Centered Theological Discipline

Hiltner's basic thesis in the *Preface* is that pastoral theology can and ought to be conceived, not as a secondary professional or academic enterprise in which theology is somehow "applied" to practical work such as care and counseling, but as a fundamental form of theological inquiry—basic research, as it were—that is focused on the empirical data of pastoral experience examined in the light of the Christian faith. "It is the thesis of this book," he says, "that pastoral theology is a formal branch of theology resulting from a study of Christian shepherding, that it is just as important as biblical or doctrinal theology, and that it is no less the concern of the minister of the local church than of the specialist."[7]

The distinctiveness of *pastoral* theology compared with the classical disciplines of theology lies solely in its "organizing principle," in the fact that it organizes theological reflection around the themes and issues presented by concrete, real-life, ongoing pastoral practice—what Hiltner liked to call (in an ill-chosen phrase from John Dewey, I think) the "operations" of ministry.[8] Thus pastoral theology, formally speaking, is an "operation-centered discipline" in distinction from biblical, historical, or doctrinal theology, which exhibit different sorts of

7. Hiltner, *Preface to Pastoral Theology*, 15.
8. Ibid., 20–24.

organizing principles. For instance, the Bible as a body of literature constitutes the organizing principle for biblical theology. These classical, scholarly disciplines of theology Hiltner grouped together (in perhaps another ill-chosen phrase) as "logic-centered disciplines" and contrasted them with "operation-centered" forms of theology, maintaining their independence.

Behind this crucial distinction lay the legacy of Boisen. Boisen contended that the study of theology and preparation for ministry would be greatly enhanced if students had "the opportunity to go to first-hand sources for their knowledge of human nature." He therefore wanted them "to read the human documents as well as books, particularly those revealing documents which are opened up at the inner day of judgment," in the fires of psychic upheaval and reorganization known as mental illness.[9] Boisen believed that such personal crises were inherently religious experiences—struggles of the soul with questions of ultimate meaning and loyalty—and hence sources of profound insight for theology and the practice of ministry. Hiltner's concept of an operation-centered discipline was, I think, his attempt to conceptualize Boisen's thesis in formal disciplinary terms. And like Boisen, Hiltner embodied the dual purpose of exploring human nature (including religious experience) and developing the practice of the care of souls.

In asserting that pastoral theology is "just as important as biblical or doctrinal or historical theology," Hiltner is registering the protest of a practical theologian against the inferior status of the disciplines of practical theology (pastoral care, preaching, administration) in modern theological faculties. Systematic theologians, for example, are said to do "real theology" while practical theologians merely apply it. But Hiltner's point is much more than a social protest. He is maintaining that pastoral operations, if properly defined and interpreted, have a valid epistemological claim to make in theology. This is not just a matter of pastoral experience causing theology to "come alive" subjectively for the pastor.[10] Hiltner's claim is the more ambitious one of Boisen—that the encounter with human nature in the practical experience of ministry can contribute to the church's basic theological understanding. To use his favorite analogy, there is a "two-way-street" between operation- and logic-centered disciplines, each contributing to the other on the "village green of theological integration."[11]

9. Anton T. Boisen, *The Exploration of the Inner World* (Philadelphia: University of Pennsylvania Press, 1971), 10.

10. Howard Clinebell, Jr., *Basic Types of Pastoral Care and Counseling*, rev. ed. (Nashville: Abingdon, 1984), 49–50.

11. Hiltner, *Preface to Pastoral Theology*, 219, 222–23.

Regrettably, Hiltner failed to clarify the full epistemological import of this analogy at philosophical and theological levels. He did not explain exactly in what sense experiential insights from contemporary ministry can provide fundamental theological knowledge, or what their limits are. But he did attempt to illustrate his claim in the "content" chapters of the *Preface* on healing, sustaining, and guiding. In the main, his view was that reflection on pastoral practice could "complete and correct" fallible human understandings of God's definitive revelation in Christ.[12]

Hiltner believed that only in this way would theology be totally integrated with pastoral practice, not simply correlated with it as an external frame of reference. Most theories about the "theology of pastoral care" or the "relation of psychology to theology," for instance, speak *to* practice from one or another theological perspective, either to guide or critique it, but they do not speak *out of* practice as an expression of theology arising from and integral to the practical context. Hiltner's hope was to create a mode of theological reflection uniquely expressing the themes, issues, problems, and insights of the practitioner, just as the biblical theologian may be said to articulate Christian faith in a mode expressing the unique historical and literary witness of the Bible, or the systematic theologian to articulate and critically examine the faith in terms of its abstract coherence, meaning, and truthfulness.

Hiltner regarded his thesis about pastoral theology as important for the whole life and work of the church and not simply for a small number of seminary experts. He hoped that ordained ministers in particular could begin to function as serious theologians in their own right through this understanding of pastoral theology, and he saw a limited role for laity as well. For reasons perhaps more historical than logical, however, Hiltner was reluctant to develop the lay dimension of his thought and has been criticized for a narrow, clerical professionalism in his vision of the field.[13] But there is no reason why his principles could not extend much more fully than he envisioned in 1958 to include lay caregiving and other ministries as sources of theological insight.

An Inquiry in the Shepherding Perspective

If one grants the possibility of operation-centered forms of theology, the next problem is how to define or categorize those operations with

12. Ibid., 221–22. Cf. Seward Hiltner, *The Christian Shepherd* (Nashville: Abingdon, 1959), 12–13.
13. Campbell, "Is Practical Theology Possible?" See also James G. Emerson, "Whither Pastoral Theology: A Look at Five Books," *Pastoral Psychology* 33 (1985): 217–20.

enough clarity and specificity, and enough profundity, to enable theological disciplines to be formed around them. Much of the *Preface* is devoted to this problem, and Hiltner's proposals, while open to question and often misunderstood, are nonetheless subtle, complex, and highly original. At the risk of oversimplifying, I would suggest that the heart of Hiltner's proposals can be seen best under three headings: the concept of perspective, the threefold structure of pastoral perspective, and the specific concept of the shepherding perspective.

The concept of perspective. Hiltner was convinced that the true practice of ministry (or the Christian life) can never be adequately grasped or described, for theological or practical purposes, solely by enumerating the outward, public, and often conventional social roles of the profession (preaching, leading of worship, counseling, administration). He therefore proposed that ministry should not be conceptualized fundamentally in these terms. Instead, through an insight derived from process philosophy, he proposed that the acts or operations of ministry be grasped by a concept combining the pastor's subjective orientation with a corresponding objective claim on the pastor from external reality. In other words, ministry is partly a matter of the pastor's aim, goal, intentionality, and faith; but it also entails a realistic response to the world's need, or more accurately, to God's call to serve the needs of the world realistically and in accord with divine will (which may not coincide with our own). The term by which Hiltner proposed to designate this fundamental structure of ministerial action was "perspective," a term perhaps unfortunately chosen in view of its strongly subjective connotations. "Dimension" would probably have been a better choice.[14]

By implication—Hiltner was inexplicit about his process presuppositions here—true ministry occurs when our subjective aim or goal, which is elicited or influenced by God, matches what God is objectively calling us to do in the world, when subjective and objective poles of the perspective correspond. Conversely, when subjective intent and objective call are *not* in correspondence, when the pastor fails to discern or properly respond to the true need of the situation as established by God, something less than true or authentic ministry is the result.[15] (Presumably, it is possible that God's will may be done despite contrary intentions by the pastor, but such occurrences would not properly be called ministry.)

At this point I should acknowledge that I have indulged in a small

---

14. Cf. Coval B. MacDonald, "Methods of Study in Pastoral Theology," in *The New Shape of Pastoral Theology: Essays in Honor of Seward Hiltner*, ed. William B. Oglesby, Jr. (Nashville: Abingdon, 1969).

15. Hiltner, *Preface to Pastoral Theology*, 68–69.

degree of interpretative license by highlighting the underlying process presuppositions and structure in Hiltner's concept of perspective. I believe this account gives a true picture of his actual intent and underlying conceptuality. One of the most serious presentational deficiencies of the *Preface* is its failure to give thorough account of this absolutely crucial concept, especially its theological rationale. Hiltner clearly speaks of the concept as combining ministerial subjectivity or "attitude" with objective "needs of the situation." But he muddies the waters by failing to state his full theological rationale, but choosing the subjectively slanted term *perspective* (which has misled critics, among them Thomas C. Oden[16]), and by ambiguously identifying the objective pole, in certain passages, with the ministerial roles or "offices" as if they, and not the concrete human situation of need, provide the necessary objectivity.[17] Roles are necessary mediating structures, but they cannot by themselves provide an adequate guide to ministerial action unless supplemented and critically applied by means of deeper subjective purposiveness and objective truthfulness to situations.

Likewise, Hiltner's failure to define "what is needed" in explicit theological terms (what *God* is calling for through the situation) has given many the misleading impression that Hiltner was equating these concepts with fallible, subjective human definitions of need which then become normative in ministerial practice. Hiltner was acutely aware that what people or groups think they need may not be what they really (i.e., spiritually) need.[18] His theological assumption was that authentic ministry must be conducted in truth, realistically responding to what is truly needed in given situations.

But whatever its presentational deficiencies, Hiltner's attempt to define ministry, for theological purposes, at a level deeper than social role (or "office," as the older pastoral theologies had it), by means of the concept of perspective, was a striking and significant innovation. Through this conceptual device he hoped to define pastoral practice in a more profound and coherent fashion than had previously been achieved, and in a way that would be sufficiently true to the depth and richness of actual practice to enable significant theologizing to occur from within the pastoral context.

The threefold structure of pastoral perspective. The second point in Hiltner's description of ministerial practice distinguishes three (and only three) fundamental perspectives. It claims that all ministerial action can be described and guided in terms of these three orientations

---

16. Oden, *Contemporary Theology and Psychotherapy*, 90.
17. Hiltner, *Preface to Pastoral Theology*, 18–20.
18. Ibid., 162–68.

and their continuing interplay and that a distinctive branch of operation-centered theology can be constructed from each of them. They are *shepherding,* in which the pastor's aim or goal is directed with "tender solicitous concern" toward the welfare of particular individuals (or small groups of persons in their individuality); *organizing,* in which pastoral concern is directed toward the corporate social and institutional needs and welfare of the church (and the wider community)—helping it become the true organism, the body of Christ; and *communicating,* in which the pastoral aim is focused on what might be called the cultural or symbolic level of need of church and world for meaning, truth, and moral vision through the articulation of the gospel.

In reality, these three forms of need cannot be separated in any categorical sense; they are mutually interdependent. But in practice, that is, from the perspective of one who must act concretely in response to the world, some differentiating and focusing become necessary. Practitioners must prioritize and concentrate their efforts in one of these directions at any given time, however much they must also keep the whole in view and be prepared to alter their dominant perspective.

I shall not elaborate further on the exact meaning Hiltner assigned to the organizing and communicating perspectives, but I do want to stress the ambiguous relationship of all three perspectives to pastoral role functions and especially the interrelationship and fundamental inseparability that Hiltner ascribed to them. A proper understanding of these relationships is crucial for appreciating the depth, subtlety, and descriptive power of Hiltner's theory as a whole.

Typically, activities of personal care and counseling express the shepherding orientation insofar as individual need and welfare are at the center of attention. Leadership functions are normally conducted in the organizing perspective because institutional need is foremost, while preaching, leadership of worship, and teaching ordinarily express the communicating perspective's aim toward noumenal, spiritual, or symbolic need. However, simple correlations of this sort do not always apply and can be highly misleading. Perspectives cannot be equated with social or functional roles. Indeed, the richness of this theory lies precisely in its distance from simple, functional role definitions and the flexibility and subtlety of analysis and guidance that such distance provides. This complexity, however, is also the source of frequent misunderstanding.

Hiltner vigorously insisted that all three perspectives are needed for understanding or guiding any particular act of ministry, but that in every concrete situation one or another of them will, upon a discerning analysis of the situation, be found to provide the primary structuring

for the ministerial event. Thus a personal conversation with a parishioner may indicate that an emotional or psychological need should
be the dominant focus rather than some programmatic, administra-
tive, or disciplinary concern of the church or some specifically spiritual need at the level of meaning, truth, or moral direction.

Yet in true ministry all three kinds of concerns are present with the
pastor even if one perspective, for the time being, is dominant. Thus
there is no situation (such as counseling) that can be adequately
defined by only one perspective or approach (such as shepherding).
Attention must be given to all three even if priority is given to one,
and the pastor must be ready to change the orientation if the objective
need should change. For example, in a conversation focused on emotional or family problems, a solution or insight may emerge which
brings forth another dimension, such as the need for an explicit hear-
ing of the gospel or the need for deepening one's relationship to the
community of faith (or to society) or the need to be disciplined or
guided by the larger body. By the same token, pastoral leadership in
an institutional context may bring forth special needs for prophetic
utterance (communicating) or for "tender solicitous care" of individuals (shepherding).

The three perspectives thus function with continuous relevance to
every situation in variously ordered priorites and with the possibility
of situationally-indicated changes in priority. This calls for true spiritual discernment on the part of the pastor and the responsible exercise of judgment in ambiguous situations. It obviously eliminates rigid
interpretations of what ministry should be in "typical situations" as
dictated by role definitions. And it allows for a rich diversity of practical emphases and orientations in response to the specifics of given
circumstances, viewed within a fundamental unity of purpose. This is
true even though Hiltner failed to specify in precise theological terms
what that unity of purpose is.

Theologically, then, pastoral theology is not simply the theology of
pastoral care and counseling defined as a theory of functional roles,
but is that theology emerging from the theological examination of any
and all acts of ministry where the shepherding perspective is dominant. More precisely, pastoral theology is "that branch or field of theological knowledge and inquiry that brings the shepherding perspective
to bear upon all the operations and functions of the church and the
minister, and then draws conclusions of a theological order from
reflection on these observations."[19] Pastoral theology in this sense is
distinguished from those operation-centered disciplines arising from

19. Ibid., 20.

the other "cognate" perspectives of organizing (ecclesiastical theology) and communicating (homiletical and educational theology).

The concept of shepherding and its "aspects." Hiltner chose the ancient image of the shepherd for his perspective related to individual care despite its anachronistic ring in the modern setting, despite its inconsistency with the less metaphorical terms given the other two perspectives, and despite certain inadequacies inherent in the image itself.[20] In taking these risks he was obviously more concerned to emphasize the biblical and historical continuity of contemporary pastoral care and counseling which has been much influenced by secular psychologies and is often unconscious of its history. He was not, however, unconcerned about the limitations of this metaphor and later sought to correct and supplement them.[21] Perhaps the simple term *caring* would have been better. In any case the basic idea remained unchanged. "Central to the content of shepherding is the shepherd's solicitous concern for the welfare of the sheep." To this attitudinal orientation Hiltner immediately added the complementary objective emphasis: "the necessary presence of some degree of recognition of need in the parishioner and some degree of receptivity to help."[22]

The latter point is especially significant. A distinctive feature of Hiltner's shepherding theory in pastoral theology and its practical implementation in care and counseling is the responsibility he assigns to the parishioner.[23] In this view, which Hiltner borrowed in large part from Carl R. Rogers but which he regarded as quintessentially Christian, the pastor facilitates the caring process in various ways but does not control or coerce it. At least insofar as pastoral care expresses shepherding and not, say, organizing, its cardinal feature is the priority it gives to the immediate needs and resources of the individual. What he did not say but clearly implied was that these needs and resources are in some sense bearers of divine grace, and not exclusively human properties or attributes; they lead one into a deeper life in the spirit. Thus, for instance, the mobilization of internal healing powers eventually moves the process beyond immediate biological and psychological healing to a deeper life in the Spirit, just as a deepening or awakening of spirituality will have ramifications for biopsychic wholeness.[24]

---

20. Cf. Alastair V. Campbell, *Rediscovering Pastoral Care* (Philadelphia: Westminster, 1981), 41–45.

21. Seward Hiltner, *Ferment in the Ministry* (Nashville: Abingdon, 1969), 92–111.

22. Hiltner, *Preface to Pastoral Theology*, 68.

23. Seward Hiltner, *Pastoral Counseling* (Nashville: Abingdon, 1949), 46–55.

24. Hiltner, *Preface to Pastoral Theology*, 98–115; cf. Hiltner's discussion of providence in his *Theological Dynamics* (Nashville: Abingdon, 1972), 55–80.

Within the shepherding perspective itself, Hiltner argued, it is possible to distinguish three (and only three) specific forms or "aspects": *healing* which aims at the restoration of functional wholeness that has been impaired as to direction and/or schedule"; *sustaining*—Hiltner's revision of the traditional concept of comforting—which is defined as the "ministry of support and encouragement through standing by when what had been a whole has been broken or impaired and is incapable of total situational restoration, or at least not now"; and *guiding*, which he initially defines as helping persons "find the paths *when that help has been sought.*"[25] Later, following a lengthy and intricate discussion, he describes guiding as an "eductive" process in which resources and directions are "educed" or drawn forth from the individual to aid in finding his or her own paths.[26]

Hiltner's argument about guiding requires an additional clarification. Guiding is defined as eductive *insofar as it is an aspect of shepherding.* Other forms of guiding (such as moral persuasion and reasoning, clarification of alternatives, or providing information), though appropriate and necessary as pastoral care in many situations, would belong to another perspective. Moral guidance is not limited in principle to its eductive form through the shepherding perspective,[27] though Hiltner did emphasize its importance polemically against the dominant historical tendency to impose corporate values on individuals without honoring and developing their "internal" capacity to participate creatively in the search for, and implementation of, moral responsibility.

Hiltner regarded the three shepherding "aspects" as perspectival in nature no less than the shepherding perspective as a whole. This point has been widely misunderstood. The confusion is perhaps best exemplified in a proposal by William A. Clebsch and Charles R. Jaekle that the rubric of "reconciling" be added to the Hiltnerian trilogy of healing, sustaining, and guiding,[28] a revision that has since become standard in the pastoral literature. Clebsch and Jaekle mistakenly equate Hiltner's shepherding perspective with the functional role of pastoral care and view its three "aspects" as its more particular roles, as evidenced in the history of pastoral care. Since this role typology does not encompass everything in pastoral history, especially its predominant emphasis on the restitution of persons from sin through confes-

25. Hiltner, *Preface to Pastoral Theology*, 90, 116, 69.
26. Ibid., 145–72.
27. Contra Don S. Browning, *Religious Ethics and Pastoral Care* (Philadelphia: Fortress, 1983), 36–38.
28. William A. Clebsch and Charles R. Jaekle, *Pastoral Care in Historical Perspective* (Englewood Cliffs, N.J.: Prentice-Hall, 1964), 9–10.

sion, forgiveness, and penance,[29] and many other forms of interpersonal and family reconciliation, it seemed necessary to add a fourth category of "reconciliation" to Hiltner's three. However, reconciling, though arguably necessary for their historical typology, is inconsistent with the individual focus of Hiltner's shepherding concept. It belongs more appropriately in the social perspective of organizing, which of course includes relationship with God, though Hiltner was not clear enough about this. (A similar confusion of perspectives with the role categories lies behind the recent suggestion to add "nurturing" to Clebsch's and Jaekle's list.[30]) Nevertheless, the Clebsch and Jaekle proposal, though misleading, points to a serious issue in Hiltner's theory—its understanding of the relation between individual, society, and culture, which has led some to criticize it for individualism and moral relativism.[31]

Critical Issues in Hiltner's Pastoral Theology

Many have commented on the historical significance of Hiltner's choice of the term *preface* for the title of his major work. Clebsch and Jaekle observe:

> The twentieth century has yet to produce anything beyond prolegomena to a badly needed, full-blown pastoral theology. . . . It may be that a necessary condition for developing a *pastoral* theology is a degree of general theological consensus and stability beyond anything reasonably to be expected in our lifetime. . . . Perhaps at best the present situation can bestow only what Seward Hiltner entitled one of his books, a *preface* to pastoral theology, and it may be a long time before historical, philosophical, and psychological developments can prepare ground more hospitable to the larger enterprise.[32]

It may be added that the situation has not much changed since this observation was made, though there have been some promising recent developments.[33]

29. Cf. John T. McNeill, *A History of the Cure of Souls* (New York: Harper and Row, 1951).

30. Cf. Clinebell, *Basic Types*, 42–43.

31. Browning, *Religious Ethics and Pastoral Care*, 36–38.

32. Clebsch and Jaekle, *Pastoral Care in Historical Perspective*, xii.

33. Charles V. Gerkin, *Crisis Experience in Modern Life: Theory and Theology in Pastoral Care* (Nashville: Abingdon, 1979); Charles V. Gerkin, *The Living Human Document: Re-Visioning Pastoral Counseling in a Hermeneutical Mode* (Nashville: Abingdon, 1984); James E. Loder, *The Transforming Moment* (New York: Harper and Row, 1981); Thomas C. Oden, *Pastoral Theology: Essentials of Ministry* (San Francisco: Harper and Row, 1983).

Hiltner himself was well aware of the difficulties in the enterprise and the criticism his own efforts had provoked. In the following pages I will focus on two of the principal questions that critics of the *Preface* have raised and will offer my own assessment of them. My aim is to pinpoint as clearly as possible the legitimate issues that require or deserve further comment and to distinguish these from certain misguided or confused criticisms that have, I think, clouded the waters of the Hiltner legacy.

The two topics are the problem of empirical method and the problem of operation-centeredness or pragmatism. I have selected these two in particular because they pertain directly to Hiltner's pastoral theological method, which is the heart and core of his contribution to the discipline. However, I do not wish to suggest that this exhausts the range of critical issues that can be considered with respect to his work. The following are other possibilities: Hiltner's implicit social theory and anthropology, particularly the question of how individuals are related to society and culture is implicit in the threefold perspectival scheme and has important implications for ethics and the practice of moral guidance and evangelism; Hiltner's soteriology or doctrine of salvation, especially the question of how psychological concepts of growth and change relate to theological categories of faith and sanctification; Hiltner's ecclesiology, which is implicit in the theory as a whole and has important implications for pastoral authority; Hiltner's ethics, particularly the question of moral contextualism and the problem of whether this theory is implicitly relativistic or, conversely, socially conservative and elitist. These and other topics deserve more attention in the pastoral theological literature than they have received. For immediate purposes, however, it seems best to limit this introductory discussion to the most central and critical topics in Hiltner's pastoral theology, those that pertain to its basic method.

Empirical Method in Pastoral Theology

Hiltner's theological method is empirical insofar as it asserts that genuine theological knowledge can be obtained from the concrete study of pastoral operations. Neo-orthodox theologians reject this view,[34] even though Hiltner is not empirical in the radical or extreme sense that some critics say. Alastair V. Campbell, for instance, asserts that "instead of the other theological disciplines laying down the norms for understanding the practical functions, Hiltner is suggesting

---

34. Oden, *Contemporary Theology and Psychotherapy*. Cf. Eduard Thurneysen, *A Theology of Pastoral Care*, trans. Jack A. Worthington and Thomas Wieser (Richmond: John Knox, 1962).

A Perspectival Pastoral Theology

that the study of the practical functions will produce some theological insights." He concludes that Hiltner "seems to have no place for the category of revelation—even in the negative sense of deliberately espousing 'natural theology.' " A similar point has been made by Oden and may well express a widely held impression of Hiltner's theology.[35]

This criticism, however, is not well founded. For Hiltner, pastoral operations do not yield theological insights unless theological questions, and the whole context of faith that they assume, are first brought to them. His pastoral theology presupposed and explicitly asserted the definitive and "final" revelation of God in Jesus Christ and limited the potential theological learnings of pastoral theology to a completing and correcting of the human understanding of that revelation.[36] This formula clearly attributes normative significance to empirical data but only in a qualified sense. Contemporary experience critically develops and corrects the human assimilation or understanding of revelation, which is always imperfectly grasped by human beings. It does not replace the historic revelation of God in Christ or function independently of it in the sense of a natural theology.

Moreover, Hiltner's principle of a "two-way street" implies a dialogical relationship between scriptural revelation and contemporary experience. In this dialogue the data of experience must also be deepened and corrected by the historic revelation of God in Christ. Though Hiltner was imprecise in conceptualizing this point and was inclined for polemical reasons to emphasize the theological authority and potential importance of empirical data, his method of doing so, as James N. Lapsley has pointed out,[37] clearly belongs to the tradition of modified or dialectical empiricism at the University of Chicago (e.g., Daniel Day Williams), not to the more radical wing of Wieland and Meland.

Clarifying the dialectical intent of Hiltner's method does not in itself solve the theological problem it poses. Hiltner's two-way street and other statements on method are agenda for continuing theological clarification that will require more precise formulation than he himself provided, if his program for pastoral theology is to have a serious theological future. These problems are obviously not unique to pastoral theology but are part of the whole complex of issues related to

35. See Campbell, "Is Practical Theology Possible?" 221–22; Oden, *Contemporary Theology and Psychotherapy*, 57, 90.

36. Hiltner, *Preface to Pastoral Theology*, 222, n. 17.

37. James N. Lapsley, "Pastoral Theology Past and Present," in *The New Shape of Pastoral Theology: Essays in Honor of Seward Hiltner*, ed. William B. Oglesby, Jr. (Nashville: Abingdon, 1969), 39.

revelation and authority in contemporary theology. While it is no dis-
credit to Hiltner to say that he did not contribute to that larger methodological discussion in fundamental or philosophical theology,
Hiltnerian pastoral theology will need to be more deeply dependent
upon discussions in those disciplines to clarify options than he himself
was, or than pastoral theology in general has been. In order for pastoral operations to yield theological insights in response to theological
questions, they must know more clearly what is meant by "empirical
data" and "experience" and what kind and degree of authority they
have in relation to a developed doctrine of revelation and theological
knowledge.

It seems to me that two particular revisions need to be made in
Hiltner's empiricism regardless of how the more basic theological
issues are resolved. First, Hiltnerian methodology needs something
like a "critical method" or "critical consciousness" in its appeal to
empirical data. There are no "uninterpreted facts" in either the natural
sciences or in the social sciences. As modern critical theory has
argued, it is philosophically essential to become aware of implicit
meanings and interpretations in all so-called neutral findings of science and what hidden interests they may serve.[38] This need not completely undermine the authority of empirical research but it does
significantly qualify and relativize its findings—more, I think, than
Hiltner's own writings typically presuppose. In particular, psychological and psychotherapeutic ideas and data need to be critiqued in terms
of their implicit philosophies and ethics, especially insofar as appeal
is made to their authority in pastoral theology.

Second, the empirical focus of Hiltner's method needs to be
expanded beyond intense concern with individual pastoral "cases" (*his*
legacy from Boisen). The empirical domain could well be enlarged to
include the more general social and cultural context in which particular ministries occur without losing the unique and important learnings that can be gained from close-up, detailed study of individual
pastoral events.

To be sure, one of the most valuable contributions of the Hiltner
legacy is precisely this insistence on the importance of the individual
case which, in its inevitable ambiguity and stubborn complexity, invar-
iably exceeds any explanatory scheme we may impose upon it and
thus challenges us to new and better understanding. Hiltner's case
emphasis was, in part, a kind of moral or spiritual principle, a check
against the hubris of the abstract theoretician or the self-interested or

---

38. See Jurgen Habermas, *Knowledge and Human Interests*, trans. Jeremy Shapiro
(Boston: Beacon, 1971), 301–17.

class-interested interpretations of the pastoral ideologist. But an exclusive focus on the "case" may well fail to detect the deeper patterns of cultural and historical life whose influence provides the very presuppositions in terms of which the case data are constructed and which may seem self-evident or unproblematical to the close-up observer. Hiltner himself was not unaware of this problem and often exhibited an acute sociological consciousness. But his formal method needs to incorporate this principle more explicitly, possibly along the lines demonstrated by Charles V. Gerkin and Don S. Browning in their recent writings.

One final problem may be noted concerning empirical method. Those who worked with Hiltner remember that he placed great stress on methodology in dissertations and the like. At the same time, he resisted student tendencies to become so immersed in abstract problems of method that nothing ever gets done by way of empirical study. There was a need to plunge into the empirical data at some point, whatever the methodological uncertainties or ambiguities. This tendency is well demonstrated in his writings and has led some pastoral theologians to conclude that Hiltner was an American activist at heart, impatient with basic intellectual questions. Oden cites Hiltner's analogy between counseling methods and the ecumenical movement where, Hiltner argues, progress on doctrine tends to follow, not precede, cooperation in mission.[39]

The question is whether this activist turn represents a failure on Hiltner's part to face the tough intellectual questions of methodology, as Oden charges, or whether it represents a defensible, even fundamental point about method itself. Hiltner was certainly correct that in the practical work of research in any field, method is subject to continuing revision as work progresses, even if this fact is not represented in the final published product where the "methodology" may appear to be fully formed at the outset of the study. The question is: Is this merely a fact of practical experience or a point worthy of elevation to a methodological principle?

The principle involved might entail recognizing a reciprocal relationship between the search for methodological clarity and the encounter with empirical data. From this point of view clarity about method is not worked out fully beforehand but is achieved gradually and indirectly through actual engagement with the data in a series of dialectical moves in which the knowing subject alternately stands back critically from the data and is in turn encountered by it. This interplay between subjectivity and objectivity, which requires the risk of con-

39. Oden, *Contemporary Theology and Psychotherapy*, 84ff.

crete empirical engagement as well as the courage of critical distanc-
ing, implies that methodology can never be wholly separated from
substantive inquiry, and likewise that the knowing subject can never
be entirely separated from the known object. We know ourselves
through knowing the world, and we know the world through knowing
ourselves. In this perspective Hiltner's empiricism in pastoral theology, his tendency to turn to pastoral data before all methodological
details were worked out, was more than an expression of American
activism. It was also an important—perhaps even a necessary—principle of method. Indeed, the question may be, not whether pastoral
theology is philosophically ready to engage in empirical research, but
whether it could *ever* become philosophically ready without *first* taking
the empirical plunge in some form.

Pragmatism and the Concept
of Operation-Centered Inquiry

Perhaps the most serious criticism of Hiltner's work pertains to its
alleged pragmatism. Oden, for instance, finds Hiltner guilty of an
"uncritical directionless activism so native to American pragmatism"
while Campbell laments the "limbo of pragmatism" into which Hiltner's theories would lead the field.[40] These and other critics are concerned, and rightly so, that an exclusive concentration on practical
principles and techniques would deprive pastoral theology of intellectual and theological content, sever it from its historical tradition, and
reinforce a social and institutional conservatism in ministry. Hiltner
is often cited as the architect and chief expression of such trends of
this kind in American pastoral care. So the question arises whether,
or in what sense, his theories espouse a philosophy of pragmatism.
This problem, as I shall endeavor to show, is finally a matter of determining exactly what is meant by the concept of operation-centered
inquiry.

To the general question whether Hiltner was a pragmatist I think
the answer must be both yes and no. There is certainly a spirit of
problem-solving practicality and a neglect of basic theological questions in his early work, *Pastoral Counseling*. But it would be misleading
to describe his later work, or indeed his work as a whole, in a similar
fashion as "unvarnished pragmatism," especially if "pragmatism" is
taken, as in popular usage, to mean either a disregard for theory or,
worse, the reduction of theory to the rationalizing of practical aims
and techniques. Hiltner's *Preface* is obviously an effort at sustained,
fundamental theory-building, and his other writings are replete with

---

40. Ibid., 84; Campbell, "Is Practical Theology Possible?" 223.

theoretical principles, concerns, and problems whose consideration he obviously regarded as central to responsible pastoral theory and practice.[41]

In a more technical sense, Hiltner did stand in a significant way in the tradition of American philosophical pragmatism, as Oden rightly contends.[42] His intellectual mentor in this connection was undoubtedly John Dewey. Dewey's influence is evident at least to the extent that Hiltner's thought shows considerable sympathy with one of Dewey's basic notions—that *thinking* always arises in a context of doubt or uncertainty, that it aims at some form of problem-solving, and that it is always subject to correction through further experience. Ideas, in this view, are not simple "copies of experience" (as in empiricism) but represent strategies for active coping with experience—"plans of action or proposals formed in context of a problem as a possible solution."[43] Hiltner, with psychoanalytic theory, believes that thinking is an activity of adaptation or of coping that functions with an inherently experimental logic. Ideas perform work. Thinking is not a matter of contemplation but of "inquiry," a term Hiltner used pervasively and undoubtedly borrowed from Dewey. Hiltner was therefore interested to know what ideas were "driving at," what their intention or function was for those who held or advocated them, and thus what any system of ideas was attempting to achieve in its historical context.

This way of "thinking about thinking" accounts for the often insightful but theologically incomplete treatment Hiltner gives to various theological doctrines in the *Preface* and more so in his later work, *Theological Dynamics*. In these discussions theological doctrines are subjected to a "dynamic analysis" in order to discern their original intuitions, guiding insights, and the functional ends toward which they somehow strive (literally or figuratively?). Such an analysis, Hiltner believes, provides important clues as to what particular doctrines are really about—that is, their basic direction—which a biblical or systematic theologian would need to consider. Hiltner himself, however, did not take up the constructive task of systematically reformulating doctrines. By and large, he was content to leave the matter at the level of functional analysis with "insights" or "implications" for other branches of theology. Hiltner's fondness for the term *insight* as a designation of truth also reveals his functionalist turn of mind. Its dynamic connotation aptly suggests the role of thought as a contex-

41. See Hiltner, *Ferment in the Ministry and Theological Dynamics*.
42. Oden, *Contemporary Theology and Psychotherapy*, 81–85.
43. See Gertrude Ezorsky, "Pragmatic Theory of Truth," in *The Encyclopedia of Philosophy*, ed. Paul Edwards (New York: Macmillan and The Free Press, 1967), 6:429.

tually embodied, forward-moving problem-solving activity and the nature of ideas and theories as projecting experimental designs upon reality.

It is an interesting question, however, whether Hiltner did subscribe, or could have subscribed fully, to Dewey's pragmatic theory of truth in its complete philosophical development. By his own profession, Hiltner was basically sympathetic with Whiteheadian process thought from which Deweyan pragmatism, though closely related, must be distinguished at precisely this point.[44] For Dewey it was meaningless to consider ideas as true or false in terms of some supposed correspondence with reality apart from, or antecedent to, the context of practical "inquiry." Ideas "become true" through experimental verification; truth is a " 'mutable concept' " which " 'happens to an idea' when it becomes a verified or warranted assertion," that is, when it works to solve a problem.[45] Truth in this view is emptied of absolute meaning and denied a principle of ultimate correspondence with reality. The Whiteheadian view, on the other hand, maintains a version of the correspondence notion of truth as "the conformity of appearance to reality"[46] and seeks to formulate universal categories to describe experience (or reality). Thus Hiltner's stated sympathy for process theory and his implicit utilization of it in his *Preface* and other writings implies a rejection of Dewey's extreme pragmatism, assuming that Hiltner was philosophically self-conscious and coherent about the question. It is hard to imagine, however, that he could have followed Dewey's thinking completely in view of his theological commitments (if nothing else), though it is clear that he was much influenced by Dewey's notion of thought as problem-solving inquiry.

The question of Hiltner's philosophical background is in one sense a historical problem that need not be further explored in this context, though it does have a bearing on the problem of interpreting certain key points in his pastoral theology, especially the concept of operation-centered inquiry (or discipline). The question is whether this central concept intrinsically or inevitably ties Hiltnerian pastoral theology to the pragmatic theory of truth. In this connection the problem is not whether Hiltner's theory implies pragmatism in the sense of practice devoid of theory, but in the sense of practice controlling or determining theory—theory as the mere instrument of problem-solving practice

44. See Hiltner, *Theological Dynamics*, 217. Cf. Bernard E. Meland, "The Future of Empirical Theology," in *Essays in Divinity*, ed. Jerald C. Brauer (Chicago: University of Chicago Press, 1969), 7:18–40.

45. Ezorsky, "Pragmatic Theory of Truth," 429.

46. John B. Cobb, Jr., *A Christian Natural Theology Based on the Thought of Alfred North Whitehead* (Philadelphia: Westminster, 1965), 104–5.

without the kind of normative checks and balances associated with correspondence theories of truth and more objectivist theories of ethics. Campbell, for instance, is concerned that the division of logic- and operation-centered disciplines *in principle* introduces a fatal division between pastoral theology as a practical enterprise and biblical, historical, and systematic theology, leading ultimately to a loss of theological orientation in pastoral practice as well.[47]

The problem is to determine precisely what Hiltner's concept of operation-centered discipline means and what it implies. Does being "centered" on operations mean the same as being "about" operations? If so, pastoral theology would be a theory of operations or, more exactly, the theory of shepherding as a practical function. At points Hiltner says something close to this: "As an inquiry what pastoral theology is systematic about is the actual process by which shepherding—healing, sustaining, or guiding—is brought about."[48] But if this is the case it would be difficult to escape Campbell's criticism, assuming (with Campbell) that an operation-centered or practical discipline would be one that essentially brackets fundamental questions (at least tentatively assuming answers to them) in order to concentrate on developing instrumental methodologies and theories. The resulting practical theory is based upon such assumptions and operates within their frame of reference. Subordinating larger scientific and theological questions would not mean totally eliminating or ignoring them, but it would deprive them of a central or critical role in the work of the discipline. And this is precisely Campbell's point: operation-centeredness deprives theology and ethics of their controlling interest in the pastoral theological enterprise.

Of course it is not necessary to assume that operation-centered disciplines need be entirely closed to questions of a more fundamental order. Indeed a second interpretation of Hiltner's "operation-centered" concept emphasizes this possibility. In this view pastoral theology "originates in" operations but is not wholly or finally "about" operations. Practical methods and problems provide the immediate occasion in which something of a more general, nonpractical nature is learned about the world or about values, meanings, and the like, transcending the initial concerns of practice. Here pastoral theology becomes a variant of contextual theology (e.g., liberation or feminist theology), differing from other types only in the topics to which it gives special attention, and in the particular slant it brings from its pastoral origins to all theological topics. Its content would *not* be organized around

---

47. Campbell, "Is Practical Theology Possible?" 222.
48. Hiltner, *Preface to Pastoral Theology*, 222, n. 15.

theories of pastoral practice, at least not primarily or essentially, but around certain enduring themes of faith and life having special relevance to practice (such as the relation of sin to sickness).

Such a pastoral theology might be said to reach down through the immediate circumstances of practice (as well as their broader historical and cultural context) into the flow or process of reality itself to gain insights into the meaning of faith and the structure of reality as revealed contextually through faith. This aim toward general truth more than practical theory or method seems to be what Hiltner has in mind in much of his *Preface,* where he asserts that "pastoral theology is not a different kind of theology [from biblical or doctrinal theologies] in terms of ultimate content . . . but its principle of self-organization is uniquely its own, just as theirs are."[49]

This definition of operation-centeredness provides an attractive alternative to the more narrow one previously cited. It could scarcely be faulted for pragmatism and is consistent with Hiltner's cardinal intention of establishing the operation-centered disciplines as fundamental contributors to theology. But there is also a problem here. If operation-centeredness means using the pastoral occasion as an opportunity to enrich or expand upon more general theological themes, it risks losing its distinctively practical character. This is because pastors are more than observers, even "participant observers." They are practitioners, persons required to take action involving the exercise of judgment, influence, and responsibility. This fact, I would contend, is of fundamental importance in shaping the way all practitioners (unlike observers) construe their situations, perceive facts, and evaluate possibilities. It is not to say that perception or judgment is necessarily distorted by the need to act; the practitioner role may actually heighten one's observational and reflective powers. But in any case it will substantially order and orient one's grasp of the situation, creating a distinctively practical frame of reference.

If pastoral theology's operation-centeredness is defined in terms of its contextual location in the situation of practice, therefore, it must fully incorporate this distinctive feature of the practitioner's frame of reference into the "organizing principle" of its emerging theology. Only in this way could pastoral theology, as a form of contextual theology, be authentically pastoral and not merely observational. The organizing principle of pastoral theology *must* express the practical orientation of the practitioner who is basically concerned with what to do and how to proceed (even if the best way forward be silence or inaction).

The final, comprehensive aim of pastoral theology, then, must be

49. Ibid., 21.

to develop theories of practice (or of shepherding), that is, *practical knowledge.* Generating such theories may stimulate insights into life, faith, truth, and goodness, but the procedure must eventually subsume and subordinate general questions to the fundamental practical one of "How to proceed?" The question can be asked in very concrete situations or in more generic terms at higher levels of abstraction. In any case, this is finally the only consistent meaning that can be ascribed to Hiltner's concept of operation-centeredness. It presupposes a discipline (or group of disciplines) whose basic, essential aim is to produce *practical knowledge* or, more exactly, practical *theological* knowledge.

We need to ask: Is there such a thing? If so, what is it like and how is it different from and related to other forms of theological knowledge? What is "practical" about it? What is "theological"? Is there a contradiction in the very concept, that is, can knowledge concerned with "what works" and "how to do it" also be inherently theological? Campbell and others who believe that Hiltner's operation-centered idea is an invitation to move down the slippery slopes of pragmatism are not without some justification. Certainly it is not customary or self-evident to suppose that the attempt to solve practical problems typically opens up visions of the good, the beautiful, and the true—much less the divine. And even if it can be shown that practical disciplines do in fact produce important knowledge transcending their practical aims (e.g., one thinks of secular theories of personality deriving from psychiatric practice, or history-changing insights into sin, grace, and God coming from Luther's struggles with medieval penitential practices), still this fact does not resolve the underlying question concerning the possibility of generating theological knowledge that does *not* surrender its practical character. If the essence of operation-centeredness lies in the production of *practical* theological knowledge, it will have to be made clear what such knowledge is and how it is possible, whatever "nonpractical" knowledge such inquiry may also produce. I shall return to this problem shortly.

The problem of defining operation-centeredness in Hiltner's thought leads to the general question of what options, if any, are available for Hiltnerian theory at this point. As Campbell notes with appropriate surprise, the problem has really not been discussed seriously by Hiltner's followers. But I would suggest that a few recent proposals in the field, though not necessarily by "Hiltnerians," may be construed as responses to this problem posed by Hiltner. Three of these may be briefly noted as a conclusion to this discussion.

First, there is Campbell's proposal itself, which may be termed "situation-centered" in contrast to Hiltner's operation-centered one.

Campbell's short article does not elaborate. What he seems to have in mind, however, is an open, heuristic, imaginative, and unsystematic discipline concerned with suggesting "concrete proposals for the restructuring of the Church's life . . . , for the style of life of individual Christians within the 'secular' structures of society, and for the renewal and reforming of the secular structures themselves."[50] Campbell is critical of Hiltner's narrow focus of the discipline on the work of the individual minister rather than the church as a whole, and his proposal would significantly shift the direction of pastoral theology from practical "operations" to social and cultural "structures." This leaves the specifically practical or operational aspect of the discipline ambiguous if not excluded, though it retains Hiltner's empirical concern with concrete "situations," coupled with a stronger emphasis on the critical function of the classical disciplines. It is an important but secondary matter whether the operational focus is limited to the individual minister (it was not so limited in principle for Hiltner) or extended to the whole church. In either case Campbell's proposal would appear to solve the discipline's problem by rejecting operation-centeredness as its definitive feature, insofar as this entails attention to problems of "how to proceed" and "how to do it."

A second, closely related suggestion comes from Browning, who proposes that pastoral theology be a branch of theological ethics whose "primary task" is to "bring together theological ethics and the social sciences to articulate a normative vision of the human life cycle." Like Campbell, Browning would broaden the scope of the field to include the work of the whole church, with an emphasis on its interaction with the public, secular order. But unlike Campbell, Browning specifically includes the aim of developing "a theology of those pastoral acts through which this normative vision of the human life cycle is appropriately mediated. . . ."[51] The emphasis of Browning's proposal, however, falls on the construction of norms and visions rather than the experimental development of practical methodologies as such. Like Campbell, he fears that an emphasis on practical method will lose sight of the moral and religious meanings by which methods are given purpose and critique. His construction, like Campbell's, would basically shift the discipline's focus from practical method to what Hiltner would call a more "logic-centered" concern for defining moral and religious meaning.

A third possibility that I have proposed, and which has some similarity to positions developed by Murray Stewart Thompson and Donald Capps, is to retain the operation-centered or practical focus of the

50. Campbell, "Is Practical Theology Possible?" 226.
51. Browning, *Practical Theology*, 187.

discipline as its distinctive feature, but to expand and partially rein-
terpret what is meant by operation-centered knowledge, drawing a
basic distinction between that and other kinds of knowing.[52] The customary meaning of practical knowledge emphasizes skills and techniques of practice. My proposal would significantly broaden the idea
beyond Hiltner's professionalist concern with "operations" to something like the "wisdom of experience." The latter concept includes
technical know-how but grasps the particulars of technique within a
larger sense of how life as a whole proceeds, and hence how the practitioner can proceed within it. Wisdom about the flow or movement
of life can be seen easily in ordinary instances of highly developed
expertise—for example, the wisdom of an experienced psychotherapist
or teacher goes far beyond merely knowing the technical "tricks of the
trade." Expanded to religious dimensions, wisdom in "how to live"
(and thus wisdom in how to love, how to care, how to heal) is wisdom
about the totality of life experienced as theological narrative or drama.
It is an ongoing quest for right and true relationship with the God "in
whom we live, and move, and have our being."

In this proposal, pastoral theology is a specialized form of religious
wisdom about how to live, specialized by its focus on the question of
how to care for others. As wisdom, it constitutes a lived unity of experience, knowledge, and tradition, and is literally but not narrowly practical. Its practicality—if that is the proper term—is not defined by its
mastery of instrumental techniques of care but by its fittingness with
the character and movement of life as a whole. It is therefore practical
in a profound way which entails a sense of the nature of human life
and of God and how best to participate in life with God. Discovering
the answers to these questions, as particularly related to the task of
caring, is in this conception the work of pastoral theology. In one
respect this is simply a broadening of Hiltner's "operation-centered"
idea, but it also entails a partial redirection of his view of the discipline. Its primary task is not to produce theological knowledge or
"insights" for common appropriation on the "village green of theological integration," though it may spark such insights, but to integrate
theological knowledge from the other disciplines (and from the secular
sciences) into a lived unity of "practical" experience and wisdom.[53] It
differs from the other theological disciplines (Hiltner's "logic-

---

52. Rodney J. Hunter, "The Future of Pastoral Theology," *Pastoral Psychology* 29
(1980): 58–69; Lapsley, "Practical Theology and Pastoral Care"; Murray Stewart
Thompson, *Grace and Forgiveness in Ministry* (Nashville: Abingdon, 1981); Donald
Capps, *Life Cycle Theory and Pastoral Care* (Philadelphia: (Fortress, 1983), 99–120.

53. Cf. M. Thornton, *The Function of Theology* (London: Hodder and Stoughton,
1968), 37–57.

centered" types) not simply by the kind of data it examines and reflects upon or by its "organizing principle," but it differs generically. It is a different order of knowledge and therefore cannot be literally or directly "integrated" with the other disciplines, even though it speaks of God and the ultimate mysteries of life and offers its own insights into them. Whether this approach can adequately solve the problem of Hiltnerian theory, however, remains to be seen.

Conclusion

In this chapter I have attempted to interpret Hiltner's concept of pastoral theology as a theory of continuing importance for the field, deserving more critical examination, development, and experimental implementation than it has received. In particular I have emphasized the importance of his concepts of perspective and operation-centered inquiry, noting certain misunderstandings that have impeded the recognition of their potential usefulness, but also noting difficulties requiring further clarification or revision.

In some respects Hiltner's basic theory may be stronger, more coherent, and more persuasive than even his own illustration and elaboration of it, and it is therefore important to make a series of distinctions between its illustrative presentation and its formal principles. The chief instances of this are two.

First, the traditional or "logic-centered" disciplines can and must speak critically to pastoral theology and the other "operation-centered" fields in keeping with Hiltner's two-way-street principle, even though he himself tends to underemphasize this aspect of his theory. Perhaps for polemical reasons, Hiltner was mainly interested in arguing the other way, that is, for the potentially constructive contributions of the practical modes of inquiry to the traditional fields.

Second, there is also a need to keep clearly in mind Hiltner's distinction between pastoral care (which may function in certain respects through all three perspectives) and the special priority given to the individual's initiative, responsibility, and creativity when pastoral care is done through the shepherding perspective. In principle, there are important modes of pastoral relationships with individuals that are not shepherding, for example, evangelical proclamation, education, liturgical participation and celebration, even various forms of corporate guidance and discipline. All of these activities can be viewed under certain circumstances as providing "pastoral care," though they are not shepherding in Hiltner's specific sense. To some extent Hiltner himself, and certainly many of his readers and critics, have tended to narrow the meaning of pastoral care to shepherding, and then found it wanting. Not only do the pastoral values of the other perspectives need to be fully recognized and developed, but their roles need to be considered more fully even when shepherding is dominant. There is much more complexity to this theory in principle than has been realized in theoretical critique and practice.

There are also fundamental problems with Hiltner's theory that need to be more fully explored. I mentioned several of them in passing, including the need to examine the theory's implicit social theory, its soteriology, and its ecclesiology. In this essay, I have concentrated on two major issues, both related to methodology in pastoral theology: the problem of empiricism in theology and its relation especially to natural theology and revelation, and the problem of conceptualizing operation-centered inquiry or practical knowledge and its relation to so-called logic-centered forms of knowing. I have tried to argue that Hiltner was not a radical empiricist but attempted to relate his empirical method to a concept of special revelation, even though he did not develop the topic theologically. With respect to operation-centered inquiry, I have tried to argue that a sophisticated form of philosophical pragmatism, and not a popular perversion of the idea, may be implicit in his work. I think this feature of his thought has the potential for profound development in terms of a discipline conceived as a form of practical religious wisdom. In any case Hiltner's guiding insight, namely, that a fundamental mode of theological reflection can be derived from within the practice of ministry, is an idea whose possibilities and limits have yet to be fully explored. Certainly it should not be dismissed as a crude form of pragmatism. In any case, the work of coming to terms with Hiltner's legacy for pastoral theology has just begun.

4

Conscience and
Christian Perfectionism

K. Brynolf Lyon

Anton T. Boisen articulated a vision of human life grounded firmly in an ideal of Christian perfectionism. Given the later fate of the relationship of ethics and pastoral care, Boisen's thought stands as a remarkable effort to develop the implications of that vision out of the context of a fully moral psychology of the person. The recent call to deepen our reflection on the moral seriousness of pastoral care provides us with an opportunity and incentive to wonder again about Boisen's work in this regard.[1] In this chapter we will study, in particular, the relationship between Boisen's ethic and his moral psychology, that is, his understanding of the dynamics of the moral life. The issues at stake in this discussion are complex and multidimensional. We must be concerned about the adequacy and appropriateness not only of the ethic itself and the moral psychology itself, but also the

---

1. Don S. Browning, *The Moral Context of Pastoral Care* (Philadelphia: Westminster, 1976); Don S. Browning, *Religious Ethics and Pastoral Care* (Philadelphia: Fortress, 1983); John C. Hoffman, *Ethical Confrontation in Counseling* (Chicago: University of Chicago Press, 1981); Archie Smith, Jr., *The Relational Self* (Nashville: Abingdon, 1982); James Poling, "Ethical Reflection and Pastoral Care, Part I," *Pastoral Psychology* 32 (1984): 106–14; James Poling, "Ethical Reflection and Pastoral Care, Part II," *Pastoral Psychology* 32 (1984): 160–70; Ralph L. Underwood, *Empathy and Confrontation in Pastoral Care* (Philadelphia: Fortress, 1986).

adequacy and appropriateness of the way they are related to one another. We can only give a sweeping appraisal of these issues. Yet, as we gain increasing insight into the variegated character of the landscape upon which a practical theology of care must be constructed, we must gain facility in addressing precisely these kinds of issues. Boisen's work provides us with a good case study through which to survey a portion of that terrain.

The theme of this chapter will be developed in three steps. First, we will critically examine the central features and tensions in Boisen's ethic. Second, we will see how his constructive ethic is related to his moral psychology, giving particular attention to the way in which the tensions that arise in his ethic are deepened in his understanding of the dynamics of the moral life. Finally, we will briefly examine some of the implications to be discerned from Boisen's work for a contemporary practical theology of care. We will find in the course of this discussion that though we cannot affirm all of the specifics of his vision, we may, nevertheless, be better able to see the importance and place of the underlying issues in our own reflection on these matters for having taken Boisen's effort seriously.

Boisen's Ethic

Regrettably, Boisen never presented his ethic in a systematic fashion in his published work. What we can gather about that ethic must be assembled from scraps of suggestive comments from a variety of his writings. We are left with the task, then, of providing a coherent order to his discussion. To organize his ethic, I will follow part of the format suggested by Don S. Browning for discerning the practical moral theology implicit in any theory of pastoral care.[2] In particular, I will address the first three dimensions of Browning's scheme of practical moral reasoning, roughly stated as the basic theological images and metaphors that contextualize Boisen's ethic, the moral principles he proposed for the ordering of life, and the central values and human needs that he argued ought to be promoted in the moral life.

Elements of the Theological Framework
of Boisen's Ethic

Boisen articulated the foundational images and metaphors that contextualized his ethic in relation to his understanding of Jesus—an understanding heavily influenced by Pauline theology in addition to his own perspective on the "problem-solving" character of crisis expe-

---

2. Browning, *Religious Ethics and Pastoral Care.*

rience.[3] While Boisen's reading of the life, death, and resurrection of Jesus may well seem to us now as articulated on dubious principles of scriptural interpretation, our focus here must be on how his understanding of Jesus contextualized his ethic. In this regard, Boisen's understanding of Jesus seems to conform largely to what James M. Gustafson has referred to as the "Jesus Christ, the pattern" model of relating Christology and ethics.[4] In other words, through Jesus the pattern for the holy and righteous life is disclosed. As Boisen put it, "[Jesus'] summons to be perfect even as our heavenly Father is perfect is therefore the basis and charter of the Christian enterprise."[5] What it meant to strive to be perfect, in Boisen's perspective, was filled out through three central images: harmony, conflict and sacrifice, and healing.

First, the *imagery of harmony* is crucial to this pattern. For Boisen, the depths of life disclose an urge toward harmony; particularly, a harmony between the personal and the social dimensions of existence. Theologically, Boisen argued that Jesus' resolution of his crisis experience in the wilderness was the supreme exemplification of this harmony. Jesus, in other words, was able to achieve a remarkable harmony between his own inner dynamics and the social world. What made sense of this interpretation of Jesus for Boisen is that the term *God* referred to "the composite impress of those who [the individual] counts most worthy of love and honor." Thus, to say that Jesus achieved harmony between his own inner world and the "social whole" is to say that he achieved harmony with God. As this related to his ethic, the harmony between the personal and the social disclosed through Jesus reveals something of the pattern we are to emulate in our own lives. In Boisen's words, "To be at one with that which is supreme in our hierarchy of loyalties, that to which men generally give the name of God, is ever essential to mental health."[6]

The pattern of life revealed through Jesus in Boisen's perspective, however, had its core in *the imagery of conflict, sacrifice, and the need for self-control.* This imagery is most clearly evidenced in Boisen's understanding of the doctrine of the cross. The cross, Boisen said, was the "heart" of the message of Jesus. As Boisen explained its central

3. See, in particular, Anton T. Boisen, *The Exploration of the Inner World* (New York: Harper, 1936), 125–41; Anton T. Boisen, "What Did Jesus Think of Himself?" *Journal of Bible and Religion* 20 (1952): 7–12.

4. James M. Gustafson, *Christ and the Moral Life* (Chicago: University of Chicago, 1979).

5. Anton T. Boisen, "Christian Perfectionism," *Chicago Theological Register* (January 1934): 10–13.

6. Boisen, *Exploration of the Inner World*, 307, 173.

meaning, "Through [Jesus] there comes to us the imperious summons to assume the same responsibility which he assumed and to give ourselves completely to the sacrificial task of bringing in the new world that ought to be."[7] The imagery of the cross, then, gave to Boisen's understanding of the depths of life a profound sense of struggle, sacrifice, and conflict which served as an ever-present counterpoint to the imagery of harmony. Indeed, the imagery of conflict and sacrifice frequently seems to eclipse the imagery of harmony altogether in his descriptions of the present reality of the human situation. Harmony, in other words, is decidedly more "not yet" than it is "already" in Boisen's thought. This predominance of the doctrine of the cross clearly underwrote the haunting overtone in Boisen's ethic on self-control. As Boisen declared, "The garden of the heart, left untended, is always taken over by weeds." Vigilance at the garden of the heart thus became the dominant mood of his ethic.[8]

The third aspect of the imagery of the pattern of life revealed through Jesus in Boisen's thought is that of *healing*. There is, Boisen argued, a healing power within nature itself.[9] These healing forces of nature may reveal themselves initially in breakdown or disruption in our lives. Yet, this breakdown may well have a healing purpose within it which may be realized if the right situation prevails within the individual and he or she is acceptable to their social group. There is a clear analogy in Boisen's thought between this understanding of the healing forces of nature and God's grace. Indeed, through the life and death of Jesus, Boisen said, we can discern that healing love which lies at the center of nature and history. Given the strenuous emphasis on the cross, of course, Boisen was implying no doctrine of easy grace in this imagery. Just as with his understanding of the healing power of nature, the reality of God's grace does not imply that now "we might be saved from the consequences of our weakness and selfishness" or that we can "escape the requirements of unconditional commitment to the making of the better world." The grace of God available to all carries with it the necessity of repentance and the giving of oneself "earnestly to the pursuit of the better life."[10] We might well wonder here whether Boisen's doctrine of grace is not only not "easy," but also not unconditional. Part of the ambiguity here may well lie with Boisen's tendency to run together the notions of grace, salvation, and jus-

7. Ibid., 140.

8. Anton T. Boisen, "The Period of Beginnings," *Journal of Pastoral Care* 5 (1951): 15–16; see also E. Brooks Holifield, *A History of Pastoral Care in America: From Salvation to Self-Realization* (Nashville: Abingdon, 1983), 246.

9. Boisen, *Exploration of the Inner World*, 53–57.

10. Boisen, "Christian Perfectionism," 13; *Exploration of the Inner World*, 293.

tification. Whatever the reason for, and extent of, this ambiguity, Boisen nonetheless affirmed a healing power at the depths of life.

The three images I have isolated in my attempt to discern the theological framework of Boisen's ethic are, of course, related to one another. The imagery of harmony in Boisen's thought has primary reference to the vision of the life toward which we are to strive. The imagery of sacrifice and self-control refers, most directly, to the nature of the path we must follow in our movement toward that harmony. And, finally, the imagery of a healing force within the world intends to convey that power in the depths of life by which we are enabled to enter onto the path. We must now move, however, to the more specific kinds of moral principles which Boisen espoused in the context of this theological framework.

Moral Principles in Boisen's Ethic

The two most obvious norms which perform moral functions in Boisen's thought are love of God and love of neighbor. As he wrote, "Jesus in his emphasis on love to God and love to one's neighbor goes at once to the heart of all religion and of all ethical systems."[11] Boisen never provided us, however, with a formal discussion of his understanding of those norms. What we can gather about his construal of them must be discerned from what he said about the requirements of love generally and the notion of universality.

The requirements of love form the *central substantive claim* of Boisen's ethic. While Boisen talked about love in both prescriptive and descriptive terms, I am here concerned simply with its prescriptive meaning. This is not always an easy differentiation to make in Boisen's work since he so frequently runs the prescriptive and the descriptive aspects of his discussion together. Yet, given the centrality of love to his ethic, an effort must be made.

The best way to approach the moral character of love in Boisen's thought is through his understanding of God's love as revealed through the crucifixion:

> That death upon the cross represents to me the Love which is ready to give itself to the uttermost for the imperfect and the erring, a Love that respects the integrity of each individual and refuses to coerce or to require obedience to the end that all may be bound together not through fear and through force but by the free response of love.[12]

Given that Boisen says we are to commit ourselves to Jesus' cause,

11. Boisen, "Christian Perfectionism," 12.
12. Boisen, *Exploration of the Inner World*, 300.

it seems reasonable to assume that the love we are to manifest toward others is to be, as far as is possible, of the same intention as God's love. Thus, our love of others is to be characterized by the willingness to sacrifice oneself for the benefit of the other, the respect of each person's integrity, and the seeking to bind persons together not by coercion but by "the free response of love." Two comments about this characterization of love must suffice at this point.

First, Boisen's emphasis on love as persuasive rather than coercive and, therefore, as respectful of the integrity of all persons is a critical aspect of his ethic. Indeed, this seems to be near the heart of the meaning of his claim that humans are "living human documents." As Charles V. Gerkin has recently noted concerning what Boisen meant by that metaphor: "Each individual living human document has an integrity of his or her own that calls for understanding and interpretation, not categorization and stereotyping."[13] While Boisen never fully explicated how respecting the integrity of persons played out in terms of more specific obligations regarding our action in the world, the general tone of his discussion suggests something like a general principle of "equal regard."[14] The integrity of *each* person must be respected in the manner appropriate to *all* persons. In other words, the integrity of persons must be treated from a universal perspective. We will later address what Boisen meant by "universal" in this context.

Second, that Boisen's understanding of love should embody a strong emphasis on self-sacrifice should not be surprising given the theological framework which undergirded his ethic. One might well wonder, however, what he saw as the moral constraints on self-sacrifice. In other words, was all self-sacrifice to be regarded as good per se, or were there moral limits on the virtue of self-sacrifice? As opposed to much of the contemporary discussion of self-sacrificial love, Boisen did not stress the role of moral obligations to the self as a constraint on the notion of sacrifice of self for others. The reason for this, however, had to do with his moral psychology. In Boisen's perspective, as we shall see more fully, the self simply *is* the internalization of the attitudes and values of the group. Thus, to further the group was, at least indirectly, to further the self. The only morally legitimate constraint on self-sacrifice, then, had to do with the expanse or "capacity for universality" of the group in loyalty to whose ideals the self-sacrifice was made.

As feminist theory has made clear, there are important problems

---

13. Charles V. Gerkin, *The Living Human Document: Re-Visioning Pastoral Counseling in a Hermeneutical Mode* (Nashville: Abingdon, 1984), 38.

14. Gene H. Outka, *Agape: An Ethical Analysis* (New Haven: Yale University Press, 1972).

involved in the idea that self-sacrifice is the pinnacle of the moral life.[15] The basic difficulty concerns the degradation, or even loss, of the self that seems to be implied in many prominent ways of understanding self-sacrifice in the Christian tradition. Interestingly, Boisen's perspective on self-sacrifice avoids some of these difficulties. However, as we shall later see, it does so because Boisen had already voided the self in important respects.

The second clue to the meaning Boisen attributed to his moral principles lies with his understanding of universality. The notion of universality embodies the *central formal requirement* of Boisen's ethic. By "universality" Boisen meant that we ought to order our lives according to something greater than our own local and particular interests. Rather, we must order our lives in accordance with our loyalty to (as he variously referred to it) God, Greater-than-self, the "social whole." In tying this moral claim to his understanding of social salvation, Boisen wrote that "social salvation will be achieved only as this Greater-than-self can become an object of devotion so universal that all men will be bound together in the bonds of a common loyalty which will have priority over the claims of family and clan and nation."[16] It is important to recognize here that Boisen's notion of universality is not identical with what is now called the principle of universalizability in ethics. The principle of universalizability, roughly stated, holds that similar situations must be treated similarly. More formally, it holds that an action which is morally right in a given situation must also be morally right in any relevantly similar situation.[17] Boisen's understanding of love seems to imply such an understanding. His idea of universality, however, has reference to something else. Influenced by George Herbert Mead's understanding of the social self, the idea of universality in Boisen's thought had primary reference to the object of our loyalty. Universality, in other words, is a characteristic of the fellowship to which we ought to be loyal. We are to be loyal to what H. Richard Niebuhr (who was also heavily influenced by Mead) would later call the universal community and, thereby, to God.[18] This is what ties together love of God and love of neighbor in Boisen's thought: love of neighbor must be grounded in the universal loyalty represented in love of God.

Unfortunately, Boisen did not sufficiently clarify how we are to

15. See, for example, B. H. Andolsen, "Agape in Feminist Ethics," *Journal of Religious Ethics* 9 (1981): 69–83; Margaret A. Farley, *Personal Commitments: Making, Keeping, Breaking* (San Francisco: Harper and Row, 1985).

16. Boisen, *Exploration of the Inner World*, 293.

17. See, for example, Alan Gewirth, *Reason and Morality* (Chicago: University of Chicago, 1978), 105–6.

18. H. Richard Niebuhr, *The Responsible Self* (New York: Harper, 1963).

make normative judgments regarding what constitutes "universality." While he says that we are to move to increasingly "higher" loyalties in this regard, he never specifies the moral grounds or criteria upon which we might know what "higher" really means in this context. To say, as Boisen did, that the ultimate loyalty was to the "social whole" is of very little assistance without substantially more normative-ethical content to (and not simply sociopsychological description of) the criteria which determine the meaning of the "social whole." In a similar manner, Boisen's understanding of universality provides little help in determining how conflicts between "lesser" and "higher" loyalties are to be mediated. He simply says that such "lesser" loyalties are to be incorporated into the more universal loyalties. As the ethicist Joseph L. Allen has recently observed, however, this way of construing the matter glosses over some of the harder realities involved in the conflict of moral claims we confront in our day-to-day lives.[19]

As a final observation concerning the moral principles which specified the implications of his theology for the ordering of life, it should be noted that Boisen thought those principles were fundamentally teleological in character. In other words, moral standards were to be judged by the relative balance of good versus evil which they produced. As Boisen put it, ethical norms "are validated by their long-run consequences in the lives of those who hold them" (p. 16). The consequences which he regarded as most important were those of, what he called broadly, survival. As Boisen wrote, "The ultimate test is the biological test, the test of survival—stated, however, not in terms of the individual but of society as a whole and the more abundant life which ought to be achieved."[20] By "survival" Boisen meant that our moral standards not only ought to provide for the continuation of sheer biological existence, but also ought to promote human flourishing, the abundant life in general. It is also important to observe from this comment that Boisen thought that the promotion of the individual's own flourishing was insufficient to regard an action or character trait as morally justifiable. Boisen was no ethical egoist. Rather, in line with his understanding of universality, it was with regard to the flourishing of all people that moral standards or norms were to be constructed and evaluated.

Central Needs and Values

Boisen's use of the phrase *the abundant life* referred to a variety of more specific kinds of values and human needs which moral norms

19. Joseph L. Allen, *Love and Conflict: A Covenantal Mode of Christian Ethics* (Nashville: Abingdon, 1984).
20. Boisen, "The Period of Beginnings," 16; *Exploration of the Inner World*, 162.

were to promote in society. These included such things as joy, peace, and stability of character.[21] However, the central aspect of the abundant life for Boisen was clearly love. As he declared, "I believe that love is the paramount human need." When Boisen used the word *love* in this context he was not referring to a moral norm, but rather to a human need. In particular, love as a human need referred to our need for response and approval by those to whom we are striving to be loyal.[22]

We shall see this understanding of love developed more fully in his moral psychology. At this point, however, it is important to note that the implication of this way of construing the central human need is that moral standards or norms are to be evaluated by their long-term consequences in promoting the satisfaction of our need for response and approval. The problem with this way of putting it is that our need for response and approval can be satisfied in any number of ways: some good, some bad. We clearly need to provide a normative constraint in our ethic on the ways in which we satisfy that human need. Yet, if, as Boisen suggested, it is the satisfaction of this need which constitutes the primary means by which we are to judge moral norms and standards, those norms must be dependent on, and not prior to, the articulation of the need. Boisen's ethic seems to require, in other words, a deontological as well as a teleological standard, that is, a standard which is not immediately dependent upon its promotion of human flourishing for its moral justification.

Having outlined Boisen's constructive ethic, we must now turn briefly to his moral psychology. We will not be examining the whole of his psychology, but rather that aspect specially concerned with the dynamics of the moral life. Our particular focus of concern will be the way in which his ethic relates to his moral psychology.

Boisen's Moral Psychology

In his monumental study *The Exploration of the Inner World,* Boisen concisely stated the core of his moral psychology:

> The problem of right and wrong thus resolves itself into a question of group attitudes. What we think is right or wrong will be determined by those whose approval we want, and what the group regards as right or wrong will determine its chances for survival in the struggle for existence and the extent to which it will achieve the more abundant life.[23]

21. Boisen, *Exploration of the Inner World,* 293.
22. Boisen, "The Period of Beginnings," 16; "Christian Perfectionism," 11.
23. Boisen, *Exploration of the Inner World,* 180–81.

Two important aspects of Boisen's perspective on the moral life are revealed in this statement. First, morality is a function of the individual's appropriation of the attitudes and values of the group. Second, the most fundamental motivation in the moral life is the desire for approval by that group to which we aspire. Since these dimensions of Boisen's thought play such central roles in his moral psychology and are so deeply related to his ethic, it will pay us to examine each more fully.

First, Boisen's moral psychology is a fully social psychology. Our moral standards, Boisen thought, are a reflection of the moral standards of some group or, as he frequently referred to it, some "fellowship." Drawing on Mead's understanding of the social self, Boisen argued that individuals achieve their definiteness through their assimilation or internalization of group attitudes. As Boisen put it, "This organization of social attitudes which the individual takes over is his character. What the individual is, then, depends upon the group which he reflects or represents and the degree of harmony or consistency which he achieves."[24] As can be seen, Boisen's way of stating this has little nuance: the individual simply *is* a reflection of a more or less complete appropriation of the attitudes and values of a particular group. As we will later see, this perspective creates serious problems for any normative ethic. Nonetheless, this way of stating the matter did permit him to recognize the social formation of the self and the centrality of the imagery of harmony, conflict, and healing to the understanding of the dynamics of the moral life.

This recognition, however unfortunately stated, seems to me to be an important contribution by Boisen to our understanding of the moral dimensions of pastoral care. Its importance lies in the attempt to provide a psychology which recognizes that morality has reference to life in community and, therefore, that one cannot legitimately separate (though one can, of course, distinguish) the individual and the communal dimensions of morality in pastoral care. We must look at this more closely.

In Boisen's perspective, people become ill precisely because they experience themselves as isolated from or in disharmony with the group or fellowship of persons which embodies the values and attitudes to which they aspire. This disharmony is located by Boisen in, essentially, a loss of control over the instinctual life. In other words, the internalized social norms, for whatever reason, cannot control or discipline the instincts.[25] The result is a sense of guilt so powerful that

24. Ibid., 172, 152.
25. Boisen, "The Period of Beginnings," 16; Anton T. Boisen, *Religion in Crisis and Custom: A Sociological and Psychological Study* (New York: Harper, 1955), 194.

the individual experiences himself or herself as isolated from the group to which he or she aspires. Recovery, then, is largely dependent upon a kind of moral restoration: restoration of loyalty to and fellowship with the group and, therefore, restoration of commitment to the ideals and values of that group. This understanding of restoration is deeply embedded in the underlying imagery of his ethic: harmony can be most fruitfully pursued only by aligning oneself, through the group, with the healing forces at the depths of life, accompanied by a restoration of self-control in the face of the conflicts of the inner world. For Boisen, the question of the possibility of moral restoration for the individual was thus inseparable from the question of the nature and conditions of community.

Given Boisen's moral psychology, then, there could be no such thing as an "individual ethic" as opposed to a "communal ethic": there was only a communal ethic which was either harmoniously or disharmoniously internalized in persons. Though his rationale for this rests more on psychological than on ethical grounds per se, Boisen could well agree with the recent reminder of Don Browning that ethics is, by its very nature, communal.[26] Since, as Browning has remarked, the effort to separate the individual and communal dimensions of ethics frequently tends to place the pastoral care of the church in an oppositional stance with regard to the rest of ministry, the intention (though not necessarily the substance) of Boisen's moral psychology stands as a needed corrective.

The second aspect of Boisen's moral psychology that deserves mention is his claim that the basic motivation in the moral life is the desire for approval by the group to which we aspire. The underlying idea, as we saw with regard to his ethic, is that what we most fundamentally need and want is the approval of those to whom we seek to be loyal, that is, from those we love. Since the moral life is essentially an effort to harmoniously embody the values and attitudes of that group to which we aspire, the need for approval by that group can be seen as the motive of morality in Boisen's moral psychology. Indeed, the need for approval, in Boisen's thought, seems to be the primary defense against isolation and estrangement from that group upon which, in a later developmental analogue to one's parents, we are dependent. While this way of putting the matter raises a host of complex problems regarding ethical reflection, it does suggest two important additional implications of Boisen's understanding of the moral life.

First, by locating the psychological ground of the moral life in the need for approval by the group to which we aspire, Boisen was able to see the moral life as not simply a product of a "push from behind,"

26. Browning, *Religious Ethics and Pastoral Care*, 37–38.

but also—and, for Boisen, more importantly—as a product of a "pull from ahead." In other words, the moral life is not to be understood simply by reducing it to the influence of our past histories. What is more important, Boisen thought, are the ideals toward which we are striving. In Boisen's words, "Not where a man comes from, but the direction in which he is moving, is for [us] the important question. The yesterdays demand attention only in so far as they are influencing the todays and determining the tomorrows."[27] It must be admitted that Boisen's moral psychology lacked dynamic sophistication on this point. Yet, his emphasis on the positive role of ideals in the moral life and the relation of those ideals to our need for approval finds some resonance in the recent work in that version of psychoanalytic thought known as self psychology, as well as in John C. Hoffman's effort to understand the dynamics of a nonmoralistic morality with regard to pastoral care.[28]

Second, since the sense of isolation is the "root evil" of non-organic mental illness in Boisen's perspective, we can see again how he ties together the dynamics of the moral life and mental health: they find their common and most fundamental ground in our need for approval by those whom we "account most worthy of love and honor."[29] Thus, mental health and morality were not antagonistic. Indeed, given Boisen's moral psychology, they could not be, since restoration to the group (a condition of mental health) *meant* moral restoration (though not necessarily moral perfection, of course).

It may well appear, however, that what Boisen has tied together in this is mental health and *conventional* morality. In other words, mental health is related to the conventional moral standards of the group to which one aspires. To a large extent, this is true. Yet, for Boisen, not all loyalties to particular groups and, therefore, not all moral standards, were equal. As we have seen in his understanding of universality, Boisen's ethic was meant to provide a means of differentiating "higher" from "lower" loyalties and, thus, better from worse moral standards. This understanding of universality had its correlate at the level of his moral psychology. Any particular group to which the individual aspired was embedded within a broader or more universal group. The child's relation to his or her parents, for example, was relativized by the fact that the parents have reference beyond them-

27. Anton T. Boisen, *Problems of Religion and Life* (New York: Abingdon-Cokesbury, 1946), 99.
28. See Heinz Kohut, *Self Psychology and the Humanities: Reflections on a New Psychoanalytic Approach*, ed. Charles B. Strozier (New York: Norton, 1985); Hoffman, *Ethical Confrontation in Counseling*.
29. Boisen, *Problems of Religion and Life*, 100.

selves to something greater. This is the psychological ground for Boisen's claim that we cannot really successfully "escape" the requirements of the moral life—we can only incorporate lesser loyalties into higher loyalties. This, in turn, is the psychological rationale for the perfectionist character of Boisen's ethic: we are so constituted that our love for others can find no rest until it finds its harmony with God.

Conscience

Boisen's understanding of conscience is, in many ways, the culmination of his moral psychology. The central themes of Boisen's moral psychology are all reiterated in this understanding of conscience: the essentially social character of the self, the desire for approval by the group, the importance of human aspiration, and the relationship of morality and mental health. As Boisen wrote:

> I believe that men have divine potentialities. The characteristic feature of human nature is social control through the internalization of social norms within oneself in the form of conscience. The human being thus has the capacity for doing the right thing through inner self-direction and not through outer compulsion or blind instinct.[30]

In Boisen's perspective, conscience is composed of precisely those values and attitudes of that group to which we aspire. In internalizing those values and attitudes we acquire the capacity for self-judgment: "We judge ourselves in the light of the organized attitudes of the group. Self-criticism is essentially social criticism and the sense of guilt is the social condemnation which the individual pronounces upon himself on the basis of what he knows of the attitudes of the community."[31]

It is important to remember, though, that when Boisen talks about conscience as internalized social judgment in this context he is referring not simply, or even primarily, to those groups to which we have belonged. While it may have its origin there, he is principally talking about the social judgment of those groups to whose fellowship we aspire. Boisen argued that this understanding of conscience permitted us to see it in a more positive light. Conscience is not essentially a manifestation of pathology. It does not arise so much on the soil of conflict as on the soil of human aspiration. Thus Boisen stated that conscience lies "on the growing edge of human nature. It represents the awareness of success or failure in maintaining one's status and one's growth. It is the artistic sense which tells us what is or is not

30. Boisen, "The Period of Beginnings," 16.
31. Boisen, *Exploration of the Inner World,* 152.

fitting in social relationships, long before our clumsy reasons are able to pronounce judgement."[32]

While Boisen said that he was influenced in this interpretation by William Ernest Hocking, the similarities between Hocking and Boisen on the understanding of conscience are not ubiquitous. Hocking did say that conscience is "an awareness of the success or failure . . . in maintaining [one's] status and growth,"[33] but he explicitly rejected the idea that conscience could be adequately understood as the internalization of social norms or customs. The reason Hocking rejected this interpretation had to do not only with the idealistic strains of his metaphysic as applied to conscience, but also because he saw that it was only by providing a way for conscience to be something more than internalized social judgment that ethics could be conceived as performing a truly critical, and not just legitimating, task in human life. Boisen, I think, meant to affirm this as well, given the psychological and ethical implications of his understanding of "universality." Yet, his continual references to conscience as internalized social control or internalized social criticism creates a profound ambiguity on this point. If conscience is only internalized social criticism, then it can serve only a rationalizing or legitimating function in relation to the group, regardless of how universal the group is conceived to be.

Nonetheless, this view of conscience as an essentially constructive force in human life was an important aspect of Boisen's moral psychology: it provided a centralized inner agency concerned with the moral life which could become embroiled in, though was not in essence derived from, psychic conflict. It is out of this understanding of conscience, therefore, that we should read his concern about not "lowering the conscience threshold" in our care for persons. To try to do so, from Boisen's perspective, would miss the point. The perfectionist drive within us is not the problem in mental illness, but a critical resource in the movement toward recovery.

Implications of Boisen's Work for a Practical Theology of Pastoral Care

In the course of presenting Boisen's ethic and moral psychology, I have noted a variety of the insights and difficulties. At this point, however, we must take a broader view and attempt to discern some of the implications of Boisen's work for a contemporary practical theology of pastoral care.

32. Ibid., 176.
33. William E. Hocking, *Human Nature and Its Remaking* (New Haven: Yale University Press, 1929), 123.

Boisen's work shows us quite clearly that the relationship between ethics and moral psychology in practical theology is intimate indeed. This, in itself, of course, is as we would expect. Yet, Boisen's work provides an illustration of the more problematic point that ethics and moral psychology are dialectically related. In other words, the kinds of terms and dynamics that are highlighted in our understanding of human moral experience will set certain conceptual constraints on our understanding of the ethic that will make sense in that light. Our normative understanding of the moral life will likewise establish certain conceptual constraints on the kinds of dynamics of human moral experience that we will find most central or important. The implication of this is that one's ethic and one's moral psychology are dependent upon one another even for their internal coherence.[34] If, as the philosopher Robert Neville has argued, *all* thinking is fundamentally rooted in valuation, this ought not to strike us as particularly surprising: even the avowedly descriptive (rather than evaluative) task of moral psychology finds its ground in valuation. Boisen himself argued much the same point (though on grounds other than those suggested by Neville) in his claim that what we count as "normal" or "average" in human life depends on its relative value in relation to what we want to accomplish. In a sense perhaps stronger than Boisen would have affirmed, his work helps us see that the normative categories derived from our ethic and the descriptive categories derived from our moral psychology are dialectically related: they suffuse one another.

My point in observing this is not to provide an invitation to moralism in pastoral care, but rather to provide a recognition of the deep structures of interrelationship and dependence that exist in the variety of dimensions of human experience that we have found helpful to distinguish in our work in pastoral care. While ethics is not psychology and psychology is not ethics, any contemporary practical theology of pastoral care must find ways to deal with the fact that they are deeply and internally related.

To have recognized the deep relationship between ethics and moral psychology, of course, is not necessarily to be able to articulate adequately the substance of that relation. A brief example from the work of Boisen must suffice to illustrate the kinds of problems we face on this point. As I have hinted throughout the course of this discussion, Boisen's way of describing the social character of the self raises serious problems for his—or any—ethic. The problem derives from Boisen's

34. For a recent argument which suggests more independence here, however, see Don S. Browning, *Religious Thought and the Modern Psychologies* (Philadelphia: Fortress, 1986).

reliance on Mead's idea that an individual's character is the internalization of group attitudes and values. This is central, as we have seen, to Boisen's moral psychology in general and to his understanding of conscience in particular. The difficulty with this way of construing the matter, as Walter F. Conn and Gibson Winter[35] have observed with regard to Mead, is that it obscures the personal dynamics of transcendence. In other words, if the self is simply the product of its internalization of group ideals, we have no way to understand what "it" is that accomplishes the internalizing or how, finally, it is possible to conceive meaningfully the self's transcendence in moving to higher loyalties. For Boisen, perhaps even more than for Mead (if Catherine Keller's recent characterization of Mead is correct), there is little ground for "the possibility of dissent from the internalized other."[36] If Boisen had identified conscience more firmly with the tension *between* the instincts and the internalized social norms (which may have been his idea in appropriating Hocking), rather than tending to identify conscience with the internalized norms themselves, he might have had an avenue out of this problem. However, he did not (or, at least, did not do so consistently). With regard to the impact of this perspective on ethics, Hocking seems to me to have been right in this: the enterprise of ethics is threatened with becoming simple rationalization of a particular group's attitudes and values of conscience is reducible without remainder to internalized social criticism. As I have said, this was not Boisen's intention, but his way of formulating the nature of conscience decidedly pushes his discussion in this direction.

This difficulty in Boisen's moral psychology also has implications for his understanding of self-sacrificial love. As we have seen, self-sacrificial love was, for Boisen, the heart of the calling to Christian perfectionism. Yet, given the fact that Boisen had essentially voided the self of critical capacity in relation to the ideals and values of the group toward which we aspire, there seems very little check on the moral justifiability of the sacrifice that the group's ideals require of us. Indeed, the general mood which permeates Boisen's ethic, vigilance at the garden of the heart in the service of the fellowship to which we seek to be loyal, compounds this sense. Again, I do not think this was Boisen's intention. His claim that every person is to be treated with the respect due the integrity of all persons (to the extent this claim also applies to the self) would seem to provide an important

35. Walter E. Conn, *Conscience: Development and Self-Transcendence* (Birmingham: Religious Education Press, 1981); Gibson Winter, *Elements for a Social Ethic* (New York: Macmillan, 1966).

36. Catherine Keller, *From a Broken Web: Separation, Sexism, and Self* (Boston: Beacon, 1986), 180.

constraint in this regard. Yet, two problems block our path in this. First, Boisen's moral psychology does not seem adequate to account for the inner capacity which would make this judgment possible. Second, if love as a moral principle is justified by appeal to the consequences it produces in terms of approval by the group, and if the meaning of the inner structure of love (that is, the meaning of "respect" and "integrity") is relative to the group's ideals, there is a disconcerting circularity that provides no relief from the central problem here.

While Boisen's position on this matter was not adequate either to the intention of his moral psychology or his ethic, the underlying issue of the relationship between the substance of one's ethic and the substance of one's psychology continues to be of great importance in the effort to articulate a practical theology of pastoral care. Browning's deconstructionist method of practical moral rationality, Hoffman's distinction between the positive and negative conscience, and Archie Smith, Jr.'s, reading of the dynamics of human experience (through Mead and Winter, by the way) out of the context of a social ethic grounded in black liberation theology suggest the continuing vitality of the discussion.[37] The issue, in other words, is rightly posed in Boisen's work, even though his attempt to address it did not finally succeed.

Conclusion

The work of Anton Boisen stands as a remarkable achievement at the beginning of the contemporary era in pastoral care and counseling. Torn between the moralistic piety of his upbringing and the brute facts of his own tormented inner world, Boisen was yet able to turn conflict to creativity. While the creativity alone was never able entirely to assuage the conflict, Boisen's legacy remains an important one. His effort to articulate a moral psychology in dialectical relation to an ideal of Christian perfectionism, while no longer tenable in many ways, is still a rich resource for discerning the complex and diverse range of issues that confront those of us who follow him in attempting to reflect thoughtfully on the moral seriousness of pastoral care.

37. Browning, *Religious Ethics and Pastoral Care*; Hoffman, *Ethical Confrontation in Counseling*; Smith, *The Relational Self*.

5

The Ethic of Sincerity and the Sincerity of Ethics

K. BRYNOLF LYON

In the therapeutic ethos of Western culture, ethics has become a matter of sincerity. Ethical reflection, for many in our time, is reduced to "clarifying one's feelings" and, consequently, truthfulness has replaced rightness as the criterion of moral discourse. As one young woman put it, "I can't tell you if this is morally *right*, I can only tell you this is honestly how I feel." Truthfulness, however, has not only become the standard by which to judge the adequacy of moral reflection for many persons; it has also become the highest virtue to be realized in moral practice. Sincerity is thus the goal and the end of the moral life. Believing it is eschewing the authoritarianism of imposed moralities, this ethic of sincerity strives for those dangerous and elusive moments of honesty in a psyche at risk of deception from within and without.[1] It should not be surprising in such a situation that the therapist should fill the cultural role in our time of Aristotle's

1. Philip Rieff, *Freud: The Mind of the Moralist*, 3d ed. (Chicago: University of Chicago Press, 1979). Jurgen Habermas has argued that truthfulness or sincerity is the appropriate criterion of the rationality of therapeutic discourse. Whether this is correct or not, I am concerned here with the expansion of this criterion to the realm of moral discourse in contemporary culture. See, in this regard, the interesting com-

99

spoudaios, that is, those cultural exemplars who have the appropriate sense of living their lives well. The therapist is, thus, a moral expert for many in our culture by virtue of her or his being an expert in the vicissitudes of sincerity.

What has this to do with pastoral care? Pastoral care is, among other things, a moral activity: implicitly or explicitly legitimating, undermining, or transforming the moral praxis of the subjects of that care and the moral ethos of the culture of which that care is a part.[2] There can be little doubt, for example, as E. Brooks Holifield has recently shown us, that the modern pastoral counseling movement in this country sought both to undermine and transform what it saw as an authoritarian moral order.[3] Yet, its reasons for seeking change seem more well-founded than some of its visions of what that moral order should be transformed into. Indeed, certain aspects of the pastoral counseling movement itself have clearly fostered the emergence of the ethic of sincerity. Thus, Don S. Browning has recently argued that pastoral care and counseling have become estranged from ethical reflection.[4] Concerned with the dangers of moralistic attitudes and practices, Browning argues, pastoral counselors have tended to develop naive assumptions about the moral dimensions of their work, and their ethical reflection has subsequently lost critical depth.

Browning's argument is, I think, quite true. Yet, we must also step carefully here. Some of the early work in the pastoral counseling movement saw quite clearly, even if inadequately, a place for ethical reflection in pastoral care. Indeed, if the pastoral counseling movement has facilitated the emergence of the ethic of sincerity, it has done so against the express intentions of many of its most vocal spokespersons. To examine the nature and fate of some of the early assumptions surrounding the relationship of pastoral counseling and ethics will, perhaps, illuminate the present prospects for restating that relationship today. In this chapter I will concentrate, in this regard, on the work of Seward Hiltner.

---

ments of Robert N. Bellah et al., *Habits of the Heart: Individualism and Commitment in American Life* (Los Angeles: University of California Press, 1985), on the "therapeutic" character type.

2. Don S. Browning, *The Moral Context of Pastoral Care* (Philadelphia: Westminster, 1976); K. Brynolf Lyon, "Moral Praxis and Pastoral Care," in *Interpreting Disciplines,* ed. L. Dale Richesin and Larry D. Bouchard (Fort Worth: Texas Christian University Press, 1987).

3. E. Brooks Holifield, *A History of Pastoral Care in America: From Salvation to Self-Realization* (Nashville: Abingdon, 1983).

4. Don S. Browning, *Religious Ethics and Pastoral Care* (Philadelphia: Fortress, 1983).

The Place of Ethics in Hiltner's Work

A concern with the relationship of ethics and theories of psychotherapy appears prominantly in Hiltner's early works. As early as 1945, for example, he sought to show how Sigmund Freud's work helped to provide psychological underpinning to Paul Tillich's notion of the "transmoral conscience." His concern with ethical issues in relation to pastoral care itself, however, became quite explicit in his *Pastoral Counseling*, published in 1949. While it may appear that his central concern in this text was with eliminating moralism in pastoral counseling, there is an underlying ethical position which focuses his discussion. Indeed, in a footnote to the text Hiltner criticized the work of Brock Chisholm for presuming that "if the underbrush of moralistic rigidity is cleared away, everything will take care of itself" and, thus, for Chisholm's failure to build "a new and superior concept of ethics."[5] Hiltner's own ethical orientation in this work was grounded in an amalgamation of what he called the "inner release" perspective, the "objective-ethical" perspective, and the Christian theological perspective on human nature.

Hiltner's methodological stance regarding the relation of ethics and theories of psychotherapy, which had remained rather amorphous to this point in his published works, became clarified in two of his writings appearing in 1953. In "Pastoral Psychology and Christian Ethics" he argued that pastoral psychology and Christian ethical reflection were (or ought to be) dialectically related. In other words, he argued that "pastoral psychology contributes to our understanding of . . . Christian ethics" just as "study of our operations as Christian ethical leaders deepens, corrects or illuminates our pastoral psychology." This same thesis underlaid his *Sex Ethics and the Kinsey Reports*.[6] It was a sensitive examination of how the Kinsey reports could both deepen Christian ethical reflection on sex attitudes and practices and how Christian ethical reflection could critique some of the underlying assumptions of those reports.

Yet, what is in many ways the centerpiece of Hiltner's critical reflection on these issues during this early period was never published. His doctoral dissertation, completed in 1952 and entitled "Psychotherapy and Christian Ethics: An Evaluation of the Ethical Thought of A. E. Taylor and Paul Tillich in the Light of Psychotherapeutic Contribu-

---

5. Seward Hiltner, *Pastoral Counseling* (Nashville: Abingdon, 1949), 255.

6. Seward Hiltner, "Pastoral Psychology and Christian Ethics," *Pastoral Psychology* 4 (1953): 23; Seward Hiltner, *Sex Ethics and the Kinsey Reports* (New York: Association, 1953).

tions to Ethics by J. C. Flugel and Erich Fromm," suggested provocative avenues of approach to the relationship of ethics and theories of
psychotherapy that were either dropped or obscured in his later works.
In 1958, for example, Hiltner's *Preface to Pastoral Theology* was published. While this work forged important new ground in the understanding of pastoral theology generally, it failed to carry forward
Hiltner's earlier insistence on the essential relationship of ethics and
pastoral care. In particular, his notion that ethics was a bridge
between theology and theories of psychotherapy—an idea developed
in his dissertation—was certainly obscured in this text. While the reasons for this are not entirely clear, it is perhaps not unrelated to his
functional separation of the "individual" and the "social" dimensions
of morality in this text.

In 1962, however, Hiltner published an intriguing article entitled
"Clinical and Theological Notes on Responsibility." While it was less
concerned with pastoral care per se than with an attempt to construct
a general image of human responsibility, it clearly furthered his earlier
discussion in important respects. Likewise, Hiltner's *Theological
Dynamics*, appearing in 1972, reasserted the notion, albeit somewhat
backhandedly, "that 'ethics' and 'care' ought not to be separated
categorically."[7]

This brief survey of Hiltner's work with respect to the relationship
of ethics and pastoral care is not exhaustive of his writings relevant
to this topic. My point, however, is simply to note that Hiltner was
obviously keenly concerned about that relationship. This alone is significant since it is often popularly assumed that the concern with the
constructive relationship between ethics and pastoral care is a new
one. What we will find as we examine the substance of Hiltner's position, though, is twofold. On the one hand, certain ambiguities in his
understanding of that relationship clearly facilitated the current
estrangement of ethics and pastoral care. On the other hand, however,
we will find that certain of his insights regarding that relationship
merit closer scrutiny.

Hiltner's Critique of Ethics

Hiltner's concern with ethics and pastoral care had both a critical
and a constructive intent. On the critical side, Hiltner was clearly

---

7. Seward Hiltner, "Clinical and Theological Notes on Responsibility," *Journal of
Religion and Health* 2, no. 1 (1962): 7–20; Seward Hiltner, *Theological Dynamics*
(Nashville: Abingdon, 1972), 195.

opposed to legalism and undialectical abstraction in Christian ethics: the first because it encouraged moralism and mediated against the emergence of a true moral concern in individuals; the second because it failed to make contact with the ambiguities and developmental potentials of persons' lives. Some further comments on this may prove clarifying.

Hiltner saw moral legalism in the light of the theological doctrine of "bondage to the law" or the "law conscience." The law conscience, Hiltner argued, was characterized less by adherence to some particular ethical doctrine than by a rigidity and demand for conformity which could accompany adherence to principle. Hiltner thought that this rigidity was a manifestation of psychic compulsion and unfreedom—"the most obvious enemies of moral action."[8] Such legalism, therefore, if it comes to be dominant in pastoral care could easily become moralistic: an effort to replace needed clarification and empathy with moral judgment. The problem with this, Hiltner saw, was that it failed to pay due heed to the personality of the individual, the subject of pastoral care; that is, it failed to appreciate the psychological context within which such judgment was to be effective. Thus, legalism in pastoral care could easily—and, in Hiltner's view, all too often did—result in blocking the moral development of the individual by reinforcing the compulsion, rigidity, and unfreedom symptomatic of the problem that led the individual to the pastor in the first place. As Hiltner wrote, "Thus, the legalistic approach, in working so hard for good behavior, tends to be deficient in helping people to increase their moral responsibility."[9]

Hiltner's opposition to undialectical abstraction in Christian ethics was grounded in the same basic theme as his rejection of legalism: Christian ethical reflection should not proceed in simple abstraction from the psychological-situational factors that contextualize the lives of persons. Hiltner argued, however, that since most of moral theology had in fact been abstract in just this sense "an immense amount of Christian ethical thought had been compensatory." In other words, Christian ethics had tended to overdramatize certain aspects of the moral life in reaction to what it most deeply feared (and most deeply misunderstood) about the nature of human beings. Given this, Hiltner thought that an undialectical Christian ethic was bound to do at least as much harm as good. As he wrote, "Any ethic which is chiefly com-

8. Seward Hiltner, "Toward an Ethical Conscience," *Journal of Religion* 25 (1945): 1–9; "Pastoral Psychology and Christian Ethics," 33.
9. Hiltner, *Theological Dynamics*, 193–94.

pensatory in character is also, at the same time, illusioned with regard to the factors which make for the realization of the good for men."[10] Thus, an undialectical abstraction in ethics obscured the ambiguities and tragedies as well as the developmental potentials for moral growth evidenced in the psychological matrix of persons' lives. For Hiltner, then, anthropology could not be superfluous—in that sense in which it is for certain of those in the Kantian tradition—in moral reflection.

In terms of pastoral counseling, both factors led Hiltner to reject "moral education" approaches to the counseling relationship. Such approaches, Hiltner felt, tended to arise more from the anxieties of the minister than from the needs of the parishioner. Subsequently, Hiltner remained for many years highly ambivalent about using such traditional terms as "discipline" and "guiding" in referring to dimensions of pastoral care. Indeed, his espousal of an eductive stance in pastoral guiding should be read in the context of his concern with legalism and undialectical abstraction in ethics: We must avoid the imposition of externals (particularly idealized moral externals) on internals so that we will not foreclose what chance we have of facilitating moral development.

Hiltner's Constructive Position

Hiltner, however, was not only a critic of ethics and morals. He also sought to construe Christian ethical reflection itself in a way that could fruitfully inform, and be enriched by, the "kind of experience that occurs in counseling."[11] Thus, the paradigm case in his reflection on ethics and pastoral care was the counseling situation. Unfortunately, Hiltner was not very systematic or clear in his articulation of his constructive position. His constructive statements are scattered throughout many of his writings. To try to put it succinctly nonetheless, Hiltner seems to have wanted to propose something like this: an aretaic (or ethic of character) version of contextual ethics grounded in a developmental theory which would mediate a reflective dialectical interplay between ethical principle and the life situation of individuals. A careful dissection of this will suggest the way in which Hiltner thought this would work.

Hiltner clearly thought that ethics should be more concerned with the character of persons than with the acts of persons. An action

10. Seward Hiltner, "Psychotherapy and Christian Ethics: An Evaluation of the Ethical Thought of A. E. Taylor and Paul Tillich in the Light of Pychotherapeutic Contributions to Ethics by J. C. Flugel and Erich Fromm," Ph.D. dissertation, University of Chicago, 1952, 432–33.
    11. Ibid., ii.

viewed in abstraction from the character of the person performing the action was, he said, "meaningless." This was not to say that actions could not be morally judged, but rather that they could not be so judged outside of their relation to the person's character. As he wrote, "Morality is a function of character. If an act is seen in the context of character, then it too can be considered morally."[12] The dynamics of character, in other words, was the dominant contextual factor to be taken into account in ethical reflection.

Within such an aretaic framework, Hiltner argued that the most important question to ask was not whether an action was morally right or wrong per se, but rather "does this act lead toward genuine moral growth on the part of this person and others involved?"[13] Hiltner thought, in other words, that Christian ethics should be concerned not only with the end-points or ideals of morality, but also with the moral development of the person:

> But a relevant Christian ethics ought to be something other than a statement of the end-points one hopes people may be able to reach. It ought, in itself, to be something that is relevant to people now struggling with these particular problems, just as it would be relevant if they made the grade. There is a "pastoral" or shepherding dimension of Christian ethics itself. Christian ethics must be something more than an end-point statement of what is desirable. If it is a Christian ethic, then God is at work, supporting, sustaining, judging, loving, throughout the process of *development*.[14]

Thus, Hiltner thought that a central interest of ethical reflection should be with whether an action expressed a general movement of character in the direction of moral growth. As he wrote in his dissertation, "The moral or ethical quality of an act by a person (or group) must be judged in the light of its ability to help that person move toward an ultimately moral end, not in the light of the superficial resemblance of the step to one's ideal image of the ultimately moral end."[15] The difficulty with this formulation of the matter, as Hiltner himself saw at least in part, was that an action leading toward moral growth for one person may still cause tremendous suffering to others involved. There was a certain naivete in Hiltner's dealing with this issue in his early writings. In "Pastoral Psychology and Christian Ethics," for example, he wrote that "increasing freedom, if genuine, is

12. Hiltner, *Sex Ethics and the Kinsey Reports*, 30.
13. Hiltner, "Pastoral Psychology and Christian Ethics," 30.
14. Hiltner, *Sex Ethics and the Kinsey Reports*, 38.
15. Hiltner, "Psychotherapy and Christian Ethics," 435.

automatically accompanied by increasing responsibility, or capacity for responsibility."[16] Hiltner went on in this discussion to argue that freedom and responsibility, if properly understood, "go hand in hand." Hiltner, however, did not adequately clarify at this point what precisely he had in mind by those concepts as moral ends and, thus, in what normative sense they "go hand in hand." This ambiguity tended to lead Hiltner in the direction of splitting off the morally good for self from the morally good for the community (even though he denied they could be categorically separated). He only compounded the problem in *Preface to Pastoral Theology* by associating the good for self with the shepherding perspective and the good for the community with the organizing perspective of pastoral theology.[17] This position could not but leave the minister (and the parishioner) in a situation of moral schizophrenia.

A few years later, however, when Hiltner addressed the notion of responsibility more systematically, he forthrightly denied that one could "bifurcate" the self and the community in terms of the meaning of responsibility. Indeed, he went so far as to argue that "the criterion of [an individual's] own responsibility is, in part, what he does to increase responsibility in his society." The good for self and the good for the community were inextricably interwoven here: "There is no sharp or basic dividing line between public and private morality . . . whether you start from one point or the other, you move over."[18]

To say that ethical reflection needs to be centrally concerned with whether an action leads toward moral growth, of course, requires that we be able to determine what constitutes moral growth. Hiltner argued that in approaching this question we needed "a casuistry, a theory of dialectical relationship between actual concrete situation and general principle."[19] He also referred to this as our need for a "systematic moral pathology." Hiltner was not very clear about what this actually meant, though. He simply argued that "we study principles through cases and cases through principles, the general or universal and the concrete together. Yet, how are we to mediate this dialectical reflection? What are the relevant axes around which we are to reflect on that dialectical movement? On what grounds do we adjudicate apparent conflicts between principles and cases? Hiltner never systematically addressed these issues in his published works. His dissertation, however, provided a potential avenue of approach to them.

16. Hiltner, "Pastoral Psychology and Christian Ethics," 31.
17. Seward Hiltner, *Preface to Pastoral Theology* (Nashville: Abingdon, 1958), 150.
18. Hiltner, "Clinical and Theological Notes on Responsibility," 16; Seward Hiltner, "Context: Yes—Abstractness: No," *Religion in Life* 35 (1966): 208.
19. Hiltner, "Pastoral Psychology and Christian Ethics," 32.

Though his remarks surrounding this are sketchy, Hiltner apparently thought that we needed a theory of moral development to ground the dialectical reflection between case and principle.[20] This is implied as well in his discussion of the importance of a "developmental ethic."[21] Hiltner never developed such a theory of moral development, however, thus leaving this aspect of his ethic curiously incomplete. Even his remarks on "the seven ages of shepherding" in *The Christian Shepherd*, while including brief comments on the development of care and concern, did not play the role in mediating principle and case that Hiltner seems to have envisioned earlier.

Indeed, in Hiltner's later writings on ethics and pastoral care, his discussion of the moral principles that were to be utilized in this dialectical reflection tended to be subsumed to the issue of responsibility. The actual content of one's ethical judgments, Hiltner often said, was less important than that those judgments were responsibly made.[22] Responsibility, in this regard, was first and foremost responsibility to God but also responsibility to others. How the pastor was to make coherent determinations of "moral growth" on this basis in pastoral care, though, was not fully clarified. To the extent that Hiltner discussed the function of moral principles, however, it was clear that he thought they should function more in an "illuminative" than in a "prescriptive" sense.[23] In other words, moral principles were useful in illuminating or disclosing certain aspects of the situation, rather than being necessarily reliable guides to right conduct or moral judgment.

The moral dimension of pastoral care in all this, for Hiltner, referred primarily to the pastor's enabling the movement toward greater personal integration and, thus, toward greater capacity for responsible action. Hiltner thought that this frequently required that the pastor reframe the moral character of the client's stated problem—whether this was directly communicated to the client or not. Pastors were to see moral issues primarily in the light of the developmental vicissitudes of responsibility rather than, as the client frequently saw them, as mistaken judgments or failures in moral rectitude (overconcern with either of which was a manifestation of compulsive legalism). Since responsibility was a dynamic feature of personality, this required a moral concern with the assessment of character as a whole in pastoral care situations.

20. Hiltner, "Psychotherapy and Christian Ethics," 32, 396, 458.
21. Hiltner, *Sex Ethics and the Kinsey Reports*.
22. Hiltner, "Context: Yes—Abstractness: No."
23. On these terms, see James M. Gustafson, "Context versus Principles: A Misplaced Debate in Christian Ethics," *Harvard Theological Review* 58 (1965): 171–202.

The Sincerity of Ethics

In *Pastoral Counseling* Hiltner wrote that "the pastor's own stand where moral and ethical questions are involved is already clear from noncounseling aspects of his work. He can, therefore, assume that the person who is willing and ready to discuss his situation with him has that fact in the back of his mind."[24] The proper stance of the pastor here was not to offer moral critique or moral reflection, but rather to listen, to understand, and to respond empathically to the inner conflict. Since the moral context was presumed to be clear, one should proceed eductively in the counseling relationship. What happens, however, when this counseling stance becomes the underlying theme of ministry per se? Exactly twenty years after his remarks were published, Hiltner expressed concern that ministers had backed too far away from the requirements of appropriate church discipline:

> Faith is not strictly a private affair in the sense that anybody's views are just as authoritative as those of anyone else . . . If there is no disciplining of the results of his inquiry—only "It's fine that you are giving thought to these matters"—then Christian faith is put in the realm of whim or fancy, and secret approval is given to the notion that anything goes if you believe it sincerely.[25]

Hiltner was dismayed by that ethic of sincerity he saw creeping into the church. The moral context had itself become obscured.

It is clear from Hiltner's constructive position on Christian ethical reflection that it was not his intention to promote the ethic of sincerity. He saw pastoral counseling as concerned with persons' honesty about themselves for the sake of increasing their freedom and responsibility. To put it another way, Hiltner was concerned less with the ethic of sincerity than with the sincerity of ethics, that is, that ethical reflection not be compensatory and, thereby, dishonest about human needs, developmental processes, and the dynamics of change. It was an ethic that was sensitive to the ambiguities and potentials of the human personality that Hiltner sought, one not naively moralistic about the dilemmas of the human prospect. Hiltner sought an ethic that was contextualized by a psychological realism, not one that ended in subjectivistic stand-offs.[26]

24. Hiltner, *Pastoral Counseling*, 50.

25. Seward Hiltner, *Ferment in the Ministry* (Nashville: Abingdon, 1969), 181–82.

26. For a helpful analysis of subjectivism and moral development, see James Fishkin, *Beyond Subjective Morality* (New Haven: Yale University Press, 1984).

We still have much to learn, I suspect, from Hiltner's general vision of this. Indeed, recent works by Don S. Browning and John C. Hoffman[27]—however much they diverge from certain of the particulars of Hiltner's position—clearly echo the sentiment of his overarching vision: Pastoral care requires an ethic informed by and sensitive to the dynamics of personality, just as ethics requires an adequate and meaningful interpretation of the dynamics of human personality to inform certain aspects of its vision of the proper ordering of life. Yet, the line separating a concern with the sincerity of ethics and the ethic of sincerity can be a fine one indeed. Certain ambiguities in Hiltner's understanding of the relationship of pastoral care and ethics illustrate this point.

Principles and Cases, Cases and Principles

Hiltner's appeal for dialectical reflection between moral principles and cases was grounded in his contention that morality was essentially a function of character and, thus, that the simple application of abstract principles to a particular life situation distorted this characterological context. Hiltner was getting at an important point in this. As the moral philosopher Stuart Hampshire has noted, our moral activities and practices are intricately woven into the broader fabric of our way of life.[28] Thus, to determine the moral adequacy of a particular action or idea requires appreciation of those other elements in that way of life to which that action or idea has reference.[29] The way to make sense of the moral dimension of the client's situation, therefore, Hiltner argued, was not simply to compare that situation with an abstract moral principle. Rather, we should read the principle and the life situation of the client in the light of each other. In doing so, Hiltner thought that our understanding of the nature of the moral problem itself would be transformed. He hoped in particular that this would lead to a more developmentally nuanced sense of how we could facilitate moral growth in pastoral care.

Yet, as I noted, how this dialectical reflection was to be disciplined was not entirely clear. This becomes additionally problematic when

27. Browning, *Moral Context of Pastoral Care;* Browning, *Religious Ethics and Pastoral Care;* John C. Hoffman, *Ethical Confrontation in Counseling* (Chicago: University of Chicago Press, 1981).

28. Stuart Hampshire, *Morality and Conflict* (Cambridge: Harvard University Press, 1984).

29. For a recent theological exposition of a similar point, see Stanley Hauerwas, *The Peaceable Kingdom: A Primer in Christian Ethics* (South Bend, Ind.: University of Notre Dame Press, 1983).

we recognize the danger of reductionism, of making ethics simply psychology writ large—which is, in fact, the confusion underlying the ethic of sincerity.[30] The way in which Hiltner often stated the form of the required dialectic (as between case and principle) did not much help, in that it confused the case itself with the psychological interpretation of the case. In practice this sometimes led to a marring of the boundaries between moral principles and psychological interpretation (which we shall see again shortly). To avoid this we must be clear about the form of the dialectic: It is not case and principle that must be dialectically related, but rather an ethical interpretation of the case and a psychological interpretation of the case. Both ethical and psychological interpretation here are "abstract" in Hiltner's sense. However, they can be related dialectically as they respectively interpret the "concrete," the life situation of the individual.

This may simply serve to underscore the problem of how we are to mediate or discipline that dialectic. Hiltner's early idea that a theory of moral development might help us in this regard seems a potentially fruitful one. A theory of moral development might enable us to determine developmental increments of moral growth relative to the moral principles such a theory encompasses. Thus, it would mediate between its guiding moral principles and its underlying psychology through its postulated developmental stages. Yet, such a theory would need to be carefully constructed for at least two reasons.

On the one hand, the sheer complexity of adequately combining psychological developmental theory and moral theory in such a way that each developmental advance is "better" on both psychological and moral grounds is fraught with many pitfalls. Lawrence Kohlberg's attempt to engage in this kind of reflection with respect to his theory of moral development serves as a helpful model of these issues.[31] Indeed, Browning has recently tried to incorporate Kohlberg's theory into an ordered schema of practical reasoning as it relates to pastoral care.[32]

On the other hand, both the psychological and the moral dimensions of the theory must be broad enough to be adequate to the task of pastoral care. There are two aspects to this. First, the psychology in which the theory is based must be integrable with the kind of dynamic understanding necessary in pastoral care. On the face of it, this would make the use of Kohlberg's theory problematic since its cognitive-developmental underpinning is not easily translatable into

30. Hoffman, *Ethical Confrontation in Counseling.*
31. Lawrence Kohlberg, "The Claim to Moral Adequacy of a Highest Stage of Moral Development," *Journal of Philosophy* 70 (1973): 630–46.
32. Browning, *Religious Ethics and Pastoral Care.*

dynamic categories. Robert Kegan's recent attempt to integrate cognitive-developmental psychology with object-relations theory, however, may prove potentially useful in this regard.[33] Second, though, the moral principles in which such a theory charts developmental increments must be compatible with a generally adequate Christian ethic. Whether, for example, Kohlberg's emphasis on justice is sufficient with respect to this is a matter of considerable debate.[34]

These cautionary remarks should not deter us from pursuing Hiltner's insight. They simply alert us to the complexity of the task we confront if we pursue this route. Hiltner, as I noted, did not do so in any systematic sense. He tended to focus his attention increasingly on the notion of responsibility as the core moral challenge confronting pastoral care. It is to that topic that we must finally turn.

The Moral Content of Responsibility

Hiltner wrote very little about particular moral principles as they related to pastoral care. Thus, we find very little discussion of love and freedom as moral principles (to mention two that he addresses in *Theological Dynamics*) in his direct discussion of the relationship of ethics and pastoral care. Rather, Hiltner tended to discuss the moral dimension of pastoral care under the rubric of responsibility. Responsibility was both a psychological concept and a religio-ethical one for Hiltner. These two dimensions of responsibility were at least partially separable. Achieving greater responsibility in a psychological sense, for example, did not necessarily guarantee achieving greater responsibility in a religio-ethical sense.

Hiltner's greater emphasis on responsibility in his discussion of ethics and pastoral care is certainly understandable, given his strenuous opposition to legalism and his belief that being responsible was more fundamental than making "correct" moral decisions in every case. Yet, the idea of responsibility threatens to become an ethic of sincerity in practice unless its *moral* content is made clear. And, in fact, in Hiltner's early writings on this there was a tendency subtly to collapse its moral meaning into its psychological meaning.[35]

33. Robert Kegan, *The Evolving Self: Problem and Process in Human Development* (Cambridge: Harvard University Press, 1982).

34. James O'Donohoe, "Moral and Faith Development Theory," in *Toward Moral and Religious Maturity*, ed. Christiane Brussleman (Morristown, N.J.: Silver Burdett, 1980).

35. Hiltner distinguished more clearly between these dimensions in certain of his later works (see, for example, "Clinical and Theological Notes on Responsibility"), though these works were generally not concerned with the relationship of ethics and pastoral care directly.

Given the emphasis he placed on the concept, however, Hiltner's interpretation of responsibility is surprisingly vague. Of course, responsibility was principally responsibility to God. Hiltner argued, for example, that an individual was exercising his responsibility "if he uses that freedom in response to God's leading him to his fulfillment." What exactly does this mean, though? Hiltner sought to clarify this in his articulation of two criteria of responsibility: "Continued contact with the source (God) to which man is responsible, and also evidence that the right Law or the right Word has been heard and heeded."[36] The first, in other words, had to do with acknowledgment of God as the One to whom we are responsible; the second had to do with the "fruits" of one's actions. While there are complications with both of these as criteria of responsibility, I will focus my remarks on the second.

Fruits can be either morally good or bad, or nonmorally good or bad. The "fruits" Hiltner had in mind here are obviously morally or nonmorally *good* fruits. To say this, however, implies some moral principle or value theory in relation to which the fruit is judged to be good. The problem is that Hiltner did not specify what moral principles of value theory he thought should be used in making such determination. This creates a complex problem in pastoral care. If pastoral care is, at least in part, a way of seeking to help persons become more responsible in both a psychological and an ethical sense, then the pastor must make some judgment with respect to whether persons are, in fact, becoming more responsible through her or his pastoral care. In its psychological meaning, the criteria for making such a judgment lie within the psychological theory the pastor uses. In its religio-ethical meaning, however, Hiltner provides us with two criteria but no general standards by which to interpret the criteria in concrete situations.

Hiltner did not specify what standards one might use because, it seems, he thought they were largely a matter of "common sense." Thus, that guidelines from history and basic moral principles such as love and freedom were to be used seemed self-evident to Hiltner. That they could be used and interpreted in any number of different ways was problematic only when they were "misinterpreted," given one's anxiety about the openness of the moral situation itself.[37] While Hiltner may not have actually meant it this way, this gives the impression that diversity in the interpretation of moral principles or guidelines from history is more a matter for psychological reflection than for moral reflection. In any event, Hiltner's failure to clarify the standards

---

36. Hiltner, "Clinical and Theological Notes on Responsibility," 14–15.
37. Hiltner, *Theological Dynamics*, 194.

that were to be used in interpreting responsibility in situations of pastoral care left the agent of pastoral care with no clear way to carry through Hiltner's underlying intention.

Conclusion

In an era dominated by psychological ideas and theories, Hiltner's concern with the sincerity of ethics seems less prophetic than it once did. We struggle less with recognizing the importance of the sincerity of ethics than with articulating a coherent alternative to the ethic of sincerity. Hiltner's emphasis tended to be more on how to incorporate dynamic understanding into a pastoral care permeated with moralistic legalism, while our emphasis today tends to be more on how to recover the moral and theological point of a pastoral care dominated by contemporary psychological understanding. Certain ambiguities in Hiltner's own work perhaps contributed to our current dilemma. Yet, in reflecting seriously on Hiltner's discussion of pastoral care and ethics, we find not simply mistakes that we must find ways to avoid, but also potentially fruitful guideposts on where we might go from here. To lose the richness of Hiltner's contribution would only be to our detriment.

6

A Psychology of Religious Experience

G. A. ELMER GRIFFIN AND
H. NEWTON MALONY

New England in the 1890s was "a veritable caldron of ideas—swirling cross-currents of new experiments in medicine, psychotherapy and mental healing."[1] During the last two decades of the nineteenth century and the first quarter of the twentieth, the psychology of religion movement was a central concern of American psychologists.[2] Several names stand out in this period: B. S. Hall, James H. Leuba, Edwin D. Starbuck, J. P. Pratt, and George Albert Coe. There can be no doubt, however, that the bold and integrative genius of William James was central to the *Zeitgeist* of this era. His *Principles of Psychology*, which included discussion of the moral causes of illness was already making an impact on contemporary psychology. By 1896, James's persistent interest in mental healing, psychotherapy, and "exceptional mental states" had taken him throughout New England. In preparation for the Lowell Lectures which would

1. Eugene Taylor, ed., *William James on Exceptional Mental States: The 1896 Lowell Lectures* (Amherst: University of Massachusetts Press, 1984), 2.
2. Benjamin Beit-Hallahmi, "Psychology of Religion, 1880–1930: The Rise and Fall of a Psychological Movement," in *Current Perspectives in the Psychology of Religion*, ed. H. Newton Melony (Grand Rapids: Eerdmans, 1977), 17–26.

prefigure his Gifford Lectures and his *Varieties of Religious Experience,* he visited various asylums in Massachusetts.[3] On at least one occasion he worked with patients from Worcester State Hospital, where Anton T. Boisen would later do his major work. James's interest in religious matters and in mental healing significantly influenced many thinkers, including William McDougall, James's friend and successor to the Munsterberg chair in psychology at Harvard. McDougall apparently held this position in 1922 when Boisen enrolled there and took his seminar on abnormal psychology.

By the time Boisen had developed his interest in the psychology of religion, the caldron of integrative ideas, although still stewing, had ceased to boil. For reasons that Boisen would point out, the psychology of religion was on the decline.[4] The narrow scientific psychology and antireligious prejudice which James had imaginatively and persistently resisted had gained an upper hand. However, the balanced and open-minded tradition of James was there to be rediscovered in New England, and it is out of this tradition that Boisen developed his own psychology of religion.

Boisen's Intellectual Background in the Psychology of Religion

As a high school student and undergraduate at Indiana University, Boisen had close relationships with two psychologists: one was John A. Bergstrom, an experimental psychologist who lived across the street from him; the other was Dr. William Lowe Bryan, a professor of philosophy and psychology to whom Boisen dedicated his autobiography and whose course in ethics was of great importance in Boisen's development.[5] In spite of their influence, Boisen chose to major in German out of veneration for his father.

In the fall of 1887, Boisen enrolled as a graduate student. He took a course in experimental psychology from Dr. Bergstrom, and under the guidance of Dr. Bryan, he read and became deeply interested in James's *Principles of Psychology.* However, he continued his studies in German. In 1898, Boisen had his first "acute conflict" induced in part by literature he was reading. Out of loyalty to his father's love, he determined to become a forester.

---

3. William James, *Principles of Psychology* (New York: Dover, 1950), vols. 1 and 2; William James, *Varieties of Religious Experience* (New York: Mentor, 1958).

4. See Beit-Hallahmi, "Psychology of Religion," 18.

5. Anton T. Boisen, *Out of the Depths: An Autobiographical Study of Mental Disorder and Religious Experience* (New York: Harper and Row, 1960), 41.

In 1905, Boisen felt called to the ministry. Three years later he entered Union Theological Seminary, where he developed a special interest in "the psychology of religion as interpreted by William James," which retrospectively he lamented had "yet found little place within the structure of theological education."[6] At Union, Boisen took all the courses offered by Coe, a professor of religious education and psychology, who later published *The Psychology of Religion*.[7] Hugh W. Sanborn observes that Coe's *Psychology of Religion* "proved to be a most significant study for Boisen because it directed his attention to the social nature of religion."[8] This aspect of Boisen's psychology, or more accurately of his sociology of religion, is best seen in his second book, *Religion in Crisis and Custom*.[9] However, Boisen disagreed with Coe's theological optimism as well as with his depreciations of mystical experience and of mental illness as an appropriate subject for the psychology of religion. These disagreements would figure significantly in his own psychology of religion.

After some work as a surveyor for the Presbyterian Church and after an assignment in a machine-gun battalion in World War I, Boisen began the quest for a pastorate in earnest. It was this pursuit which precipitated his journey "into the depths." In 1922, after a prolonged psychiatric hospitalization, Boisen entered Andover Theological Seminary and Harvard as a special student. At Harvard he took part in a seminar in "The Psychology of Belief" with Dr. Macfie Campbell. He also took a seminar on abnormal psychology from McDougall, "a great admirer of James." As Sanborn notes, "In the tradition of James, both McDougall and Campbell expressed interest in the relation of religious factors to human development." Sanborn further indicates that in Campbell, Boisen found someone who was critical of all forms of reductionism and who took seriously the role of values in personality integration. In McDougall, he found a psychologist "who approached the mind from a purposive, dynamic orientation without neglecting the social environment."[10] Elements of McDougall's "purposive psychology" also seem evident in the nondeterministic, nonmechanistic tone of Boisen's work.

In 1923, when Boisen was forty-seven years old, he formulated his

6. Ibid., 60.
7. George Albert Coe, *The Psychology of Religion* (Chicago: University of Chicago Press, 1916).
8. Hugh W. Sanborn, *Mental-Spiritual Health Models: An Analysis of the Models of Boisen, Hiltner, and Clinebell* (Lanham, Md.: University Press of America, 1979).
9. Anton T. Boisen, *Religion in Crisis and Custom: A Sociological and Psychological Study* (New York: Harper, 1955).
10. Sanborn, *Mental-Spiritual Health Models*, 18.

project for the study of the interrelationship of religious experience and mental illness. By 1924 he had begun work on it at Worcester State Hospital, where James had visited and had reportedly treated several patients suffering from "functional disturbances."[11] Boisen's research at Worcester, which eventually became *The Exploration of the Inner World,* was conducted on the same, then extraordinary, premise: that certain types of mental illness are functional and therefore treatable by nonmedical intervention. As Charles E. Hall, Jr., observed, this interpretation of mental illness as psychogenic came at a time when most physicians thought it was due to organic causes.[12]

By the time *Exploration of the Inner World* was published, Boisen had a thorough knowledge of the field of psychology of religion. He makes direct citation and evaluations of many important works, including Leuba's *Psychology of Religious Mysticism* (1926), Coe's *Psychology of Religion* (1916), Starbuck's *Psychology of Religion* (1899), and of course James's *Varieties of Religious Experience* (1901–1902).[13]

Boisen had also developed a clear sense of the trends in, and the problems of, the psychology of religion. By 1951, he concluded that the movement had "spent itself." It had diverted its energy to religious education or had become too dependent on Freud, Jung, Adler, Frank, and Kunkel and thus did not have enough basis in controlled, empirical observation. What empirical work was done tended to deal with peripheral factors rather than those of central significance, while the more penetrating studies relied too much upon general observation and armchair reflection instead of on hard data. It was James who provided what Boisen found lacking in the psychology of religion of his day. "In James . . . Boisen found an investigator who recognized the significance of the problem of mental illness for the study of religious experience. Furthermore, James stated explicitly that he only dealt with half of mysticism in his study of the religious mystics [the insane were neglected]. . . . Boisen began at this very point where James left off in *The Varieties.*"[14]

11. Taylor, *Williams James on Exceptional Mental States,* 3.

12. Charles E. Hall, Jr., "Some Contributions of Anton T. Boisen (1876–1965) to Understanding Psychiatry and Religion," *Bulletin of the Menninger Clinic* 31 (January 1967): 42–52.

13. James H. Leuba, *The Psychology of Mysticism* (New York: Harcourt, Brace and World, 1926); Coe, *Psychology of Religion;* Edwin D. Starbuck, *Psychology of Religion* (New York: Charles Scribners Sons, 1899); James, *Varieties of Religious Experience.*

14. Anton T. Boisen, "The Present Status of William James' Psychology of Religion," *Journal of Pastoral Care* 3 (1953): 157.

Boisen's Psychology of Religion

Methods

As one might expect, Boisen sought to do work that was empirically credible. He valued research competence and praised "true scientific detachment." He was never taken in by scientific pretense, for he understood very early the limitations of the scientific method as applied to problems of the psychology of religion. An entire chapter of *Exploration of the Inner World* is dedicated to this problem. Boisen points out the limited meaning of objectivity and the impossibility of scientific disinterestedness; he argues that the application of strict scientific principles to the study of human nature is "like surveyors whose assignment calls for the use of compass and pacing, but who give their measurements in tenths of inches and meantime, all too often, they lose sight of what is distinctive in human nature."[15] Boisen sought to model a methodology that was responsible scientifically yet capable of engaging the profound questions of human nature. He was disenchanted with a scientific psychology that restricted itself to statistical analysis and sought to extend the boundaries of the discipline.

As Paul W. Pruyser has pointed out, Boisen extended James's vignettes approach into "full-fledged case studies with longitudinal perspective." Henri Nouwen also credits Boisen with extensive and insightful use of the "human document."[16] In extending James, Boisen was following G. S. Hall, who used a biographical method. His extensive use of clinical and historical cases, such as that of George Fox, is so pervasive and developed that it can be argued that Boisen anticipated Erik H. Erikson's psychohistorical studies of Luther and Gandhi, both of which are well within the field of the psychology of religion. In using and extending James's method, Boisen went far beyond empirical analysis and was able to include historical and contextual factors in his psychology of religion.

Content

Because of the thematic and consistent nature of Boisen's work, it is not difficult to isolate the central theoretical elements of his psychology of religion. His primary concern was to demonstrate that mental illness, "sickness of the soul," has religious significance. In the

15. Anton T. Boisen, *The Exploration of the Inner World: A Study of Mental Disorder and Religious Experience* (New York: Harper, 1936), 96, 190.

16. Paul W. Pruyser, *A Dynamic Psychology of Religion* (New York: Harper, 1968), 218; Henri Nouwen, "Anton T. Boisen and Theology through Living Human Documents," *Pastoral Psychology* 19 (1968): 49–63.

tradition of James, Boisen held that the study of relgous experience is central to a profound understanding of human nature. The religious significance of the functional mental disorder lies in the fact that it is an attempt to settle ultimate questions about one's life. When confronted with the challenge of this crisis, one can either drift or withdraw, deny responsibility and transfer blame, or attempt a reorganization of one's personality around ultimate values. Other things being equal, a successful resolution depends on the degree to which patients are willing to exercise their capacity of volition and responsibility, and avoid concealment and transfer of blame. This insight was Boisen's primary concern throughout his career.[17]

Boisen's psychology of religion was occupied secondarily with an attempt to understand the nature of religion. He was not content to see to it that religion was granted a legitimate place in the study of human nature, but he also concerned himself with examining religion in the light of psychiatry and psychology. For him, it was not just a matter of what religion and religious experience can tell us about human nature. He was also concerned about what psychology and psychiatry can tell us about religion and theology. For example, in an article entitled "Theology in the Light of Psychiatric Experience," he analyzes theological concepts such as sin and guilt in light of psychological knowledge. Here and in other publications, Boisen brackets questions about the metaphysical reality of God and other religious constructs in order to understand their psychological function. He discovers that "the idea of God and the laws of the spiritual life are derivatives of the social nature of man . . . the idea of God is the symbol of that which is supreme in the individual and social system of loyalties. . . ."[18]

Boisen's openness to psychology allowed him to develop a dynamic model of interaction between the self, God, and the social world. Sanborn calls this model "a personality-in-social-field model." He says that it is "best described as a progressive or constructive socialization-unification model because it focuses on the dynamic interrelations between personality as a developing socio-psychological self and that part of the total social environment in which the individual identifies at any point in his/her life."[19] Through this model, Boisen puts an emphasis on the spiritually healthy person as being primarily defined in social relation. He subjects the idea of God to clinical-

17. Boisen, *Religion in Crisis and Custom;* Nouwen, "Anton T. Boisen and Theology."

18. Anton T. Boisen, "Theology in the Light of Psychiatric Experience," *Crozer Quarterly* 18, no. 1 (1941): 47.

19. Sanborn, *Mental-Spiritual Health Models,* 57.

phenomenological analysis and scrutinizes it for its mental and/or therapeutic value.[20] In our estimation, this kind of model is genuinely integrative and therefore allows for a more interactive psychology of religion.

Boisen's psychology of religion can not be fully understood unless one takes into account his position in regard to the psychoanalysis of religion. When Boisen explored the psychological function of religion, he did not find that religion is an "escape from reality," as Freud maintains. Instead, he said, "religion is to be understood as an attempt to face and grapple with the realities of life, not to escape from them."[21] In spite of his understanding of the psychological and sociological functions, Boisen does not succumb to the "hermeneutic of suspicion" which is exemplified, as he sees it, in the Freudians.

In "The Present Status of William James' Psychology of Religion," Boisen gave an appraisal of the field which, as he saw it, "has often been content to accept psychoanalysis as authoritarian doctrine. . . ." He maintains that Freud and his followers have been interested chiefly in "reductive interpretations" of religion. In contrast, his work, his psychology of religion, and the clinical training of the clergy which grew out of it was "a return to William James and an attempt to take up where he left off."[22] Like James, Boisen advocated a balance between science and religion at a time when religious themes were falling into disrepute. He avoided medical materialism by emphasizing the healing power of experience. He expanded the boundaries of the discipline by extending a methodology which would engage the formative and ultimate issues of human experience.

Boisen's Influence on Contemporary Psychology of Religion

Seward Hiltner, in a seminal article entitled "The Psychological Understanding of Religion," concluded that "perhaps the most unique work in this field in America has been done by Anton Boisen." Hiltner suggested that Boisen's empirical studies of "religious experience in psychotics as well as his dynamic study of eruptive forms of group religious experience" have made significant contributions to the psychological study of religion. But Hiltner also noted that Boisen had not received the attention he deserved "because of Boisen's own psy-

20. Ibid., 65.
21. Anton T. Boisen, "The Psychiatric Approach to the Study of Religion," *Religious Education* 23 (1928): 202–3.
22. Boisen, "The Present Status," 157.

chotic experience and certain preoccupations in his thinking."[23] In an attempt to ascertain the extent to which Hiltner's conclusion are valid, we traced references to Boisen in textbooks on the psychology of religion from 1950 to the present.

Gordon W. Allport, writing three years after Hiltner's comment, failed to mention Boisen. His failure would seem to support Hiltner's claim that Boisen was neglected by later writers, but it is worth noting that Allport in *The Individual and His Religion*[24] was not writing about the same issues as Boisen did. Allport wrote about religion among healthy mature persons whereas Boisen wrote about religion in emotionally disturbed and suffering persons. Allport wrote about individuals; Boisen studied the mentally ill.[25]

We find that Allport virtually ignored James's concern for the "sick mind" and left unattended the relationship between faith and psychopathology. Perhaps Boisen's conclusion about Henry Nelson Wieman is also applicable to Allport, namely, that Wieman ". . . assumes that in mental disorders we are beyond the pale of religion."[26] Besides, Allport may have known little about Boisen's work, since Boisen was a hospital chaplain and a seminary practicum teacher, and not a psychologist, and some of Boisen's studies, for example, his study of the religion of Pentecostals, was published five years after Allport's book.

Paul Johnson's *Psychology of Religion,*[27] which was published in 1955, does not represent a change in the recognition given to Boisen's ideas. Boisen is included in a meaningless list of twenty-one authors who had, according to Johnson, "enriched" studies of the psychology of religion in the 1920s and 1930s. Of peculiar interest is the fact that Johnson was a Boston University School of Theology professor who should have known about Boisen's contribution while Boisen was chaplain at Worcester State Hospital. Boston is geographically near Worcester, but, more significantly, Boisen and Johnson were both concerned about pastoral care and the training of ministers. Nevertheless, Johnson's book virtually ignores the issue of religion in mental illness and Boisen's contribution to it.

The only exception to this trend is Carroll Wise's *Religion in Illness*

23. Seward Hiltner, "The Psychological Understanding of Religion," *Crozer Quarterly* 24 (1947): 3–36.

24. Gordon W. Allport, *The Individual and His Religion* (New York: Macmillan, 1950).

25. Boisen, *Exploration of the Inner World*; "The Psychiatric Approach to the Study of Religion."

26. Boisen, "The Psychiatric Approach to the Study of Religion," 201.

27. Paul Johnson, *Psychology of Religion* (Nashville: Abingdon-Cokesbury, 1955).

and Health, published in 1942.[28] At the time, Wise was occupying Boisen's old position as chaplain of Worcester State Hospital and was heavily influenced by Boisen's legacy at that institution. Wise's book had little impact on the psychology of religion, maybe because he was a chaplain and not a social scientist, but it guaranteed the continued influence of Boisen's ideas in the pastoral counseling movement.

The late 1950s represent a turnaround, notably in Walter Houston Clark's pivotal volume entitled *The Psychology of Religion*, which contains more than twenty references to Boisen. Clark's book went through eleven printings and is considered the most important volume in the field since James's *Varieties of Religious Experience*. Clark gives credit to Boisen for his valuable suggestions regarding the dynamics of mental illness and for providing insightful analyses of the psychodynamics of famous religious figures. He says that Boisen's *Exploration of the Inner World* "makes the bold yet reverent speculation that the knowledge of psychotic experience may help in the understanding of Jesus himself, particularly with regard to his messianic consciousness, even though Boisen does not believe that Jesus was unbalanced."[29] Carl Gustav Jung had suggested earlier a positive role for religion in the treatment and understanding of mental illness, but Clark credits Boisen with providing a clearer model of why the two are related. Taking his cue from James's "sick soul," Boisen contended that in the search for absolutes in life some people are plagued with doubt as to what is worth pursuing and to what loyalties they should give themselves. Religion with its demands as well as its promises is an option for disturbed persons as they struggle through life crisis. The dilemma they face is whether to give themselves to selfish egoism or to unselfish sacrifice. Intense suffering often results, according to Clark's presentation of Boisen.

The decision of sufferers to give themselves to faith is a testimony to the power of religion in human life. In affirming Boisen's observations, Clark concluded, "Under no other form can the human mind project an aim so ultimate, all-embracing, and profound than in his conception of the divine." According to Boisen, the process works in the following way: "As long as his [the patient's] attitude toward the crisis is a responsible one, no matter how distorted some of his ideas, there is hope that he may get back in touch with reality and so recover. Indeed his stability may be firmer than before. But if the crisis breaks

---

28. Carroll Wise, *Religion in Sickness and Health* (New York: Harper, 1942).
29. Walter Houston Clark, *The Psychology of Religion* (New York: Macmillan, 1958), 14.

him and he gives up, he may become a 'drifter,' like the simple schizophrenic, or utilize the delusion of persecution to excuse himself, as
in paranoid schizophrenia, or, worst of all, degenerate into the silli-
ness and complete disorganization of hebephrenic schizophrenia."[30]
Boisen concluded that taking the religious rather than the psycho-
pathological route out of suffering often results in a grandiosity that
has both eccentric and creative features, as the prophet Jeremiah and
the charismatic leader George Fox illustrate.

Of import for the development of the psychology of religion was
Clark's strong emphasis on the psychopathology of religion and his
conviction that Boisen provides a creative elaboration of James's theory of the sick soul in his dynamic model of the relation between
religion and mental illness. These themes have had a lingering influence on the development of the field.

In 1968, Pruyser, late professor at The Menninger Foundation, published *A Dynamic Psychology of Religion* and called Boisen's *Exploration of the Inner World* profound. He said that Boisen's ideas "stress a
dimension that is much needed in psychology of religion,"[31] especially
his practice of placing both religion and psychopathology within the
framework of the "life crisis."

According to Pruyser, Boisen saw mental illness, at least catatonic
schizophrenia, as an attempt to reorganize the personality in terms of
optimal potentialities and ultimate loyalties. In this sense, mental illness and religious experience are related, and religious experience is
placed "at the nexus of the holistic, integrating tendencies of the
organism."[32] Boisen testifies to this truth when he says of himself, "If
I have recovered, as I think I have, I cannot ascribe it to the methods
of treatment, but rather to the curative forces of religion. . . ."[33]

Pruyser recognizes a second significant contribution that Boisen
made to the psychology of religion: Boisen's reliance on his own experience to inform theory. Clifford Beers, in *The Mind That Found Itself*,[34]
pioneered the method of reflecting on one's own mental illness, but
Boisen went one step further and formulated a theory of schizophrenia
on the basis of his experience.

A book related to the psychology of religion but written by a soci-
ologist appeared in 1970—J. Milton Yinger's *The Scientific Study of*

30. Ibid., 182, 348.
31. Pruyser, *Dynamic Psychology of Religion*, 12.
32. Ibid., 12.
33. Boisen, *Out of the Depths*, 99.
34. Clifford Beers, *The Mind That Found Itself* (New York: Longman Green, 1908).

FIG. 1 **Individual Tendencies and Needs Relevant to Religion**

	General	Variant
Normal	How handle the fact of death? (Malinowski)	How deal with persistent loneliness? (Fromm)
Abnormal	How deal with repressed hostilities? (Freud)	Does religion help control neurosis? (Boisen)

Religion.[35] Considered a classic, it includes seven references to Boisen. In a chapter on "Religion and Character," Yinger compares four major theorists who saw religion functioning in human life. Boisen is one of them. Figure 1 shows how Yinger compared the way in which Malinowski, Freud, Fromm, and Boisen saw religion meeting different needs in people.

The diagram indicates that, for Malinowski, religion helps people deal with death (a normal and universal need); for Freud, religion helps people deal with repressed hostilities (a universal but abnormal need); for Fromm, religion helps people deal with loneliness (a variant of a normal need); and for Boisen, religion helps people deal with mental illness (a variant and abnormal need). A text in the psychology of religion by Daniel C. Batson and W. Larry Ventis uses a similar spectrum to clarify the function of religion in life: ". . . the views of psychotherapists on the relationship of religion and mental health cover a very wide spectrum. They run the gamut from Freud's contention that religion is a form of mental illness, through Boisen's contention that mental illness is potentially religious, to the contentions of Jung and Allport that religion, conceived broadly, is necessary for mental health."[36]

In Yinger's interpretation the use of the word *neurosis* is interesting. It is probably an imprecise term for what Boisen really meant, for he was referring to something more serious than neurosis and yet something less serious than a complete psychotic breakdown. Boisen felt that religion could be restorative in moderate disturbance where the person was experiencing identity and loyalty confusion and where there was an option of giving up on life or reaffirming it. This is close

35. J. Milton Yinger, *The Scientific Study of Religion* (New York: Macmillan, 1970).

36. Daniel C. Batson and W. Larry Ventis, *The Religious Experience: A Social-Psychological Perspective* (New York: Oxford University Press, 1982), 215.

to what James termed the outlook of the "sick soul." In these cases, catatonic schizophrenia being the prime example, there is much suffering and the real possibility of giving in to the psychosis. At the same time, the possibility of resolving the crisis by religious dedication is also a possibility. Yinger confuses the issue by terming the struggle "neurosis."

In another section, Yinger notes correctly that in his study of 173 hospitalized mental patients Boisen found a small but significant percentage of patients who used religion to reconstruct their lives. Yinger notes, however, that ". . . Boisen does not explore the conditions in which one may hope for the visions of a Fox instead of the illusions and delusions of a disturbed person."[37] A closer reading of Boisen shows that he felt strongly that prior religious involvement was the deciding feature when the religious option was chosen.[38] Culture and previous experience are also important. And as Yinger himself notes, Boisen was one of the researchers who in the second quarter of this century explored the importance of economic hardship for understanding religious sect development. He follows in the tradition of the "deprivation hypothesis" insofar as he suggests that extreme forms of religious expression are often compensations for poverty.

A year after publication of Yinger's book, Merton Strommen edited a volume called *Research on Religious Development: A Comprehensive Handbook.*[39] In an overview article on "Psychological Interpretations of Religious Experience," Peter Bertocci discusses Boisen along with James, Otto, Freud, Erikson, Jung, Fromm, Maslow, Allport, and Nuttin. Obviously, Boisen is listed with significant notables!

In the same book, Bernard Spilka and Werme discuss Boisen and suggest that religion may function four ways in psychopathology. First, it may be the symptom of underlying disturbance because of its susceptibility to diversity and uniqueness. Second, it may be an agent for controlling deviation and suppressing pathology. Third, it can by focusing attention on an afterlife or compensatory ideology, become a haven from crisis. Finally, it may be the occasion for a constructive handling of stress.

Spilka and Werme note that Boisen felt there was a thin line between the first and the last function. At times, misinterpretations may go both ways: on the one hand, bizarre constructions may be construed as pathological symptoms (function 1) when they are, in

37. Yinger, *Scientific Study of Religion,* 200.
38. Boisen, *Out of the Depths.*
39. Merton Strommen, ed., *Research on Religious Development: A Comprehensive Handbook* (New York: Hawthorn, 1971).

fact, reconstructive attempts (function 4); at other times, religion may seem constructive when it is, in truth, symptomatic of disturbance. Thus the writers accord to Boisen a sensitivity that might be missed by casual readers of his material, if they see him as suggesting that any and all religion among the mentally ill persons is integrative.

The most recent text in the field, one by Spilka, Ralph W. Hood, and Richard L. Gorsuch, continues to recognize Boisen's importance. Two significant themes emerge: first, the authors explicitly relate Boisen to O. Hobart Mowrer; second, they relate Boisen to William James.

Spilka, Hood, and Gorsuch maintain that Boisen may have had a significant influence on Mowrer's emphasis on conscience in religion and psychopathology. Mowrer felt that mental illness was due to an overly weak, rather than an overly strong, superego. Guilt was not false, as Freud had suggested. The voice of conscience and the importance of confession and restitution are important for a return to health, according to Mowrer. Spilka, Hood, and Gorsuch cite Boisen and Mowrer in support of their idea that "both private and public confession can be used to gain a sense of forgiveness and to make a commitment for constructive behavioral change." They also like Boisen's statement that "when insights achieved in mystical experiences are integrated into a new and valuable social self that a truly religious basis for positive psychological growth occurs."[40] In any case, they see that Boisen and Mowrer have much in common.

Regarding the relationship between James and Boisen, Spilka, Hood, and Gorsuch conclude that James "insisted that what all religious experiences share in common is a resolution to a previously experienced uneasiness." They maintain that Boisen would agree with this statement, citing his comment that "a religious experience marks the successful resolution to an inner conflict." In a later discussion, it is clear that they see Boisen as building on James's distinction between the healthy and the sick mind in religion.[41]

Conclusion

This chapter has attempted to relate Anton Boisen to the tradition of William James by considering his intellectual heritage, his elaborations of James's contention that religion is an essential part of

---

40. Bernard Spilka, Ralph W. Hood, and Richard L. Gorsuch, *The Psychology of Religion: An Empirical Approach* (Englewood Cliffs; N.J.: Prentice-Hall, 1985), 195, 305.

41. Ibid., 156, 173.

human nature, his construction of a theory that builds on the idea of the "sick soul," and his continuing and significant influence on current psychology of religion. We have maintained that Boisen is a theorist and a methodologist whose ideas are still worthy of note for the field. His understanding of the way in which religion is related to psycho-pathology will continue to inform the psychology of religion for some time to come. In this form, and in others, the thought of William James remains alive.

7

A Paradoxical Understanding of Persons

HERBERT ANDERSON

In an essay written for *Theology Today* in 1963, Seward Hiltner lamented the absence of a systematic Christian anthropology. Systematic theologians like Niebuhr, Barth, and Brunner were, he said, correct in pointing away from "humanistic, or legalistic, or rationalistic distortions of Christian anthropology," but none of them established anthropology as a systematic perspective within Christian theology. Because the divine-human relationship is the concrete datum of all theology, Hiltner insisted that "the genuinely basic content of theology proper should be the same as the basic content of anthropology, soteriology, eschatology, and ecclesiology."[1] Even a thoroughgoing Christocentrism should not render the study of humankind irrelevant and meaningless.

Although Hiltner did not present a fully developed theological anthropology, he was intent on articulating clearly and truthfully the nature of human nature. The beginning context for that study is the divine-human relationship revealed in Christian scriptures. Self-

---

1. Seward Hiltner, "The Future of Christian Anthropology," *Theology Today* 20, no. 2 (1963): 244, 252.

conscious and disciplined thought from a Christian perspective neither can nor should ignore the priority of special revelation. At the same time, Hiltner believed that one must be able to take into account anything genuinely relevant that turns up from any source. As long as one remains faithful to the normative vision of humanity revealed in the person of Jesus, it is desirable and even necessary to examine all possible data from the human sciences that might illumine our understanding of humankind. Truth about the human condition cannot be confined to special revelation.

The Eclectic Character of Hiltner's Personality Theory

This chapter is in two parts. The first part examines the sources of Hiltner's theory of personality. Because he was willing to "take into account" data about the human person from a wide variety of sources, his personality theory is eclectic. It is shaped by three primary sources: the psychoanalytic movement, Kurt Lewin's field theory, and the self theory of Carl R. Rogers that is implicit in the therapeutic method that Hiltner adopted. The second part considers Hiltner's paradoxical anthropology. One must always say at least two things that frequently appear to be in contradiction about human nature. Part of the genius of Hiltner's methodology was his ability to regard theological and psychological perspectives with equal seriousness.

Sources: The Psychoanalytic Movement

The psychoanalytic movement provided Hiltner with a basic dynamic approach to the understanding of personality. At a time when the church was suspicious of psychology in general and Freud in particular, Hiltner consistently and courageously maintained that Freud's contributions were too significant to be lost in criticism. Although he found the term *unconscious* etymologically problematic, Hiltner agreed with Freud that there are indeed intrapsychic forces influencing human behavior that are outside awareness. "The dynamic facts which Freud present are what matter, and these are that there are moving and vital parts or aspects of the personality ordinarily not in consciousness which nevertheless influence conduct, including thought."[2] The interaction of those moving and vital parts is marked by "conflicts among energy dimensions, the tensions and counterbalances among forces, and a variety of equilibriums."[3] Hiltner consistently regarded the person in dynamic rather than static ways. As a

2. Seward Hiltner, *Pastoral Counseling* (Nashville: Abingdon, 1949), 73.
3. Seward Hiltner, *Theological Dynamics* (Nashville: Abingdon, 1972), 14.

consequence *no one* ever arrived. What mattered to him was that one was on the way in the right direction.

A dynamic approach to personality meant for Hiltner as well as the Freudians that conflict is a permanent part of life. "Dynamic psychology shows us that various claims made upon us tend to become internalized as aspects of personality; insofar as these conflict in the world outside, they conflict also in the world inside."[4] Conflict is both internal and external. Hiltner was careful not to equate internal conflict with unexpressed biological needs, although he insisted that those needs have a truth and reality that must be dealt with. And yet psychic life is deep, energetic, in conflict, and full of self-deception about values, needs, and wants. It was Freud's claim regarding the unconscious that led to the assertion regarding the dynamic character of psychic processes. The fundamental truth about conflict is that it is inescapable because life has depth not always apparent.

This conclusion that the person is inescapably conflicted affected how Hiltner defined the goals of pastoral counseling. The pastoral task is to help people find ways of living through conflict. Personality growth proceeds through this constructive handling of conflict, not through the absence of it. This truth, Hiltner ruefully observed, is one of the easiest points in dynamic psychology to see in general and one of the most difficult to believe in particular.

The neo-Freudian perspectives of Karen Horney and Erich Fromm shaped Hiltner's personality theory in significant ways. He found that both of them understood the person in ways that reflected the social and communal aspects of Christian anthropology. Their psychodynamic approach to the human situation helped to determine Hiltner's own interpretation of the creative and destructive processes in human life and society. The health of the whole society and the health of each individual are inextricably linked together.

Hiltner was particularly appreciative of Fromm's willingness to use the depth insights of psychoanalysis to examine issues that Christianity had always regarded as basic. "Men who accept the fact of their freedom, instead of fleeing in panic before the responsibility it brings, will set about reconstructing themselves and their society without minimizing the evil and destructive forces within and without, that constantly threaten them." Both Fromm and Hiltner used the tools of the psychoanalytic tradition to probe human evil. And yet this probing did not eventuate in despair about human possibility. Hiltner agreed with Fromm that there was something more to humankind beneath the evil. "Far from becoming discouraged about man's potentialities through the revelations of rationalization, repression, and all the other

4. Hiltner, *Pastoral Counseling*, 76.

automatic psychic defense mechanisms that man uses, Fromm has said repeatedly that it is the positive core trying to move toward fulfillment that impresses him."[5] Throughout his long and significant career, both in theory and in practice, Hiltner remained relentlessly realistic and yet constantly confident about human possibility.

Sources: Kurt Lewin's Field Theory

Although Hiltner regarded Freud's dynamic psychology as a highly illuminating perspective on the development and functioning of the person, he looked to more biological metaphors in order to move beyond the mechanistic aspects of Freud's position. In all organic life, including human life, the dynamics are far from being mechanical. As a single unity the human organism always behaves as a unified whole and not as a series of undifferentiated parts. The biological perspective, which emphasized both functional differentiations and organismic unity, significantly influenced both Hiltner's theory of personality and his understanding of the healing process.

Hiltner was most interested in identifying how the various differentiated aspects of the human person are interrelated. For that task, Kurt Lewin's field theory was an invaluable resource. Personality, body, and environment are all regions of one life space. The person is not only dynamic or conflicted but also organismic and intricately interdependent. Hiltner follows Lewin's field theory closely in identifying the person as a complex energy field, motivated by psychological forces, and behaving selectively and creatively. The person, according to Lewin, is at the same time separated from the rest of the world by means of a continuous boundary and yet included within a larger reality. These themes of differentiation and relatedness that are central to Lewin's personality theory are consistently present in Hiltner's thought as well.

In the *Preface to Pastoral Theology,* Hiltner modified field theory to disclose his understanding of healing the human person. The healing process is defined by Hiltner as "the restoration of functional wholeness that has been impaired as to direction and/or schedule. . . . What is restored is not, theoretically, a vision that once actually existed 'fullgrown,' so to speak. It is restoration only in terms of process and direction." The wholeness of the organism is functional and dynamic. It comes about because of the constructive integration of differentiated intrapsychic processes. Hiltner concluded, because of the dynamic character of life, that redemption was also directional.

---

5. Seward Hiltner, "Erich Fromm and Pastoral Psychology," *Pastoral Psychology* (1955): 11–12.

Because the human person is an interdependent organism, healing is also of a piece. In the imagery of field theory, "no aspect of the field is categorically separated from any other or from the focus."[6] For the Christian, the movement toward wholeness cannot be defined apart from the individual's connection with God who is the ultimate ground and meaning of existence. With that, Hiltner reaffirmed his conviction that theological anthropology can never be far from the divine-human relationship.

Both the impairment of the organism and the integration of differentiated processes into a psychobiological unity imply the action of the individual as decision-maker. The activity and creativity of the self is of central importance. Hiltner borrowed the metaphor *participant-observer* from Harry Stack Sullivan to describe the role of self-consciousness in the integrative process. Consciousness and decision-making are both essential to the organism's movement from unity to differentiation to a higher level of complex unity or organismic integration. However, the capacity to decide may itself be impaired. The impairment which most needs healing, Hiltner observed, is that which seems to be most inaccessible to decision, and yet it is precisely to that area that decision must be applied if there is to be healing.[7] The way out begins with the emergence of a genuine conviction of sin. The self, because it is free, is capable of sin. The sinful self, when it is fully conscious of its sinfulness, is also an agent in healing.

For Hiltner, field theory is not as much about a theory of personality as it is a way of understanding the influence of the gospel in relation to the influences of human knowledge in general. It is a metaphor for describing the interaction of the saving truth of gospel with other terms of truth in the healing process. In reference to the study of the person, Hiltner was willing to take into account anything relevant from any source. That same openness is present in Hiltner's understanding of healing. If healing is all of a piece and all in the same field, then "any healing, brought about by whatever means, may have religious dimensions or move toward religious depth. It is its effect upon the production of functional wholeness that indicates the degree and kind of its religious dimension and depth."[8]

Sources: Carl R. Rogers's Self Theory

Hiltner's emphasis on the responsible, decision-making, conscious self points to yet another influence in the development of his theory

6. Seward Hiltner, *Preface to Pastoral Theology* (Nashville: Abingdon, 1958), 99–100.
7. Hiltner, *Preface to Pastoral Theology*, 97.
8. Ibid., 100.

of personality that is more implicit than explicit. Although the influence of Carl R. Rogers is more apparent in Hiltner's counseling methodology than in his personality theory, the two are not easily separated. In a footnote in his early book on *Pastoral Counseling*, Hiltner acknowledges the need for more consideration of the self "which is of equal importance to psychological studies on the one hand and to philosophical and theological studies on the other."[9] The self as decision-maker is related to factors affecting development on the one hand and to that which makes for impairment or healing on the other hand. Some of these factors are conscious, some are not. Even when the factor of choice or decision is limited and difficult to exercise, the individual is always a deciding self.

There are three principles in Rogers's self theory that are also present in Hiltner's thought: the organism is the total environment; the phenomenal field is the totality of experience; and the self is a differentiated portion of the phenomenal field. Every individual exists in a continually changing world of experience of which he or she is the center. As a result of interaction with the environment, and particularly as a result of evaluational interactions with others, the structure of self is formed. It is an organized, fluid, but consistent conceptual pattern of perceptions of characteristics and relationships of the "I" or the "me," together with values attached to these concepts. The focus of Hiltner's book on *Self-Understanding* is the liberation of the creative powers of the self. The structure of that self transcends mere adjustment. The self must look within to understand itself but it must also "look beyond the within, to that which binds all selves together, to the God who sustains [an individual] when he seeks his true human destiny."[10]

In a chapter on freedom and destiny in *Theological Dynamics*, Hiltner examines self-direction, self-fulfillment, and self-transcendence as three principal ways in which theology has approached the question of freedom. His conclusion is that self-transcendence is a more comprehensive way of understanding human freedom than either self-fulfillment or self-direction. Self-transcendence enhances human freedom because it makes it possible to perceive ambiguities accurately and to be clear-eyed about limits and possibilities in a particular life situation. This discussion on freedom and destiny depends on an understanding of personality not unlike that of Rogers, in which there is a basic congruence between the phenomenal field of experience and

9. Hiltner, *Pastoral Counseling*, 263.
10. Seward Hiltner, *Self-Understanding* (New York: Scribner's, 1951), 171.

the conceptual structure of the self. Although it would be inaccurate to describe Hiltner strictly as a self theorist, his theory of personality presupposes responsible agency that is intent on fulfillment and has the capacity for transcendence.

The sources that have been identified point to three aspects of Hiltner's personality theory. *The person is dynamic and therefore conflicted, organismic and therefore interdependent, and a self and therefore responsible.* These sources, however, do not exhaust all of the factors shaping Hiltner's theory of personality. Anton T. Boisen and Paul Tillich were significant intellectual companions whose understanding of the human situation profoundly influenced Hiltner. What is most evident from this survey of sources influencing Hiltner's theory of personality is his willingness to take into account anything genuinely relevant from whatever source. He was not always explicit about the criteria for defining relevance. He was determined not to be confined by traditional categories or anything like parochial thinking. Because of his openness to truth wherever it is to be found, it is not surprising that Hiltner's theory of personality is eclectic. Truth cannot be confined. Hence no one theory will do.

Toward a Constructive Anthropology

Despite Hiltner's determination to take into account a wide variety of resources regarding the person, he is equally determined that the behavioral sciences must not be allowed to control either the thought forms or assumptions of the church's care of persons. Hiltner transformed the material from his sources in order to construct a theory of personality that was compatible with his understanding of Christian anthropology. In 1949, Hiltner wrote, "What we need is a view which is more realistic, which can take fully into account the dark and evil and even self-defeating aspects and potentialities in human nature, and which at the same time places full value upon the tremendous powers for creativity, for socially useful self-direction, and for responsible and free productivity."[11] Two major themes from that early quotation reflect Hiltner's constructive anthropology: the human potential for evil; and the human potential for inner creativity, self-direction that is socially useful, and the assumption of human responsibility. One must always say two things about humankind. Hiltner's understanding of personality did not waver from this fundamental paradox throughout his career.

11. Hiltner, *Pastoral Counseling*, 258.

The Human Potential for Evil

Part of the appeal of the psychoanalytic movement was its realism about the dark and self-defeating potential of human nature. "The unique fact about psychoanalysis, one might say, is that it has found unparalleled tools for probing the evil in man.[12] Getting down to cases for Hiltner always meant being realistic. The way to avoid superficial, quick results is to "take seriously the 'case history,' with emphasis upon the conflicted and energetic factors in the development of the person in his relationships, and never upon the 'case' as something impersonal."[13] Hiltner was relentless in his demands for a realistic assessment of a life situation. Truth was the supreme value even when it meant uncovering the darker side of a personality that had been hidden from awareness. He was also aware, however, that his search for the truth about one's person was an act of heroic honesty that required courage.

The examination of gratitude in *Theological Dynamics* is an illustration of Hiltner's determination to probe the darker side of all life. Gratitude is not always good. Reactive gratitude, which may begin with the honest expression of appreciation, eventually turns to resentment at the power of the giver and the infantile dependence produced by the gift. Pseudo-gratitude from the outset seeks to redirect an individual's focus away from a particular problem that needs to be confronted. Because of the duplicity of the human heart, Hiltner concluded with characteristic candor, "even genuine human gratitude is never pure and unmixed."[14] Understanding this "darker side of gratitude" led Hiltner to the surprising conclusion that being against gratitude at one time may be a friend rather than an enemy of authentic gratitude that might emerge later.

Hiltner was appropriately cautious about oversimplifications regarding the relationship between sin and sickness. Most theories, he thought, missed the mark because they were not ambiguous enough. "The fact is that sin and sickness are related and not related in very complex ways."[15] Merely regarding sickness as evil is not sufficient because it ignores the meaning of an illness. It is a voice of the personality of the victim that must be taken seriously. Illness may be an unconscious self-relevation of human finitude. Borrowing from the work of Gotthard Booth, Hiltner was "almost" tempted to say that "the

12. Hiltner, "Erich Fromm and Pastoral Psychology," 11.
13. Seward Hiltner, "Contributions of the Behavioral Sciences to Pastoral Care and Counseling," *The Princeton Seminary Bulletin* 62, no. 3 (1969): 39.
14. Hiltner, *Theological Dynamics*, 49.
15. Ibid., 106.

evil in much illness cannot be successfully circumvented unless one gets acquainted with it, and even 'makes friends' with its intention in order to redirect that intention into more appropriate channels."[16] One must look at the whole person even in the darkness.

"Making friends" with the human potential for evil was an urgent matter for Hiltner. It was, in a profound sense, the way of salvation. When he wrote *Self-Understanding* in 1951, the need for self-reflection had been made urgent by the appalling social consequences produced by those who followed fascism or Nazism. The defense against such evil must include reflection and a deeper sense of self-knowledge and self-consciousness. Everyone, Hiltner believed, is capable of moving in the direction of self-understanding. "To cultivate that capacity within the limits of one's courage and ability is essential if one is to achieve stature as a human being."[17]

Hiltner was intent on looking directly and unflinchingly at human evil not only because he believed that the recognition of sin was the beginning of healing. He was also confident that even bad decisions in human life are not beyond repair. "Since sin is not a message of doom but one showing where we can take hold, this is not a bad but a good feeling. It offers more opportunities for us to exercise freedom and get well."[18] Seeing more is seeing better. The truth, he would hold, sets people free. The news of sin is good news. Self-understanding makes possible the expression of inner creativity and responsible action.

The Human Potential for Creativity, Social Usefulness, and Responsibility

Realism about the human potential for evil did not lead Hiltner to a one-sided pessimism. In contrast to the prevailing theological pessimism of his time, Hiltner may have been regarded by some as inordinately optimistic. Pastoral counseling would be a hopeless enterprise if human transformation were not possible. "If, on the other hand, in far-reaching knowledge of the evil depths of human potentiality we can nevertheless emotionally affirm God's movement for positive transformation in human life, we are eductive, and counseling has point and meaning."[19] Hiltner was quick to make a connection

16. Seward Hiltner, "Illness: Product of Personality," *Pastoral Psychology* 13, no. 2 (1962): 9.

17. Hiltner, *Self-Understanding*, 6.

18. Hiltner, *Theological Dynamics*, 106.

19. Hiltner, *Pastoral Counseling*, 259.

between our understanding of the nature of human nature and counseling methodology.

That same confidence in the human potential for constructive
behavior was reflected in Hiltner's *Self-Understanding*. The person, he
said, can be transformed, if not completely, at least enough to turn
uselessness into productivity, aimlessness into creative expression,
thoughtlessness into concern, and misery into happiness. It is never
an easy process, but it can happen. *People can be transformed through
psychotherapy, friendship, and personal religion.* On occasion, Hiltner
linked this essential creative self with the operation of the Holy Spirit
or the grace of God. At other times he labeled this deeper potential
self within every person as the ethical conscience. "The ethical conscience is progressive, stands on the deepest reality of the inner life,
and its whole purpose is corrective."[20] The potential for good and the
potential for evil are both present within each person. The emergence
of the ethical conscience or potential for good is not entirely of our
own conscious making, however responsible we might be for movement toward healing, but the result of God's Spirit acting in human
life. What we work hard for happens in spite of our efforts.

The liberation of the creative human spirit *will lead human beings
to act in the interest of community.* Hiltner believed that true self-
interest could be distinguished from selfishness because it seeks for
the common good. One cannot escape being involved in the complexity of society's life in community, nation, and world. The inward look
is as essential for the welfare of society as for that of the individual.
Self-interest and social concern are never mutually exclusive. Genuine
responsibility begins with responsibility for the self. "Any attempt
categorically to separate individual and social responsibility, or to dis-
claim one or the other, is itself a mark of irresponsibility." Individual
and community are inextricably linked.

Although Hiltner *regarded responsibility as an essential mark of the
person,* he was realistic about the limits to genuine responsibility. It
can be subverted by exaggeration, by the obsession of perfection or
scrupulosity. It can be subverted by assuming exaggerated responsibility for other things and people, or by secret self-pity, or even more
by secret hostility. In a way that is consistent with his relentless realism, Hiltner uses clinical criteria to disclose the ways "in which an
apparent exaggeration of responsibility subverts its intent."[21]

From the clinical perspective, human responsibility is a directional

20. Hiltner, *Self-Understanding*, 119–20.

21. Seward Hiltner, "Clinical and Theological Notes on Responsibility," *Journal
of Religion and Health* 2, no. 1 (1962): 16, 9.

phenomenon rather than a trait of character. It is more like a product than it is like a trait. Responsibility is not a quantum detached from either the characterological or the environmental contexts. The clinician looks at responsibility contextually, motivationally, and situationally. The advantages of this clinical perspective on responsibility are threefold: it is realistic, particularly about motivation; it shows that responsibility is not something to be possessed apart from the environmental context; it is more concerned about understanding the past as a springboard for present and future responsible action than judging the past.

From the theological perspective any assertion about responsibility is first of all an inference about the divine-human relationship. A large part of both Judaism and Christianity may be seen as efforts to help individuals become or remain responsible. "That basic responsibility is to God ('Against thee, and thee only, have I sinned'); but since God wills the fulfillment of the self and other persons, being irresponsible to God means, automatically, being irresponsible to the self and to others as well."[22] Although Judaism and Christianity differ on how human beings are restored to responsibility or helped to maintain it, both presuppose that it is God's intention that humankind might respond to God and to others. "Thus responsibility is fundamentally to God; and when this is exercised, and only when it is exercised, there is human fulfillment for both persons and society."[23] The self, understood clinically and theologically, is always a responsible self.

Summary

An address entitled "Theological Perspectives on Humanness" is Hiltner's clearest and most systematic presentation of his anthropology. He explicitly identified his understanding of humankind as paradoxical. No adequate statement can be made about being human except one of apparent contradiction and hence continuing tension. "Thus humankind is indeed not only full of evil but also of sin, the latter term implying complicity in producing the predicament and also, therefore, provided that proper help can be found, some chance of reconstructing the existing situation."[24] Evil or badness is not the whole or even the most basic truth about humankind. There is a deeper quality, an essential self that contradicts what we perceive as

22. Ibid., 15.
23. Ibid.
24. Seward Hiltner, "Theological Perspectives on Humanness." Unpublished paper for the Ohio University Conference on Humanness, p. 3.

the human predicament. One must always say two things about the nature of human nature.

There is a second paradox identified in this address on humanness that is consistent with Hiltner's earlier writings about human sexuality. Humankind is both living as animated bodies and living in accordance with special qualities granted by the Creator. The person cannot escape being body. And yet, human beings, created in the image of God, have a capacity for freedom and love, which is itself finite and limited in the conditions of existence. We are bodies and we transcend being bodies. Hiltner regarded the Pauline concept of spirit (which included body but not as a human possession) as a bold step in showing the proper relationship between humankind as animated bodies and humankind as made in the image of God.

The third paradox that Hiltner noted as characteristic of humanness has to do with being and becoming. The metaphor of pilgrim (as in *Pilgrim's Progress*) was a "foretoken of modern developmentalism" and the title *saint* was a way of reminding us that process is in the interest of a fully functioning self even if that goal is never achieved.

> The two ideas of pilgrimage and sanctification have been discussed primarily to show that, long before modern views of development and process had evolved, the Western theological tradition had insisted that any conception of desirable humanness, to use our current vocabulary, would be meaningless if the quality were seen only cross-sectionally, as simply present or absent, instead of as a paradox involving the whole living of a life.[25]

Even though we are sure that we never arrive at perfect humanness, it is impossible to imagine being human without articulating stages in the process of development.

Hiltner used the theological metaphor of the kingdom of God to identify a fourth major paradox that is essential to humanity. Although it should be said that Hiltner's primary focus was on the inner world, the self is always social. True humanness is never disconnected from community. "Precisely as the view of Jesus did not and could not separate the individual from the social dimensions, so I believe we must reason today."[26]

The genius of Hiltner's anthropology was his ability to uncover the ambiguities of the human situation as demonic and to articulate the paradoxes of humanness as normative. Whether the images used to

25. Ibid., 15.
26. Ibid., 19.

describe humankind came from psychological or theological sources, paradox was evident. Our misunderstandings about humanness arise when a basic paradox is broken in either direction. "To take the situation as genuinely paradoxical is, on the one hand, to be prepared to live with its tension, but it is, on the other hand, to strive for untangling at any point where that is possible. There is active seeking without, however, the illusion that the search will ever break the tension. Thus, the acceptance of the big paradox may lead to resolution of many smaller paradoxes."[27] The capacity to think paradoxically without being immobilized into passivity is what makes it possible to strive to achieve an unrealizable goal. The ability to think paradoxically is also a healthy corrective to any inclination to think one-dimensionally about the person. We might have been able to avoid some of the excesses of the modern pastoral care if we had heeded Hiltner.

Hiltner insisted that a theory of personality that is consistent with a Christian theological anthropology cannot begin either with God or with humanity, but each must be seen at all times in the light of the other. Humanity is the context for thinking about God. With characteristic candor, Hiltner observed that no complete theological anthropology has emerged that maintains the paradox in proper balance. Hiltner himself erred on the side of the human dimension. He was a courageous advocate for diverse sources of truth about the nature of human nature. Sometimes his passion for taking psychology seriously led him to equate psychology with theology much too readily. And yet, throughout his career, he was in principle determined to keep the paradox alive. Hiltner's challenge to generations of pastoral theologians who follow after him is to continue to develop a theological anthropology that maintains the paradox of tension and mutual support even though we know too, paradoxically, that can never be achieved. What matters is that we are on the way in the right direction.

27. Ibid., 24.

8

A Ministry
of Reconciliation

RALPH L. UNDERWOOD

What was Anton T. Boisen's vision of Christian ministry and what is its significance for Christian ministry today? Though Boisen's own ministry entailed much work with ordained ministers and persons seeking to become ordained ministers of the Christian faith, these questions are not addressed to the ordained ministry alone but to the ministry of all Christians. Boisen's own ministry grew out of his personal encounter with mental illness and with the mental illness crisis in Western civilization. The problem of mental illness in today's culture is still very much with us, yet we are increasingly conscious of additional problems. Since Boisen, we have entered the nuclear age and its threat of human annihilation. While we still puzzle over the strange territory of the personal psyche, we also encounter, as never before, the strange territory of many cultures more intensely exposed to one another in educational, political, economic, health, and religious dimensions. Do such developments enhance or diminish the significance of Boisen's vision of Christian ministry?

My thesis is that, for Boisen, the essence of Christian ministry is the task of understanding guidance toward the ends of reconciliation, including ultimate unification with God, and social participation. This statement does not encompass all that Boisen assumes or says about Christian ministry, but it interprets the core of his message. The emphasis on guidance underscores Boisen's belief that Christian ministry is primarily addressed to human problems and a person's efforts to solve these problems. Crises were the pristine example, for Boisen, of problem-solving in human affairs. He understood crises to be turning points shaped and directed by human decisions. Hence, guidance with respect to crises and decisions is central to the task of ministry.

Very little of Boisen's writings are on Christian ministry as such. Even then, so much of what he writes adopts a social-scientific viewpoint and is not explicitly theological. In another sense, however, almost everything Boisen has written is about Christian ministry. If ministry is not the overall topic addressed, assumptions about ministry inform the topic at hand. Accordingly, the approach for examining my thesis will be to analyze the basic published writings which Boisen has left us from the perspective of the major sources which generated his vision of ministry. My intent is to analyze sources in order to uncover key concepts which underlie an elusive topic. The sources which will receive extended consideration are his liberal theological heritage which emphasized a social gospel and included social self theory; his personal encounter with mental illness and his interpretation of its meaning; his philosophy of education, especially as it was informed by thinkers such as John Dewey, and by Boisen's own upbringing; and his theory of religion and experience of the religious. Analysis in each area entails some overlap with others, yet each discloses distinctive features of Boisen's understanding of Christian ministry. Taken together, these sources lay the foundation for Boisen's insights regarding Christian ministry. Finally, an assessment of Boisen's vision of Christian ministry will be proffered.

The Social Gospel and the Social Self

The importance of the first two sources, social interpretations of reality and crisis theory, are pointed out in the way that Boisen's *Religion in Crisis and Custom* begins: ". . . religious experience is rooted in the social nature of man and arises spontaneously under the pressure of crisis situations."[1]

Boisen's professional life was fueled by the intellectual ferment in the United States at the time. Two developments which influenced his thinking greatly were the vision of the social gospel and a new understanding of the social self. Boisen was reared in a pious, Reformed family. During his undergraduate days he was impressed with an eth-

---

1. Anton T. Boisen, *Religion in Crisis and Custom: A Sociological and Psychological Study* (New York: Harper, 1955), 3.

ics professor and went on in seminary to assimilate a liberal framework as the context for his religious and ethical interests. The rhetoric of the social gospel was compelling. While at Union Theological Seminary, Boisen was introduced to ministry on New York's lower West Side.[2] Though he was unsuccessful as a young pastor, he consistently emphasized community involvement. He believed that the church's influence is tied to family solidarity and community service.[3] At the heart of his creed one finds the affirmation of social salvation: "To believe in the possibility of a redeemed society and to commit oneself to that belief is the essence of religious faith in this modern world; to disbelieve in this is the unpardonable heresy."[4]

Because of this commitment to societal redemption, Boisen studied not only individual crises, but also social traumas; for example, economic crises and war.[5] The extended attention he gave to ministry with the mentally ill cannot be detached from this vision. For Boisen, to minister is to serve in the midst of problems encountered in contemporary life; and to minister in these ways is to contribute to social salvation.

Boisen adhered to a theory of the self that coheres well with his version of the social gospel. George Herbert Mead's theory of the social self enabled Boisen to reflect on the relations of the individual and society. Furthermore, it undergirded his vision of ministry, including the aims of ministry. Also, Mead's theory supplied him with his basic metaphors for the reality of God. Accordingly, Boisen defined personality as "the internalization of the organized beliefs and attitudes of the group." He concluded that ". . . the idea of God stands for something which is operative in the lives of all men. . . . It is the symbol of that which is supreme in the interpersonal relationships and corresponds closely to what Mead has called the 'generalized other.' " Boisen liked the phrase *fellowship with the Greater-than-self,*[6] and spoke of God as friend and guide.[7]

Given this understanding of the self, it is no surprise that Boisen constructs a diagnostic schema based on styles of social adjustment.

2. See Anton T. Boisen, *Out of the Depths: An Autobiographical Study of Mental Disorder and Religious Experience* (New York: Harper and Row, 1960), 60–61.

3. See Anton T. Boisen, *The Exploration of the Inner World: A Study of Mental Disorder and Religious Experience* (New York: Harper, 1936), 232.

4. Anton T. Boisen, *Problems in Religion and Life: A Manual for Pastors* (New York: Abingdon-Cokesbury, 1946), 138.

5. Boisen, *Religion in Crisis and Custom.*

6. See Boisen, *Religion in Crisis and Custom,* 177, 64, 77; see also *Problems in Religion and Life,* 122.

7. See Boisen, *Exploration of the Inner World,* 197.

Nor is it surprising that the church and its ministry are understood primarily in terms of fellowship: "The church is in this view no mere body of doctrine or ceremonies by a fellowship, and its central task is the perpetuation and re-creation of religious faith from mood to mood and from generation to generation."[8]

By virtue of their social nature, according to Boisen, persons construct an inner community, mental representations of persons they love, value, and idealize the most. One's concept of God, then, is the supreme representation of these love objects, and religion seeks union with this "idealized other-than-self."[9] This framework generates commentary on many topics. Concerning marriage, for example, Boisen writes:

> According to Hocking, the idealizing tendency, which Rank recognizes as of the essence of love, represents the fact that the lover seeks that which is beyond the finite love object, and no love relationship is complete until the lovers have made a place for the eternal fellowship of which their own relationship is an expression. Herein we may find the explanation of the ceremonial sanction required in marriage among men of all times and all races.[10]

Moreover, this approach establishes for Boisen what is the nature of the basic human problem to which ministry is to be addressed. The fundamental problem is one of alienation or isolation from one's idealized community, "the fellowship of the best." Boisen saw ordained ministers and psychotherapists as representatives of such a community, and he understood the purpose of their work within this framework. Thus one finds remarkable comments such as the following: "Restoration to 'mental health,' the modern term for 'salvation,' is conditioned therefore not so much upon the resolution of intrapsychic conflict as upon the sense of being received back into the fellowship of the best."[11] For Boisen, isolation is death, and the principal aim of human helping is inner reconciliation and restoration to community.[12] He claims that forgiveness is the "essence of all good psychotherapy and the essence also of the gospel of Jesus and of Paul," and he frames this forgiveness in the context of reconciliation: "The unsocialized, and

---

8. Boisen, *Religion in Crisis and Custom*, 46–47, 210; see also *Problems in Religion and Life*, 83.

9. Boisen, *Out of the Depths*, 199.

10. Boisen, *Religion in Crisis and Custom*, 225–26.

11. Ibid., 208.

12. Boisen, *Exploration of the Inner World*, 196; *Out of the Depths*, 197; *Problems in Religion and Life*, 76–101.

hence unassimilated, interest must be resolved and the sufferer must be able to feel himself restored to the fellowship of the best."[13] Out of reflection on his own experience, Boisen understood guilt as estrangement caused by desires and impulses which one either cannot renounce or acknowledge.[14]

At the heart of psychotherapy, the ordained ministry, and all Christian ministry, in Boisen's vision, is the act of confession and forgiveness. Even so, this act is not the sum total of such ministry. For example, Boisen states that cure is the result not only of confession but also of socialization. One can see how such inferences are faithful to the fundamental concept of the social self. Also, Boisen's emphasis on the quality of interpersonal relationships as primary in human helping, and consequently in all ministry, is a necessary corollary of this vision.[15]

In summary, then, the self is social in origin and structure. Others' values and beliefs are internalized and idealized in the process of forming an internal community. This internal community, the social self, maintains an ongoing dialogue and constitutes the standards to which one is loyal, by which one values oneself and on the basis of which one makes decisions. At the same time ongoing life and new social experience expose one to new ideas and values. Conflicts develop and need to be addressed. If one is to be restored to community, externally and internally, forgiveness and reconciliation are primary requisites. In addition, socialization exposes one to new experiences which may challenge one's present self-understanding. Consequently, at any given time personal wholeness is only relative and is part of an ongoing, dynamic process. Implicit in Boisen's vision is the understanding that while individual wholeness has its own value, it is not to be elevated in isolation from social concerns. Mental healing restores one to functioning in the community so that one can participate in it and contribute to the community. The ultimate goal of such reconciliation and participation is union with God.

By adding social self theory to the social gospel, Boisen attempted to rescue the gospel from neglect of the individual. By wedding the social self and the social gospel, Boisen sought to help mental-health workers and ministers avoid the distortions of individualism. In the course of this project he relativized differences between secular psychotherapy and religious ministry by positing an essential purpose

13. Boisen, *Religion in Crisis and Custom*, 50–52.
14. Boisen, *Problems in Religion and Life*, 75; see also *Religion in Crisis and Custom*, 144.
15. Boisen, *Exploration of the Inner World*, 244–45.

held in common. This interpretation of how Boisen employed the understandings of the social gospel and the social self underscores the significance of reconciliation as a function of ministry. But is it possible to relate this task of ministry to the notion of "understanding guidance," also in my thesis? This question will be explored in the discussion of crisis and mental illness as well as the discussion of Boisen's philosophy of education.

Mental Illness

The second major source of Boisen's vision of Christian ministry to be examined is his understanding of mental illness and crisis. Contrary to what virtually everyone assumes about Boisen, he was not much interested in mental illness. What he was fascinated with was one kind of mental illness: mental illness as a crisis that disclosed to persons their own neediness. He was not interested in organically based mental illness nor in chronic mental illness. He was interested in his own episodic psychoses and the meaning they had for his life and vocation. Along with this he was interested in others' similar experiences.

The kind of mental illness Boisen loved to study was the outcome of a personal crisis. "Crisis" means turning point or time of decision. It is a juncture in the human journey when some telling decision or decisions are made. Because decisions are involved, guidance is an appropriate and vital form of ministry in connection with crises. A crisis intensifies thinking and feeling and is an opportunity which may have a constructive or a destructive outcome.[16] It is important to note that for Boisen mental illness represents a failure to assimilate new experiences and make decisions.[17] At the same time, in the crisis type of mental illness, problem-solving activity continues. Furthermore, this kind of mental illness may be the cost entailed in one's taking risks to make social contributions. "Sanity in itself is not an end in life. The end of life is to solve important problems and to contribute in some way to human welfare, and if there is even a chance that such an end could best be accomplished by going through Hell for a while, no man worthy of the name would hesitate for an instant."[18] This is one reason why Boisen does not see mental illness as an individual matter.[19] The kind of crisis that leads to religious experience, mental illness, or both represents a deep and intense encounter with life's fundamental issues, and, thereby, is religious in essence.

16. Boisen, *Religion in Crisis and Custom*, 68–69.
17. Boisen *Exploration of the Inner World*, 194.
18. Boisen, *Out of the Depths*, 132.
19. Boisen, *Exploration of the Inner World*, 289.

On the basis of his own experience Boisen portrayed the crisis type of mental illness as a personal failure. He struggled to control sexual impulses and felt he could not acknowledge his problem to others in the community he cherished. Analyzing his difficulty and similar experiences of others, he concluded that when persons accept consciously or unconsciously social judgments which threaten self-esteem, these persons suffer from a sense of personal and moral failure and become isolated. He understood this to be the primary difficulty in the battleground of character: "This sense of inner disharmony between what actually is and what ought to be . . . becomes malignant only in so far as it is attended by the sense of isolation in that it has to do with something that makes one feel oneself despicable in the eyes of those he loves and unfit for their company. In other words, it is the sense of moral failure and guilt which appears as the primary cause of difficulty.[20]

Out of his own experience, personal and professional, with the crisis of mental illness, Boisen chastised the church for her neglect of the mentally ill.[21] He audited the liberal church of his day and found it to be bankrupt because it had neglected people who were struggling with issues of spiritual life and death. He believed that clergy without first-hand experience and clinical supervision are hardly able "to speak with authority regarding the way either to individual or to social salvation."[22] Though the change from revealed religion to empirical faith had caused much confusion, Boisen advocated that the church proceed further and more radically in the empirical direction. He envisioned mental illness of the crisis kind as the strange territory which must be captured, the ultimate confusion to be resolved:

It is furthermore my conviction that the remaking of the outer world and the cure of the desperate sickness which now threatens to destroy our civilization is inseparably associated with the problems of the inner world and that out of the efforts to understand and help the mentally distressed should come a new vision of the great Reality to whom we give the name of God, in whom alone we are to find the end and meaning of personal and social life and the sources of power and of renewal.[23]

In one sense, for Boisen, certain members of the mentally ill population represent the confusion and crisis of an entire age. Boisen recognizes the hand of God in all persons who join these distressed persons in caring ways, and he calls on the church to dare to enter

20. Ibid., 28, 149.
21. Ibid., 219–23.
22. Ibid., 248.
23. Ibid., 237.

this ministry and thus recover authority. What this says about Christian ministry is that faithfulness in the hour of crisis is essential to any long-term hope. Certainly Boisen recognized the importance of religious practice and ministry in ordinary life. He spoke to this in terms of the church's task of preserving the insights of faith in customs which preserve the values of faith from one generation to another. Yet he saw in crisis an opportunity to rescue customary religion from stagnation. Accordingly, he advocated special attention to ministry in the context of human crises, the crisis of mental disturbance in particular, as the royal road to recovery of the gospel.

This is the vision of a person who attempted to remind us of the dynamic interaction of personal and societal life. Though he focused much attention on the plight of the suffering individual, he forbade a bifurcation of personal and social salvation. From his ethical sensitivities he modeled a ministry that attends to vulnerable persons and populations, a ministry that hopes to rediscover the presence of God in the midst of human suffering. Such ministry of presence brings reconciliation to alienated persons, since it resocializes them. At the same time, these persons who wrestle with spiritual demons and angels restore to ministering others a sense of their own depths.

It should be clear, then, that the significance of crisis for Boisen's vision of Christian ministry is very much related to the social gospel and social self themes, for the crisis is depicted as one of alienation and isolation, and the resolution entails reconciliation and restoration. Still, if a crisis is a turning point which involves a decision or decisions, and if the crisis type of mental illness is a problem-solving process, something more must be discerned about ministry as guidance. Thus far, the significance of guidance is evident only in the very meaning of the crisis concept. For further help on this issue we turn to Boisen's philosophy of education.

Philosophy of Education

In Boisen's day enthusiasm for the social gospel was matched by live interest in the pragmatic philosophy of John Dewey. As Boisen acknowledged his indebtedness to Mead, so he acknowledged his reliance on Dewey. It was their empirical philosophy which he embraced when he criticized the liberal church as not sufficiently radical in understanding the task of ministry. The philosophy of learning by doing was in the air, and Boisen breathed deeply of it. He came to his conclusion about crisis mental illness as a sense of personal failure to maintain social loyalties by applying Dewey's definition of scientific inquiry. Dewey's philosophy of inquiry was a technique for discovering and solving the problems people faced, and as such was superior to the use of personal influence through the power of suggestion.[24] Boisen pictured the mental hospital as a laboratory for experiential learning about human personality and ordinary human tendencies.

Just as scientists discover laws of nature, Boisen believed, psychotherapists and ministers aim to discover and understand the laws of inner life. In Dewey's philosophy Boisen discerned a partner to the cause of faith. In part this was due to the fact that learning by doing matches so well a vision of learning by serving. Thus Boisen wrote, ". . . service and understanding go ever hand in hand. Without true understanding there can be no effective service in that which concerns the spiritual life. And only to those who come in the attitude of service will the doors open into the sanctuaries of life."[25] Accordingly, the first teacher in Boisen's model of education is the patient whom the chaplain visits and aims to serve. In the process of listening and serving the patient, the chaplain discovers the laws of the inner life.

Following Dewey, Boisen's model of education called for cooperative inquiry. The second teacher, then, is the peer group of chaplains. In the process of reflecting together on their ministry, these ministers teach one another. This cooperative learning serves as a corrective to individualism. These two teachers in the process, the patient and ministry peers, demonstrate that ministry is learning and learning is ministry.

Clearly Boisen understands that ministry as education harbors a religious dimension. Broadly defining means of grace as "those procedures and practices by which religious faith is perpetuated and recreated," he lists various types of such means. These range from the sacramental and devotional to the legalistic, and among them Boisen includes educational means of grace: "Where the holy life is found in the location, and the virtues of discipline and industry are stressed, education comes to be recognized as a means of grace." Also, Boisen associated the creativity of Hebraic and Christian faiths with cooperative worship and inquiry.[26]

To this point, however, the one who serves is the one who learns. Is the model of education and guidance, then, completely eductive? To advance our understanding, we shall examine Boisen's key metaphor for empirical inquiry, the image of "living human documents," and also his personal understanding of supervision. Since Boisen understood ministry to be learning by serving and interpreting

24. Ibid., 182, 245, 256.
25. Ibid., 252–53.
26. Boisen, *Religion in Crisis and Custom*, 135–42, 167–69, 256.

people's problems, he ingeniously compared ministry to the exegesis of texts. For him theological education was largely a matter of learning to exegete historical texts and to exegete or understand people. Hospital patients were "living human documents" and clinical pastoral education helped ministers to learn to read these documents "in the original." Obviously the analogy serves to legitimate empirical inquiry as both ministry and theological education. At the same time, Boisen did not advocate that ministers abandon historical texts, for they represent the accumulated wisdom of the past.[27] Boisen seems to acknowledge that the past constitutes a significant portion of the minister's inner community. He required students to translate psychiatric jargon into the language of ancient wisdom.[28] He claimed that religion evokes "the far look, and that look extends both into the past and into the future."[29] This must mean that Boisen does not see a basic contradiction between historical and empirical approaches. Does this imply that guidance, at least guidance with reference to the ordained minister, is both eductive and inductive? Clearly, the minister's faith and understanding are informed by the historic texts of the faith and by the process of discovery. Both are understood as interpretive disciplines.

Another perspective on the question of guidance is afforded by Boisen's comments about the teacher, which reflects his theory of supervision. He sees the teacher as an active explorer and guide, not only a listener.[30] Of course, the minister is as well a listener and a trusted friend. Here it helps not only to keep in mind Dewey's philosophy but also to recall Boisen's parents as models. He respected his father, who was a teacher and who died when Boisen was a young child, as a tutor, especially as a guide to the world of nature.[31] Exploring new territory is a key metaphor for Boisen of the learning process. The teacher is the explorer-guide. Boisen remembered his mother as a friendly persuader. These models underscore guidance as a process founded on a personal bond and trust between teacher and student. Additionally, they highlight guidance as an eductive process of discovery. At the same time, the guides' or tutors' knowledge of the past enables them to be active and suggestive. The model of teacher or supervisor, then, envisions an educational process that is largely eductive but that has room for some inductive elements.

27. Boisen, *Problems in Religion and Life*, 38, 149.
28. Boisen, *Exploration of the Inner World*, 262.
29. Boisen, *Religion in Crisis and Custom*, 258.
30. Boisen, *Out of the Depths*, 186–87; *Problems in Religion and Life*, 139–40.
31. Boisen, *Out of the Depths*, 21–28, 102.

This conclusion corresponds with Boisen's counsel that ministers are to help people interpret life and its problems.[32] It also provides a framework for reading the epilogue to his autobiography: "I would surely be a man of little faith if I did not recognize in this story the guiding hand of an intelligence beyond our own."[33] It is for this reason that this essay speaks of "understanding guidance." The guidance envisioned is largely a presence at time of crisis, a presence that socializes and leads to reconciliation. This guidance proceeds through a process of inquiry and interpretation, a process that strengthens the bond of trust, educes understanding, and employs resources which help people to understand and resolve their problems. In this model, Christian ministry is addressed primarily to persons in crisis with the aim of restoring them to the best available human fellowship and to union with God through a process of caring inquiry and guidance.

Thus far three main sources of Boisen's vision of Christian ministry have been examined. They are the social gospel and social self theory, from which Boisen developed an image of God as Friend; the crisis of mental illness, which helped Boisen envision an image of God as mysterious Presence; and a pragmatic philosophy of education, which enabled Boisen to interpret God as Guide. The model of Christian ministry drawn from these sources now will be reexamined from yet another angle: Boisen's understanding of religion and religious experience.

Religion and Religious Experience

For Boisen, religion originates in one's relationship with parents and early guides and aims at ultimate loyalties. Religion is "an attempt to raise one's values to the level of the cosmic or universal and to establish and maintain right relationship with those to whom one looks for response and approval, those whose composite impress is represented in the idea of God."[34]

Religious experience entails constructive transformations of persons, a synthesis of crisis and ordinary life experiences which produces inner unification and social adaptation on a universal basis.[35] This concept of a universal, all-inclusive basis is essential. For Boisen all human growth and education call for the exploration, unassimilated experience, and the assigning of the new to an appropriate place

---

32. Boisen, *Problems in Religion and Life,* 91.
33. Boisen, *Out of the Depths,* 210.
34. Boisen, *Exploration of the Inner World,* 53.
35. Ibid., ix.

in one's structuring of experience. People may react to unassimilated experiences in a variety of ways. People are religious when they progressively unify previously unassimilated experiences on a universal basis and not merely on contemporary and local bases.[36] Religion represents an inner world which is both personal and universal; it gives expression to the deepest loyalties and most inclusive communities people can imagine. This overarching perspective on religion contains several motifs, some of which we already have encountered: being universal, religion is social; religion unifies social loyalties into a supreme object of loyalty through processes of idealization and organization; and religion is ethical.

The social nature of religion has already received comment. Here one only needs to acknowledge that for Boisen religion represents "the collective interest." To represent this interest religion must be organized, have ritual, creeds, and leaders.[37] When Boisen became a chaplain he set out first to provide a suitable book of worship for patients.[38] His recognition of the importance of this task is evidenced by his persistence in producing four editions of this book.

Also for Boisen, religion has to do with the ideal; it envisions the world that is not yet. With William James he viewed religion as a function of the ego ideal. Rooted in the influence of parents and early guides, religion embraces and transcends them through such idealization. Because religion lifts up the best, Boisen opposed attempts to gain mental health by means of lowering the expectations of conscience.[39] His vision of ministry does not offer cheap grace. Boisen believed that people seek the infinite love relationship through encounter in human relationships, and no more poignant example exists than his own idealization of the human love of his adult life, Alice Batchelder. Part of the dedication of *The Exploration of the Inner World* reads: "To her I dedicate it in the name of the Love which would surmount every barrier, and bridge every chasm and make sure the foundations of the universe."

Out of this dynamic of the realistic (organizational) and idealistic dimensions of religion is born the ethical character of religion. Boisen claimed that religious geniuses have in common "a will to righteousness and moral achievement."[40] The end of a mysticism is not ecstasy but personal transformation. Religion produces a morality that entails continuous, dynamic growth, not static morality of goodness. Boisen

---

36. Ibid., 151–53.
37. Boisen, *Religion in Crisis and Custom*, 212.
38. Boisen, *Exploration of the Inner World*, 255.
39. Boisen, *Out of the Depths*, 46, 196.
40. Boisen, *Exploration of the Inner World*, 81.

summarizes the socializing and ethical dynamics of organized religion: "There seems to be a law in human nature which forbids us to have secrets and impels us to share our important insights, that which we are afraid to tell creates an area of low pressure and causes mental disturbance. And the new vision which comes in the flow of religious experience must overflow into outgoing activity."[41] In other words, religion has an inner nature which is fulfilled in outward expression.

Boisen's reflections on religion and religious experience confirm earlier comments, which suggest that ministry aims at human isolation in a caring, guiding spirit for the purpose of restoring persons to community, to harmony with God and the universe, and to lives of productive service. In addition, they enhance an understanding of his vision of ministry by affirming religious symbols, organization, and leadership. For Boisen, the task of Christian ministry is the task of helping persons discover and maintain contact with the deepest streams of aspiration so that they will have the capacity and readiness to continue throughout life to explore God's never-ending mystery. He outlines four tasks for the church and her ministry: provide for broad inclusion in services of worship; organize extensions of understanding and good will; revitalize the message of salvation, including attention to the critical needs of individuals; and develop believers' groups.[42]

Assessment

From today's perspective, Boisen's understanding of Christian ministry is not so much outmoded as it is underdeveloped. This is to say that much of his vision speaks well to our situation. Despite the popular image of Boisen devoting all attention to the lone individual, his approach to ministry assumes a vital relationship between social and personal salvation. His examination of economic and military crises was not unlike a case analysis. Of course, the case study analogy hardly seems adequate for reflection on social ministry. The point is not that Boisen provides an adequate method, but that he approaches ministry from a valid principle: God wills to save societies and individuals. In his day, Boisen's writings helped remind ordained ministers and others who were committed to social well-being not to neglect the complex needs of persons. In our time, his vision is a poignant reminder and challenge to discern the needs of society reflected in personal needs and to discern which social ministries promise to serve best the needs of vulnerable and marginal persons.

Likewise, Boisen's understanding of the place of reconciliation in

41. Boisen, *Problems in Religion and Life*, 135–36.
42. Ibid., 127.

Christian ministry is sound. Though our society is less focused on personal guilt, the problems of alienation and the need for conflict resolution and reconciliation are felt keenly today. He astutely insisted on the inner nature of this reconciliation, yet located its significance in a social framework. This social framework is constituted by a dialectical process of interaction between one's inner, ideal community and exposure to social reality. It seems to me that this conceptual model anticipates later developments familiar to us now, such as Ivan Boszormenyi-Nagy's model of the family as a system which processes inner loyalties across generations.[43] Though Boisen did not have the benefit of systems thinking, his appropriation of the thought of his day was presentiment of ways to link intrapsychic dynamics and systems theory.

Boisen's intuitive grasp of the inner world and its conflicts helps to account for his appreciation of symbol, a basic unit in the language of the inner life. Boisen understood worship to be Christian ministry. In addition to his attention to a suitable worship-book project for mentally ill persons and his occasional comments on worship, one should not forget that Boisen and Alice Batchelder created a ceremony as a covenant of friendship.[44] Partly because of his own rhetorical emphasis on learning by doing and partly because he never developed his insights in this area, the place of symbol and worship in Boisen's vision of Christian ministry have not received much recognition. As a consequence, the modern pastoral care movement has been slow to develop constructive insights into the transformative and reconciling power of religious symbols, symbolic action, and worship. Instead, this movement has relied on the person and interpersonal relationships as means of grace. It is understandable that the leaders of this movement have concentrated their energies on dialogue with the psychodynamic disciplines. Clearly, the early pastoral care movement of this century, in which Boisen played a key role, was a renewal movement in the life of the church. Since then many persons have discovered personal, spiritual, and professional renewal by becoming part of the clinical pastoral education process. Also, it is clear today that the liturgical renewal movement is beginning to function in a similar manner. In fact, I believe that there is much promise both for renewal in present-day pastoral care and for advancement of this field through

43. Ivan Boszormenyi-Nagy and Geraldine M. Spark, *Invisible Loyalties: Reciprocity in Intergenerational Family Therapy* (New York: Brunner/Mazel, 1984); Ivan Boszormenyi-Nagy, *Foundations and Contextual Therapy: Collected Papers of Ivan Boszormenyi-Nagy* (New York: Bruner/Mazel, 1987).

44. Boisen, *Out of the Depths*, 165.

dialogue with the liturgical movement. The increased ecumenical diversity among leaders in clinical pastoral education and the pastoral care movement means that exposure to and appreciation of worship and liturgy are growing. This is a new moment in the history of modern pastoral care. Boisen and others simply did not lead the way in this area. Still, he was not without appreciation for the power of worship. Even though Boisen sensed the power of idealization and the inner community, he did not envision fully the extent to which social relations are guided by symbols and images. He tended to forget that crisis encounters are not the only way to renewal before God.

Boisen's vision of Christian ministry provides a model that is good-hearted, spontaneous, and open to the other, but it does not address adequately the question of the nature and authority of ministry. With the increased presence of diverse cultures, east and west, in the United States today, openness to the stranger in our midst, as well as within our own psyches, is even more relevant today than it was in his time. Personal availability and the giving of ourselves in ministry to others are as vital for today's ministry as they were in the birth of the clinical pastoral education movement. Even so, if Christian ministry entails the sharing of self, it entails as well the sharing and communication of who and what one represents. This takes place through symbolic action as well as personal presence. Is reflection on encounters with "living human documents" adequate to account for ministry and to construct a fundamental understanding of Christian ministry? Though Boisen gave lip service to the role of the classical disciplines in theological education, he did not provide a model for how such knowledge is to be brought to bear in substantive ways on the analysis of acts of ministry, including case studies. Certainly facile translations of psychiatric nomenclature into Christian symbols do not yield the kind of self-understanding in ministry which we need! To note this is to point out the limits of pragmatism and pragmatic guidance. What is required for more nearly adequate understanding of Christian ministry is analysis and a synthesis which are more critical in nature. Boisen's account of Christian ministry lacks the critical dimensions that theological, ethical, and some sociological disciplines pursue. For example, while Boisen envisions a ministry of reconciliation that restores social participation for the benefit of others as well as oneself, he articulates no theory of justice to provide discerning judgment and direction for such participation. His suggestive vision of ministry fails to spell out a clear system of checks and balances as well as to identify a final court of appeal for a practical theology of ministry. Today we are becoming more aware that Christian ministry calls for guidance that is both eductive and inductive. Because we care, we are compelled both to listen and to help provide knowledge where it is lacking. Christian ministry assists persons to read their own hearts, and it assists persons to hear what the Word is saying to their heart. Likewise, Christian ministry serves societal and cultural understanding through dialogue and helps societies and cultures to understand what true Christian faith contributes to their situation.

I make these comments as one who feels deeply indebted to Boisen and to the clinical pastoral education movement. It is imperative that we hold onto his insights, wisdom, and dedication. It is equally imperative that we undertake the unfinished task of formulating a practical theology of Christian ministry which is faithful to the apostolic witness to Jesus Christ and responsive to the Spirit ever present in our midst.

9

Physicians of the Soul

> JOHN PATTON

What Anton T. Boisen's work can contribute to the theory and practice of pastoral care and counseling is not immediately apparent. He made very few direct contributions to the way pastoral care and counseling are practiced and would seldom be thought of as a father of modern pastoral counseling. Unintentionally, however, he made a number of contributions which have significantly influenced what pastoral care is becoming today. His oft-quoted phrase, "the living human document," has been used as a text for a number of important developments in modern pastoral care, most notably the clinical pastoral method and, most recently, Charles V. Gerkin's hermeneutical theory of pastoral counseling.[1] Although Boisen's work has often been used more as a text and taking-off point for an author's own concerns than as a theoretical resource for the pastoral care field, I believe that Boisen, in fact, made a fourfold contribution to pastoral care and counseling: in his claiming a place for the pastor in the treatment of the mentally ill; in his breaking down some of the rigid barriers between illness and health; in his theory of crisis; and in his concern for a genuinely empirical theology.

---

1. Charles V. Gerkin, *The Living Human Document: Re-Visioning Pastoral Counseling in a Hermeneutical Mode* (Nashville: Abingdon, 1984).

A Place for the Pastor

"In all my efforts," Boisen said, "I rely upon a simple principle derived from my theological training which seems to me far too little understood. I refer to the view that *the real evil in mental disorder is not to be found in the conflict but in the sense of isolation or estrangement.*"[2] In this affirmation he unintentionally echoed the views of Harry Stack Sullivan who, like Boisen, was most influenced in the development of his views by his attempt to understand schizophrenia. In a striking passage from Sullivan, which begins in his typically matter-of-fact way, he comments, "Anyone who has experienced loneliness is glad to discuss some vague abstract of this previous experience of loneliness. But it is a very difficult therapeutic performance to get anyone to remember clearly how he felt and what he did when he was horribly lonely. In other words, the fact that loneliness will lead to integrations in the face of severe anxiety automatically means that *loneliness in itself is more terrible than anxiety.*"[3]

The words *loneliness is more terrible than anxiety,* in my judgment, express the primary dynamic for the development of Sullivan's interpersonal theory and Boisen's work in establishing mental hospital chaplaincy. Anxiety and the pathological ways in which human beings defend themselves against it do not, he believed, rule out the relevance of a pastor for persons who are experiencing such things. Rather, the desperate loneliness which these patients experience in their efforts to cope with and work through their anxiety actually called for the presence of a minister. Thus Boisen used his own loneliness to motivate himself to establish chaplaincies with the mentally ill—persons who, in his time, were thought to be "too sick" for pastors to be with. "Instead of allowing the psychiatrist to remain the exclusive keeper of the lower regions," Boisen said, "I am hoping and laboring for the day when the specialists in religion will be able with his help to go down to the depths of the grim abyss after those . . . in whom some better self is seeking to come to birth."[4]

Whether or not Boisen would approve of the function of either ministry or psychiatry today is an interesting matter for speculation. One would suspect that he would see much of the use of the psychiatric drugs today as destructive to the process of personal change which was so important to him. Boisen was convinced that the voice of illness must be allowed to speak, and much of today's psychiatric

2. Anton T. Boisen, *The Exploration of the Inner World: A Study of Mental Disorder and Religious Experience* (New York: Harper, 1936), 268.

3. Harry Stack Sullivan, *The Interpersonal Theory of Personality* (New York: Norton, 1953), 262. Italics added.

4. Boisen, *Exploration of the Inner World*, 266–67.

use of drugs mutes or destroys that voice in the interest of symptom relief. One might suspect, further, that although he would strongly approve the increased place of clergy in the care of those who are mentally disturbed, he would view ambivalently the specialization in pastoral counseling which has taken place under the auspices of the American Association for Pastoral Counselors.

I would speculate, and it is only speculation, that Boisen would fear that pastoral counseling specialization would cause the clergy to over-identify with the person and practice of the psychiatrist and become so involved in the therapeutic enterprise that they would forsake their particular contribution to the mentally ill—helping them find the meaning in their illness. Whatever his judgments might be about our present situation, it seems clear that Boisen's contribution to the development of mental hospital chaplaincy and clinical pastoral education has made possible a more significant place for the pastor in the care of those in psychological distress. Persons in Boisen's day seldom thought of their minister as a resource in time of emotional distress. In our day, on the other hand, they quite often view the minister as the first person to consult about their psychological hurts.

Breaking Down the Barriers

In addition to bringing the clergy into the mysterious province of the mentally ill, Boisen helped to break down the walls between the mentally ill and other human beings. Mental illness was not just a disease or dysfunction to be corrected but a meaning to be discerned and discovered. In his valuable book, *Schizophrenia: A Source of Social Insight*, Brian W. Grant points out that Boisen's attempt to discover and interpret the meaning of his own mental illness was "plainly Jamesian."[5] William James, in his *Varieties of Religious Experience*, had suggested that the fact that a person's experience may be labeled as evidence of mental illness does not disqualify that person from being taken seriously and her or his experience being judged as having value and importance. James offers three criteria for assessing the value of such experiences: *immediate luminousness, philosophical reasonableness*, and *moral helpfulness*. If Saint Teresa's theology can stand these tests, he says for illustration, "it will make no difference how hysterical or nervously off balance Saint Teresa may have been when she was with us here below."[6]

Boisen took James's pragmatism and applied it with existential seri-

5. Brian W. Grant, *Schizophrenia: A Source of Social Insight* (Philadelphia: Westminster, 1975).
6. William James, *Varieties of Religious Experience* (New York: Mentor, 1958), 32.

ousness to his own illness. Armed with an educational background which focused more strongly upon society than the individual, he insisted that the meaning he found in his own illness was important not just for himself but for church and society as well. Boisen's type of mental illness, as he understood it, was a problem-solving experience. The problem to be solved by the illness was one which seemed too shameful to be dealt with externally; therefore, the person worked on it internally through the process of his or her illness. Most typically the shame involved actual or perceived rejection and a consequent perception of worthlessness. Boisen interpreted the experience, further, as involving the failure to socialize a particular experience or type of experience, usually sexual, and the shame resulting from it's being powerful enough to drive the shamed person from contact with external reality. (I am using the term *shame* here for a phenomenon that Boisen described as guilt. The understanding of shame which has developed since the time of Boisen's writings clearly identify the phenomena he was describing more as shame than guilt, because of the pervading sense of unworthiness and perception of social rejection rather than having committed an act condemned by society.[7])

In the separation from external reality which was mental illness, Boisen believed that a person regressed to a point where the shame could be dissociated completely from the self or, optimally, reworked and assimilated as an acceptable part of life. When this occurs (and here I use Grant's summary of Boisen's views), "the individual typically can share it with strength and lucidity, calling the community to recognize that either its overrigid norms or its method of responding to them is so inhuman as to cripple life itself." In that process the "prophet-schizophrenic's" role changes "from that of a lonely outcast burdened by the inhumanity of his culture to that of a prophet with a clear status in his community. Or at least Boisen wished to see it that way."[8]

I have not used the term *schizophrenic* before because of the change in psychiatric nomenclature which took place with the advent of the *Diagnostic and Statistical Manual of Mental Disorders III* (DSM-III)[9]. As schizophrenia is now understood and diagnosed, it could no longer be called (as in Grant) "a source of social insight" or (as by Boisen) a "moral struggle." Schizophrenia, according to DSM-III, cannot be

7. Edith Jacobson, *The Self and the Object World* (New York: International University Press, 1964), 145–46. See also John Patton, *Is Human Forgiveness Possible? A Pastoral Care Perspective* (Nashville: Abingdon, 1985), chapter 2.

8. Grant, *Schizophrenia*, 23.

9. *Diagnostic and Statistical Manual of Mental Disorders III* (Washington, D.C.: The American Psychiatric Association, 1980).

diagnosed until what Boisen called the moral struggle is over and the illness has become chronic rather than acute. If his illness occurred today, during the time of his "moral struggle," his medical record might say, "diagnosis deferred," in order to determine the chronicity of the illness. Another possible diagnosis would be, "schizophrenic disorder (provisional)," or some variation of the "bipolar disorder" diagnosis. In the majority of psychiatric hospitals he would be given drugs which would make impossible "moral" or any other type of struggle. It is fortunate for the modern pastoral care movement that Boisen's illness came when it did.

Psychiatry's current hermeneutical theory, however, is not our major concern. Whatever his diagnosis, Boisen was able to find meaning in his illness and, like the forester he had literally been, was able to commit himself systematically to examining the phenomena of life as a symbolic forester in the "forests" of his own and others' human struggle. In keeping with James's pragmatic concern to discover the "fruits" of an experience, the clear implication of Boisen's work was that the dividing line between who was sick and who was well was less clear and less important than society thought it was.

Boisen himself did not directly attack this dividing line. Instead of addressing the issue of who was sick and who was well he emphasized the contribution of those who were sick in conveying the revelations of their illness to society as a whole. Moreover, as a clergyperson and not a physician he was not seen by society as having authority on such matters of illness and health. As a physician, one who had not been socially defined as a patient, Harry Stack Sullivan could say some of the same things that Boisen did and develop a following for his views of health and illness. Boisen, on the other hand, as one who had been a mental patient and who was viewed as a layperson in matters of health and illness, had to be content to work toward developing a mental hospital chaplaincy without strong support for his theoretical reason for doing so.

My claim that Boisen contributed to pastoral care and counseling by breaking down some of the rigid barriers between illness and health is problematic in the light of the barriers that Boisen himself established between patients whom he viewed as engaged in a moral struggle and particularly worthy of the minister's time and energy and those who were not. His views of mental illness and ministry to the mentally ill were as rigid as those which his work challenged. He believed that meaning could be found in illness and that the patient's struggle and search was important, but this applied only to a certain type of patient—those who seemed to be in an acute struggle to integrate a dimension of their experience into their life and world. The majority of mental patients, in Boisen's judgment, had given up the struggle, and the chaplain, like the physician, needed to focus his or her effort where there was still hope.

Boisen's own dividing line between the worthy and less worthy patients was never generally accepted, even by his own students. Neither was his argument that Jesus and many of the saints were psychiatrically ill. His work did, however, make a partial erasure of the dark line between illness and health and, perhaps more importantly, raise important questions about the uncritically accepted practice of excluding persons who were seen as psychiatrically ill from the world of relationships and meaning. Boisen's message that illness might be more than just something to be gotten rid of made some impact in his time and made a significant impact later on.

What this means for pastoral care and counseling today is that the ministry of the church to persons who are ill and in some way excluded from society cannot be understood simply as comforting the sick until they return to a more favorable condition under which "normal" ministry may take place. Care and counseling should seek to help persons hear the voice of their illness. Here Boisen is echoing, from a different point of view and with a different patient population, some of the affirmations of psychoanalysis. Beyond searching for meaning in the context of human life, however, his work suggests that illness has a religious meaning. He interprets his own illness in terms of the words of the story of Joseph and his brothers, "And now do not be distressed, or angry with yourselves, because you sold me here; for God sent me before you to preserve life" (Gen. 45:5 RSV). Illness in life may have a meaning in the context of God's providence. The human calling is to find that meaning and share it in a useful way. Boisen's work insists that the work of the pastoral counselor involves considerably more than making people feel better. It may—and usually does—involve making them feel worse, but for a purpose. Pastoral care and counseling, when it follows Boisen, intends that persons not simply get over their pain but exact a blessing from it that will be useful to themselves and others.

Boisen's Theory of Crisis

"My thesis," said Boisen, "is that religious experience is rooted in the social nature of man and arises spontaneously under the pressure of crisis situations. . . . As one stands face to face with the ultimate realities of life and death, religion and theology tend to come alive."[10]

10. Anton T. Boisen, *Religion in Crisis and Custom: A Sociological and Psychological Study* (New York: Harper, 1955), 3.

Boisen's understanding of the function of crisis in the life of persons, which was central to his work during his lifetime, can also contribute significantly to the practice of pastoral care and counseling today. For Boisen, crisis could be a tragedy or an opportunity, the making or breaking of a person, the discovery of possibility and direction in life. I note here some of the central features of crisis as they appear in *The Exploration of the Inner World,* in which he described his personal struggle with mental illness. Those that I identify seem to me not only to apply to the crisis of mental illness but also to be useful in interpreting virtually all human crisis.

First of all, Boisen understood crisis as involving the disorganization of a person's world. Something has happened "which has upset the foundations upon which his ordinary reasoning is based."[11]

Second, the acuteness of the crisis is a positive feature which reveals strength, struggle, and search. "The more sudden the onset and the more acute the disturbance, the more likely the patient is to recover, provided he can be protected from self-injury and from physical infection and exhaustion."[12]

Third, suffering is a remedial part of the crisis. "As long as there is suffering," says Boisen, "there is hope. When hope departs pain and suffering also leave."[13]

Fourth, at best crisis involves an appreciation of the seriousness of life's struggle and a search for meaning in it. "Most persons in these periods of crisis feel that their eyes have been opened to unsuspected meanings and possibilities in their lives."[14]

Fifth, acceptance of responsibility for oneself and the crisis which one is in brings suffering, but there is also the possibility of positive resolution of the crisis which brings a person to a higher or more integrated level of being. Boisen identified groups of persons in terms of their response to crisis. The first group "merely follow the line of least resistance, allowing their difficulties to accumulate. This course tends toward disintegration and destruction. The second group is composed of those who have resorted to some of the many concealment devices in order to preserve their self-esteem and escape the sense of personal failure." The result of this kind of deception of oneself, according to Boisen, is "arrested development." "Finally," he says, "we have found those who in attempting to face their difficulties become much disturbed. Among these there were not a few who recovered. There were also those who went hopelessly to pieces. We concluded

11. Boisen, *Exploration of the Inner World,* 11.
12. Ibid., 56.
13. Ibid., 15–16.
14. Ibid., 192.

therefore that such disturbances were not in themselves evils but were rather analogous to fever or inflammation in the physical organism. They were attempts at cure or reconstruction, which tended to make or break."[15]

Sixth, the person of the therapist and the relationship between therapist and patient is the most important feature in the positive resolution of human crisis. "The fact is," said Boisen, "that psychotherapy is far less dependent upon technique than it is upon the personal relationship between physician and patient. Wherever the patient has come to trust the physician enough to unburden himself of his problems and wherever the physician is ready to listen with intelligent sympathy, good results are likely to follow regardless of the correctness or incorrectness of the physician's particular theories or procedures."[16]

The implications for pastoral care and counseling of these features of human crisis which Boisen identified seem clear. I offer only a few words of elaboration. For the pastor, crisis in the life of a parishioner or counselee may, as Boisen put it, "be a tragedy or it may be an opportunity."[17] It is a time when the usual defenses have broken down and when a person may see things about herself or himself that ordinarily would not be perceived. Because crisis breaks down defenses, a time of crisis is one in which the pastor needs to be particularly careful of what is said and how it is said to the parishioner or patient.

The acuteness of an emotional crisis often reveals the strength of the person involved in it and, rather than driving the pastor away, can encourage him or her to stay with the parishioner in the pain and loneliness of the crisis experience. That same acuteness can also underscore for the pastor the importance of doing pastoral work in depth only with adequate consultative backup from medically and psychiatrically trained health professionals. Saying simply to the client or parishioner that the pastor has been in consultation with a psychiatrist who can prescribe drugs or hospitalize if needed, can be supportive and facilitate working through the crisis if the pastor also conveys that this consultation can probably make it possible to work through the crisis without such external intervention.

Most parishioners and pastoral counseling clients are unfamiliar with what is usual in a crisis situation and in-depth pastoral counseling as well. It is important, therefore, to convey to them in some appropriate way that the suffering they are experiencing is to be

15. Ibid., 202.
16. Ibid., 240.
17. Ibid., 1.

expected and is, in fact, necessary for achieving their hoped-for goals. Pastors need to be able to say in a nonpatronizing way that "it's likely to get worse before it gets better." If persons know that pain is normal in such a situation it is easier to endure. Learning to convey this fact in appropriate ways is a significant part of what it means to be a seasoned pastoral counselor.

Just as Boisen has noted that persons in periods of crisis may have their eyes opened to unexpected meanings, the pastor can teach persons through relationship the possibility of discovering new meanings for life. In listening for many years to tapes of pastoral counseling, I believe that I can hear on an audio tape when a person moves from just trying to solve his problem or getting relief from her pain to what I like to call "the exploratory mode." In the midst of the crisis a person can become curious about what his or her particular life is all about and thus become more concerned with meaning and purpose than with relief.

In my book on pastoral counseling I followed Boisen, without really being aware of it, in describing the importance of the counselee's locus of the problem. An external location places the blame for the problem on a particular circumstance or someone other than one's self. Internal location of the problem places the responsibility primarily upon the person who can do something about it, namely, oneself.[18] Similarly, Roy Schafer describes the process of psychotherapy as moving through increasingly responsible and useful constructions of reality from an essentially passive one to one in which the patient is seen as a mover and changer of things.[19]

Harry Stack Sullivan described the "expert in interpersonal relations" as one who was able to relate with sensitivity, convey security, and speak with simplicity, accuracy, and realness about what was going on.[20] What the pastor offers in the vast majority of her or his general pastoral work and in pastoral counseling is not answers or cures but relationship to who the pastor is and what he or she represents. The pastor's call is to break into the loneliness of whatever the parishioner is going through with a ministry of presence. Boisen's contribution to the development of a mental hospital chaplaincy was motivated primarily by his awareness of this need. Although Boisen might not say as directly as I have that what heals in pastoral coun-

18. John Patton, *Pastoral Counseling: A Ministry of the Church* (Nashville: Abingdon, 1983), 142–43.

19. Roy Schafer, *Language and Insight* (New Haven: Yale University Press, 1978).

20. John Patton, "Harry Stack Sullivan's 'Expert in Interpersonal Relations,' " *Journal of Religion and Health* 9, no. 1 (1971): 162–70.

seling is relationship,[21] his theory of crisis seems to me to point strongly in that direction.

A Genuinely Empirical Theology

Many persons deeply involved in pastoral care and counseling today would be hard pressed to articulate Boisen's theological point of view. The most accurate category for describing him would probably be "empirical liberal." A recent study of American theology by William Dean uses that category to describe one who has "rejected the nature-spirit duality typical of pietistic liberalism, accepted a nature-spirit unity, and consequently become more thoroughly historicist, placing God as well as the religious self within the dynamics of history. . . . God had to work within the world of natural and social history or not work at all.[22] Boisen's identification of his work with that of William James is probably enough to justify the use of such a category in describing his theology, but whatever category we use, Boisen made a significant contribution to pastoral care and counseling by affirming the possibility of a genuinely empirical theology.

In spite of his emphasis on human sin and frailty, Boisen's theology was liberal in its vision of human possibility. It was also liberal in its theological method. Boisen believed that theological convictions should be changed when they do not take into account the facts of human experience. He did not, as must be done today, distinguish between fact and interpreted fact, but even if fact is understood to be interpreted within a particular frame of meaning, the principle of modifying traditional beliefs on the basis of present-day experience can still be a central feature of theological method. What Boisen has most clearly contributed to pastoral care and counseling has been the conviction that the events which occur in pastoral care and counseling have theological significance along with the more traditional elements in theological construction. And, more indirectly, because the discovery and integration of meaning had been essential for him in the achievement of his own mental health, Boisen could affirm that theological theory based on experience could contribute to the actual practice of ministry.

In his preface to Boisen's *Religion in Crisis and Custom*, Seward Hiltner stated that Boisen had "a methodological thesis. He believes that rigorous but imaginative methods of science should be applied

---

21. Patton, *Pastoral Counseling*, 167–94.
22. William Dean, *American Religious Empiricism* (Albany: State University of New York Press, 1986), 8–9.

to religious phenomena, that no holds should be barred in our study of religion in persons and in groups. He believes that theology should be more concerned with study of this kind." Boisen understood the scientist to be one who looked behind appearances and "back of the obvious and superficial to underlying causes." He identified the principles of scientific procedure as involving empiricism, in which the raw material of experience in all its complexity was taken as the starting point, and inductive reasoning, which proceeded from the concrete to the abstract.[23]

In her recently published study, *Ministry after Freud,* Allison Stokes noted that what "continued to strike Boisen throughout his life was that liberals attempt to deal with the central problems of the Christian faith while making little effort to attack these problems empirically." She commented further that "Boisen made an extensive survey of liberal literature (journals and books), which he found deficient in the empirical method."[24] In his own attempts at doing theology empirically, Boisen followed the revelation of his own experience and studied the experiences of the mentally ill. He found in the persons he studied a belief in the revelatory power of experience.[25] He also found confirmation of his own pain and struggle with darkness. "Radical evil is a terrific reality and the fears we see in the disturbed patient are not without foundation." Boisen stated on the basis of his empirical study that there "*is* such a thing as disintegration and damnation" and, moving from the concrete to the abstract, comments that "no philosophy of life which fails to take account of that is really facing the fact."[26]

Following James, Boisen attempted to look behind appearances to the function of particular religious and ethical beliefs. Boisen pointed, for example, to the way a mother's devotion "may hang as a dead weight around her son's neck, preventing him from achieving maturity." As Boisen puts it, "devotion to a finite love object may become a substitute for that loyalty to the highest which is indispensable to mental health both personal and social."[27]

In addition to emphasizing the reality of sin and evil and the importance of examining beliefs functionally, Boisen's theology strongly emphasized the importance of social dimensions of experience. The powerful dynamic of loneliness, which seemed to motivate Boisen in much of what he did, clearly suggested the importance he placed upon a person's finding acceptance in a significant group. Two of his criteria

23. Boisen, *Religion in Crisis and Custom,* xi, 183–84.
24. Allison Stokes, *Ministry after Freud* (New York: Pilgrim, 1985), 64, 200.
25. Boisen, *Exploration of the Inner World,* 192–93.
26. Ibid., 193.
27. Ibid., 207.

for assessing the validity of a religious faith are social acceptance and social consequences. Again, like James, he insisted that it was the "fruits which a religion brings forth" which determine its value. What matters is the extent to which its beliefs and practices enable its followers "to survive in the stern struggle for survival and to achieve a more abundant life as measured by quality and breadth and complexity."[28] Or, in describing the church, Boisen saw it as "a group of imperfect persons united on the basis of an ideal which they are seeking to realize in their own lives and in the social order." The church, "despite its weaknesses and shortcomings," is where persons "confess their weaknesses and sins with the assurance of social understanding and support and yet without any lowering of standards."[29]

I will not pursue the content of Boisen's theology further, but simply suggest two important implications of it for pastoral care and counseling. The first is that the pastoral practitioner has immediately at hand in his or her practice of ministry a major source for doing theology or reformulating the concepts of faith. Pastoral events are to the pastoral theologian what a manuscript in its original language is to the biblical scholar. Clinical pastoral education has, correctly I think, focused its theological concerns primarily upon the doctrine of ministry and how the emerging professional and personal identity of the theological student and minister are related to the understanding of ministry received by the church which he or she represents. There are, however, significant contributions to the formulation and reformulation of other theological concepts which may be found in the stories of patients and parishioners as these are revealed through pastoral relationships. Pastoral theologians differ as to whether experience actually modifies doctrine or simply reinterprets it. Whichever position one takes, Boisen helped us see the richness which may be found in the examination of the crisis experiences of human life. And as far as pastoral care and counseling is concerned, if I as pastor can hope to find something which may deepen my life and faith in my relationship to parishioner or counselee, the vitality of my practice has been significantly enhanced.

A second implication of Boisen's theology is in some ways a variation of the first one, but it seems important to me to state it in a somewhat different way. It is that the religious quest involves not only the study of religion but also the study of life, not only the study of religious communities but also the study of persons estranged from those communities. The subject of study for one engaged in pastoral

28. Boisen, *Religion in Crisis and Custom*, 188.
29. Boisen, *Exploration of the Inner World*, 214–15.

care and counseling is persons detached or estranged by life crisis from their community of faith, the ones who wonder—if they ever knew the song in the first place—"How shall we sing the LORD's song in a strange land?" (Ps. 137:4 KJV). Anton Boisen was a pioneer in the conviction held by many of those who are deeply involved in pastoral care and counseling that there is something particularly important about lost sheep. I quote from an editorial I wrote for *The Journal of Pastoral Care*:

> I remember years ago hearing a layman complain about his pastor, "Since he was in training at that mental hospital, you have to be crazy to get his attention." I'm fairly clear that there's some truth in that accusation about me also, although the craziness I'm speaking of is not so much pathology as it is an in-touchness with depth. The lost, crazy and lonely bring out something in me that seems real and important in a world and a church that often appears to be drowning in trivia.[30]

I was not particularly aware of Boisen's influence when I wrote that, but as I reflect now upon what I said, it seems quite evident. It is also evident in John Foskett's book on pastoral care and counseling, *Meaning in Madness*.[31] Foskett, who is chaplain at Bethlehem Royal and Maudsley hospitals in London and who is not as hesitant about quoting Americans as are some of his British colleagues, begins a chapter on "Theological Meaning in Madness" with these words of Boisen: "The more I deal with the experience of the mentally ill, the more I am convinced that in so far as we attain to any true understanding of them, so far shall we be able to see the meaning and end of human life, both individual and collective."[32]

Whether or not that statement is accurate, Boisen did contribute significantly to our current practice of pastoral care and counseling. I have suggested that his contribution was fourfold: in claiming a place for the pastor in the treatment of the mentally ill; in breaking down some of the rigid barriers between illness and health; in his theory of crisis; and in his concern for a genuinely empirical theology. In the same editorial to which I referred earlier I recall some other words which I now see as "Boisenian" in character:

---

30. John Patton, "There's Something about Lost Sheep," *Journal of Pastoral Care* 34, no. 4 (1980): 217.

31. John Foskett, *Meaning in Madness* (London: S.P.C.K., 1984).

32. Charles E. Hall, Jr., "Some Contributions of Anton T. Boisen (1876–1965) to Understanding Psychiatry and Religion," *Pastoral Psychology* 19, no. 186 (September 1968): 40–48.

I feel committed to two things: (1) that pastoral care and counseling is a ministry of the church and must maintain a dialogical relationship to the church if that care and counseling are to continue to be ministry; (2) that relationship to the church does not just mean relationship to the parish, but to an ecclesiastical structure with a more inclusive theory and practice of ministry and community. I believe that the lost sheep was onto something and that the pastoral care ministries involved with those who are separated from the more traditional ecclesiastical structures continue to have something important to say to the church about both sin and salvation. There's something about lost sheep.[33]

33. Patton, "There's Something about Lost Sheep," 218.

10

Shepherds of the Needy

KENNETH R. MITCHELL

Those who know Seward Hiltner through his writings—and he was a prolific writer—know that he expressed himself in a clear and ordered way, providing example after example of "how to" and "how not to." Those who sat in his classes and wrestled with his ideas day in and day out have the added privilege and burden of writing about him on the basis of the memories of those personal contacts. That fact changes the picture slightly, for in those meetings Hiltner proposed ideas, argued cases, and took positions which never saw print.

All but a very few of the graduates from his doctoral programs at the University of Chicago and, later, at Princeton Theological Seminary have become academicians or full-time clinicians. Hiltner often expressed his disappointment about that; over and over he argued that *the* place to use what he was teaching was the parish. He envisioned ministers with advanced degrees forming a cadre of pastors who would practice responsible pastoral counseling in their parishes but who would also lead worship, preach, participate fully and faithfully in their church judicatories, and, to use a phrase from his own Presbyterian background, "bear rule in the church." That cadre never came into existence, much to Hiltner's sorrow.

Inseparable from that disappointment was his sharp, even angry, criticism of the notion that there could be a specialized profession

173

called pastoral counseling. For Hiltner, pastoral counseling was not a profession but an activity undertaken by every practicing pastor.[1] To be a counselor was to engage in a particular activity at a specified time, not to practice a specialty. Hiltner made his case in articles and editorials in which both his passion and his logic showed clearly. The passion was even more visible in blunt letters to, and frank conversations with, former students. Eventually, Hiltner became a critical friend to the "pastoral counseling movement," but he never joined it, preferring to think of his work as part of the "enterprise" of theology and personality. The question is not, Hiltner insisted, whether one is a pastoral counselor or not; that question is settled by ordination. The question is whether one does pastoral counseling well.

Hiltner lived out that conviction in his writing. We can learn a tremendous—one hears his familiar voice saying "tre-MEN-juss"— amount from the personality sciences and from practicing psychotherapists. His students were required to read exhaustively in psychodynamic and psychotherapeutic literature. But when one reads Hiltner's own writings about pastoral counseling, one recognizes that he never wrote as a psychologist to pastors but as one preacher to another. The psychodynamic theory was all there, but it had been integrated into the work and the style of the man or woman serving a local church.

Whether one drew one's theoretical underpinnings from psychodynamic theory or from some other source, the theoretical underpinnings were absolutely essential. Hiltner disdained a "hints and helps" approach to pastoral counseling, advice which was not demonstrably based on sound theoretical understanding. "A practice without a theory is uncorrectable," he wrote. "A theory without a practice is irrelevant."[2]

The Decade of the 1950s

When Hiltner taught his students to analyze theological data and assess theological positions, he admonished them to look at theological assertions with an eye to discovering what they were trying to protect or defend. What was the climate in which the theologian worked and wrote? Any assessment of Hiltner's own writings about pastoral counseling should attend to that admonition.

Three of Hiltner's books focus directly on questions about pastoral counseling: *Pastoral Counseling, The Counselor in Counseling, The*

1. Seward Hiltner, *Pastoral Counseling* (Nashville: Abingdon, 1949), 95.
2. Ibid., 7.

Christian Shepherd.[3] The first is an introductory survey of pastoral counseling; the second, a discussion of specific problems encountered by pastoral counselors as they go about their work; the third, a consideration of the broader field of activity which encompasses pastoral counseling: pastoral care.

These books represent Hiltner in the decade of the 1950s. *The Counselor in Counseling* was essentially written across that decade, appearing first in the pages of *Pastoral Psychology.* During that time Karl Barth was active, and Paul Tillich taught at the University of Chicago. Pastors, many of whom had seen service in World War II, were raising questions about pastoral counseling. They were clearly dissatisfied with the authoritative stances once taken by the "Herr Pastor," and many tended to reject advice-giving, finding it an inappropriate form of pastoral work. At the same time, the nondirective or client-centered work of Carl R. Rogers had captured the imagination of many counselors, both secular and pastoral.[4] Hiltner's own background and interests led him to a deep sympathy with the Rogerian style and approach. Fascinated with classical theology but drawn by Tillich, he attempted to evolve a method of pastoral counseling that avoided the authoritarian style of previous pastoral generations, was grounded in sound psychological knowledge, and was readily available to the practicing parish pastor.

Hiltner also aimed to ensure that pastoral counseling was grounded theologically, and was therefore a legitimate arena for theological inquiry. In many theological seminaries pastoral counseling was taught by a visiting professor, often a practicing pastor, who gave practical suggestions which Hiltner disdainfully called "hints and helps." Hiltner insisted that good pastoral counseling should proceed from thorough attention to method, which in turn was to be grounded in both psychological and theological theory. His work throughout the decade of the 1950s was an attempt to carry out that program.

In the second half of that decade I first came to know Hiltner personally. At the time, he was finishing two major scholarly tasks that overlapped. One was the writing of books to guide pastors in their day-to-day practice of shepherding; the other was the writing of his central work, *Preface to Pastoral Theology.*[5] (Actually, the *Preface* was

3. Ibid.; Seward Hiltner, *The Counselor in Counseling* (Nashville: Abingdon, 1950); Seward Hiltner, *The Christian Shepherd* (Nashville: Abingdon, 1959).

4. Carl R. Rogers, *Counseling and Psychotherapy* (Boston: Houghton Mifflin, 1947); Carl R. Rogers, *Client-Centered Therapy* (Boston: Houghton Mifflin, 1951).

5. Hiltner, *The Counselor in Counseling; The Christian Shepherd;* Seward Hilter, *Preface to Pastoral Theology* (Nashville: Abingdon, 1958).

published before *The Christian Shepherd,* making *Shepherd* a significant bridging book. On the one hand, it was the last of the "practical handbooks," and, on the other hand, it illustrated richly the concept of shepherding propounded in the *Preface.*)

The Eductive Approach

Hiltner's essential understanding of pastoral counseling is summarized by the label he gave it: an "eductive" approach. The label referred to the pastoral counselor's effort to understand, accept, clarify, and consolidate, while avoiding such common blunders as coercing, moralizing, generalizing, and diverting. Success in these tasks will be marked by drawing or leading from the help-seeker inner resources, as symbolized by the Latin root *educare,* "to lead out."

Despite Hiltner's powerful grasp of Freudian, Jungian, and other psychotherapeutic theories, his counseling method was very much aligned with the work of Rogers, whose "client-centered" counseling was for some years the most powerful influence from the personality sciences upon pastoral counseling. The blunders listed previously are borrowed from Porter's *Introduction to Therapeutic Counseling,* a detailed "how-to" book using the client-centered approach.

Many of Hiltner's students at Chicago undertook internships at the counseling center which Rogers directed, and were supervised by the staff there. Hiltner and Rogers were acquainted, and Rogers occasionally sat in on Hiltner's classes. The profound influence of Rogers on Hiltner's counseling method is obvious. And yet a flat identification of the "client-centered" method of Rogers with the "eductive" method of Hiltner is a mistake. The value orientations behind the two approaches were significantly different, a difference which was important to both men. Rogers had a profoundly optimistic view of the nature of human beings, believing in their essential goodness and capacity for self-healing and growth, if the right conditions are provided. He was deeply suspicious of any approach based upon notions of serious flaws or negative impulses in human beings. To use classical theological language, if Rogers had a "doctrine of sin," it was so radically different from Jewish or Christian notions of sin as to be unrecognizable.

Rogers posited a set of conditions under which he believed therapeutic change was bound to take place. They included two human beings in relationship to each other, one of whom (the client) was experiencing incongruence or lack of matching among feelings, behavior, and knowledge, while the other (the counselor) was, at least inside the relationship, experiencing congruence. If the counselor experienced unconditional positive regard and empathy for the client, and successfully communicated those inner attitudes to the client, therapeutic change was bound to take place. Receiving the "messages" of unconditional positive regard and empathy would release the forces of growth and health within the client.

Hiltner was a Presbyterian minister and carried within himself a classically Calvinistic understanding of humankind. He was far more at home with Freud's personality theory than with that of Rogers. Thus, his eductive approach made maximum use of a person's own inner resources for growth and healing, but it never assumed that those inner resources were without flaw, or that providing the proper conditions for therapeutic change was all that was necessary for the counselor.

As we shall see in the next section of this essay, Hiltner's understanding of pastoral counseling included the use of spiritual and theological resources.[6] Rogers could never countenance the use of such resources, not simply because they represented a theological point of view to which he could not agree, but more powerfully because they represented the use of an "external frame of reference." Even a position with which Rogers agreed was not to be used as an external frame of reference, as an imposition of the counselor's value system upon the client.

The very use of the name *eductive* signals a difference between Hiltner's understanding of counseling and that of Rogers. The root meaning, "leading out," already implies that there is a kind of leadership being exercised by the pastor, and moreover that the pastor may know something about the client that the client is avoiding or hiding. A good Rogerian counselor would be resolved not to know any such thing, and not to exercise any kind of leadership. The client-centered therapist of those days "knew" only what the client had expressed in the counseling hour, nothing more.

Precounseling

In defining a complex process one usually runs across issues which require special care. As Hiltner struggled to define pastoral counseling, he reminded his readers of some issues that would be critical and introduced some terms of particular importance. He paid careful attention, for example, to the fact that pastoral counseling often grows out of a *prior relationship* between pastors and parishioners, in which the pastor has been exercising ongoing pastoral care. In the context of such an ongoing pastoral relationship, "much of the pastor's personal work is dealing with people who have not yet come to the

---

6. See Hiltner, *Pastoral Counseling.*

point . . . of realizing the conditions under which the pastoral counseling process itself could proceed."[7] Hiltner recognized that proper management of this kind of work could lead to pastoral counseling process, and insisted that such *precounseling* needed to be carried out with the same eye to principles and careful methods as counseling itself.

Long-term versus Short-term Counseling

What most counselors now call long-term and short-term counseling were referred to earlier as extended and brief counseling. The terms are interchangeable. In these days when one of the prerequisites for consideration as a member of the American Association of Pastoral Counselors is at least one relationship that has covered thirty hours or more of work together, it is interesting to note that Hiltner strongly advised restricting one's work to a total period no longer than a few weeks. That is, extended counseling is rarely if ever a part of the pastor's regular practice.

His reasons were utterly practical. First, the pastor does not have the time to devote to extended counseling. Second, the pastor is rarely trained to practice extended counseling. Third, extended counseling is not merely a longer form of brief counseling, but involves powerful emotional phenomena (such as the transference) which do not appear in brief counseling. For most pastors, extended counseling is either inadvisable or impossible.

Referral

It is natural under such circumstances that Hiltner would give particular attention to referral: when and how to make referrals, in particular. He advocated that every pastor should build relationships with mental-health professionals in the surrounding community and should know with clarity and depth what each of these other professionals could and could not do. Having someone to whom one was ready and willing to make referrals for long-term help was, for Hiltner, one of the hallmarks of a responsible pastor.

The insistence sometimes provoked a reaction from Hiltner's students. Hiltner's background and thinking patterns were certainly urban in most significant respects. His insistence on referral may have been partly dependent upon the fact that he had always lived and worked where referrals were accomplished with relative ease. In a University of Chicago class, Hiltner once took a student to task for intending, in a counseling situation Hiltner had "invented," to handle

7. Ibid., 80–81.

the case himself. "How could you think of doing that and not sending this man to see a psychiatrist?" asked Hiltner. "That's easy," said the student, a relatively experienced pastor. "I live in Broken Pelvis, Nebraska, and the nearest psychiatrist is more than two hundred miles away." "Broken Pelvis" was the student's fanciful name for a town far from urban resources and has remained a symbol to members of that class ever since.

Actually, Hiltner was keenly aware of the problem. Although he insisted on the pastor's having a mental-health professional to whom to make referrals, he knew that a pastor "may find that he does not have access to such a person except perhaps for diagnosing roughly the degree of the difficulty." Thus, the pastor may be justified in undertaking extended counseling, or even obligated to do so "when a therapist is not physically or psychologically available."[8]

Shepherding

As Hiltner worked out the implications of what he had written about the practice of pastoral counseling, he was at the same time working on the *Preface to Pastoral Theology,* which was to become his most important book. The concepts worked out in the *Preface* were already a part of his working assumptions; they influenced his thinking about pastoral counseling profoundly. Central to the *Preface* as well as to Hiltner's understanding of pastoral counseling was the metaphor of shepherding. That metaphor brought Hiltner a significant dose of negative criticism. Although he was aware of the problems posed by the use of such a metaphor, he was never willing to withdraw it as a principal tool for the understanding of ministry.

The objections were many. The metaphor was a relic of rural, agricultural times, unfit for use in modern urban society. Besides, sheep are notoriously unintelligent, stubborn animals; the comparison of intelligent human beings to stupid sheep is insulting and inaccurate. The metaphor involves the assumption that there is a person who knows what is good for the sheep far better than do the sheep themselves. That may be true with sheep, but it is a dangerous, ill-founded assumption to make about relationships between pastors and parishioners. The shepherding metaphor in fact involves coercion, and Hiltner had expressed himself as being against coercion; he couldn't have it both ways.

Hiltner's first reaction to all this criticism was to point out that a metaphor is designed to be suggestive rather than literal. Most of his

8. Ibid., 90–91.

critics were trying to make the analogy exhaustive, creating a straw man that is easily demolished. Meanwhile, such attacks on the similarities and differences between sheep and human beings were unconsciously designed, he said, to permit the critic to avoid taking seriously what Hiltner had to say by means of the metaphor.

The entire concept of shepherding helps to draw a significant boundary between Hiltner's eductive approach to pastoral counseling and Rogers's client-centered approach to counseling. In a class at the University of Chicago, a graduate student used the phrase *internal frame of reference* once too often for Hiltner's taste. "Look!" the teacher growled, "a sheep that works entirely from its own internal frame of reference gets eaten by wolves." Hiltner was in fact convinced that a responsible, dedicated pastoral "shepherd" could see dangers from an external frame of reference that a parishioner, left to his or her own devices, might not see.

The perspectives within which a pastor works in shepherding include *healing, sustaining,* and *guiding.* Later, prompted by the suggestion of William A. Clebsch and Charles R. Jaekle, Hiltner was happy to add *reconciling* to the list. But these are not simply perspectives within which the pastor works; they are also the aims of pastoral counseling. In the earlier books one can see the four perspectives of pastoral work prefigured. In part, they form the dividing line between Hiltner and Rogers. Pastoral counseling always includes the possibility of guiding; there are times in a counseling relationship in which the pastor's guidance is what is called for. That could never be the case with client-centered therapy.

Such counseling principles as valuing freedom over compulsion, following the help-seeker's lead, being alert to expressed feelings, understanding, and the communication of understanding are fundamental to Hiltner's understanding.[9] They are essential to the eductive method. Yet by the time he published the *Preface,* Hiltner seems to have been seeing things in a slightly different way. The difference may be accounted for by another shift which took place in Hiltner's thinking in the 1950s. He began the 1950s with a classical "office" conception of ministry, one which permits sharp differentiation between the various acts and processes in which a minister takes part. To lead worship is very different from counseling; preaching is a task entirely different from that of church administration. For centuries—at least since Richard Baxter's *Reformed Pastor*—this office conception of the ministry held sway. The minister turned, emotionally, spiritually, and

9. Hiltner, *The Counselor in Counseling,* 187.

practically, from one task to the other, and almost became a different person in the different offices.

By the end of the 1950s Hiltner had developed the perspectival understanding of ministry which was to alter his approach to everything radically. He later said that if one did not understand his perspectival stance one did not understand much of anything about him. The intent of this stance was to unify all the various activities of ministry into one activity—the work of the pastor. Within that work, one perspective might stand out at any given moment: shepherding, communicating, or organizing. But the other perspectives never disappear! They are always present in addition to the primary one. Thus a pastor who is sustaining a parishioner through intense grief is engaged primarily in shepherding, but at the same time he or she is communicating the gospel and organizing the church fellowship, even if those perspectives are not dominant at the moment. This view of the total work of the minister engendered a significant shift in Hiltner's understanding of counseling, one which had not been reflected in his earlier books.

I vividly remember one of Hiltner's most effective pastoral counseling interviews. It took place in a class at The Menninger Foundation, where Hiltner served as a consultant forty days per year for many years. Hiltner, as pastor, was dealing with a middle-aged parishioner who had lost his wife to cancer and who was having grave difficulties working his way through the grief process. Hiltner stayed with the grieving man's feelings, not challenging them, not telling the man what to do or how to do it. Most of the interview could have been analyzed from the point of view of Hiltner's eductive theory or Rogers's client-centered theory with approximately the same outcome. But the alert listener would have been aware that Hiltner was using biblical language more and more as the interview progressed. Finally, he noticed tears coming to the man's eyes and being suppressed. He then said something that was classically Hiltnerian and quite un-Rogerian. "Do you suppose you could summon the courage to cry openly?" he asked, gently placing his hand over the parishioner's. And the man wept openly.

What Is Pastoral about Pastoral Counseling?

A pastoral counselor operating in a purely Rogerian style is immediately confronted with the question: What is pastoral about what you are doing? A Rogerian purist, as we have seen, would use no religious resources. What then is pastoral? The question so fascinated one of

Hiltner's University of Chicago students, Lowell G. Colston, that he developed with Hiltner a research project in which the same counselor worked with help-seekers in both a church and a secular counseling agency. The ultimate result was *The Context of Pastoral Counseling*, bearing both Hiltner's and Colston's names.[10] The point of the book was that the church setting in and of itself seemed to produce expectations on the clients' part different from those produced by the secular setting. Although the research interested Hiltner, his own view of pastoral counseling was not truly Rogerian, and the problem of the pastoral nature of pastoral counseling was not a significant problem for him.

The problem of the pastoral nature of pastoral counseling belongs to the 1970s and 1980s. If it was a serious problem in the 1950s, Hiltner never seemed to think so. For him, pastors were pastors and were expected to use the resources of their office. Many currently practicing pastoral counselors would shrink from the frank use of religious resources taken for granted by Hiltner. In his chapter on religious resources, he makes it clear that pastors as counselors are expected to use prayer, the Bible, religious literature, the sacraments, and other specifically religious resources.[11]

Hiltner often challenged the form in which questions were asked regarding the identity of pastoral counselors. In fact, one of the marks of his genius was his insistence on asking the right question before trying to come up with an answer. His long critiques on students' essays, which were usually written in red ink, often asserted that "on the whole" the student had worked responsibly to answer a question, but that unfortunately the question itself had been the wrong one. Hiltner applied this critique to the oft-asked question: "What's pastoral about pastoral counseling?" The question is wrong if it approaches the generalities of practice. It is right only if it asks of a particular piece of work, "What is pastoral about *your* pastoral counseling in this instance?" The focus must be on a given exchange between a pastor and a help-seeker. Only then is it the right question.

The same principle is true in terms of religious resources. The question is not *whether* to pray, read the Bible, prescribe a "therapeutic" dose of Thomas Kelly, or whatever, but it is *when, under what circumstances, and for what purposes* the counselor would do these things. "Blanket questions lead to blanket answers," he once wrote me in a letter, "and the effect, by and large, is that of a blanket: comfort and security without any provision for growth."

---

10. Seward Hiltner and Lowell G. Colston, *The Context of Pastoral Counseling* (Nashville: Abingdon, 1961).

11. Hiltner, *Pastoral Counseling*, chapter 9.

In a given situation, prayer may or may not be appropriate. If it *is* used, it "should not be a way of getting out of tight situations, or a way of getting authority behind points [the minister] has failed with in the counseling . . . situation."[12] Hiltner immediately moves us away from blanket use of prayer or blanket avoidance of it. It is obvious to him that there are times when a responsible pastoral counselor will pray with a help-seeker. (Incidentally, Hiltner would not countenance the use of the word *patient*, nor was he happy with the word *client* as used extensively by Rogers.) It is not simply use, but discriminating use, of prayer that is important.

Biblical resources come under the same rubric. "There can be no question that the pastor will use the Bible in counseling. . . . But this is not the same thing as saying the words 'the Bible' or quoting Scripture."[13] If a parishioner has a question about a biblical passage, one does not avoid the question or give a nondirective response hoping that the parishioner will "go deeper." One listens and may respond eductively in order to understand the parishioner better and to evoke deeper understanding on the part of the parishioner. But one also uses one's exegetical skills, employing something akin to form criticism. Recording a good pastoral conversation, Hiltner has a pastor say:

> Do you notice the various steps [the psalmist] takes as the psalm proceeds? First he faces the fact of how he feels. He doesn't just say, "I feel bad, but I know I shouldn't; therefore I don't." He admits it. . . . So next he realizes there must be something about himself, his own sin. So he tells the Lord he is a sinner. But in the next breath he says his enemies follow evil, while he actually follows good. He asks the Lord not to forsake him.[14]

Hiltner asks whether this response is counseling or education. He answers that it could be both but that it is really pastoral counseling. "If we had only a mechanical interpretation of the eductive approach, we should consider it to be violated in this contact, for [the pastor] does some expounding. But, and this is what counts, he does not moralize, generalize, coerce, or divert. Instead, he understands, accepts, clarifies, and helps to consolidate."[15]

Hiltner's method is actively in use to this day. The Dutch pastor Nico Ter Linden, whose training at The Menninger Foundation brought him into contact with Hiltner in the early 1970s, seems to have developed a remarkably "Hiltnerian" style in his pastoral work.

12. Ibid., 193.
13. Ibid., 202.
14. Ibid., 205.
15. Ibid., 207.

One of Ter Linden's books has recently been translated into English under the title *In the Lord's Boarding House*.[16] In one of the essays, Ter Linden approaches a help-seeker's dream in an eductive way (clarifying, consolidating, not coercive), but at the same time he draws upon the story of the apostle Peter's dream as recorded in Acts 10:9–16. His way of working with the help-seeker, an imprisoned felon, was precisely the kind of approach that Hiltner taught. I refer to Ter Linden here in order to undercut any notion that Hiltner's approach may have been appropriate twenty or thirty years ago but that it is no longer to be considered good pastoral counseling.

Individuals and Families

It is striking to note the theories of personality and of therapy on which Hiltner continued to base his understanding of pastoral counseling throughout his life. Hiltner was essentially a Freudian, but he also appreciated the theories of many other persons. He understood Carl Gustav Jung thoroughly and made occasional forays into Jungian theory as a way of understanding human behavior that was otherwise incomprehensible. (A *Pastoral Psychology* editorial after Dwight Eisenhower's election to a second term as president had a thoroughgoing Jungian base.) Hiltner's attraction to much of the methods of Rogers has already been mentioned. He made himself deeply knowledgeable about the developmental theories of Erik H. Erikson, though he sometimes castigated his students for too much dependence upon Erikson. In later years, he read with interest the work of Heinz Kohut.

One is immediately struck by the fact that all these writers—Erikson is in part an exception, because of his bio-psycho-social approach—are concerned with the development, the health, and the treatment of the individual.

If we look back at the way in which psychological theory has had an impact on pastoral counseling, we can discern three moments of special significance. The first is the impact of psychodynamic theory in general: Freud to begin with, and then others. The second, taking place in the period in which Hiltner wrote about pastoral counseling, was the impact of Rogers. Unlike Freud's psychoanalytic theories and therapies, client-centered therapy was grasped and used by pastors with relative ease. The third moment of significance is the emergence of family-systems theory: a way of approaching therapy which suggests that problems in living are deeply related to the intimate systems

16. Nico Ter Linden, *In the Lord's Boarding House: Stories of Caring for Others*, trans. Kenneth R. Mitchell (Nashville: Abingdon, 1985).

in which human beings grow up, and in which they live in adult life. Hiltner was conversant with, and deeply influenced by, the first two "psychological impacts." The third was of little interest to him, even though he had a keen interest in the family as such.

> The notion of the person as an isolated unit, enclosed by mental, as well as physiological skin, cannot possibly be sustained. We become human and remain human because of our relationships. These relationships are not external, to be understood merely as part of environment. They are the very stuff of which our selfhood is made. Those we love and those we hate are part—an essential and not an accidental part—of our selfhood. Of all the social relationships that enter into the creating and sustaining of the form of our selfhood, those of the family are the earliest and the most powerful.[17]

The chapter from which this quote is taken does not carry out the promise implied in its opening statement. For its time, it is a forward-looking essay, still worth considering today, but Hiltner did not participate in the great expansion of knowledge about the family that occurred in his time.

Conversations with Hiltner over the past fifteen or so years, as family therapy was making its impact upon pastoral counseling, revealed that he was suspicious of its approach to human problems. I was never sure why, and at least one of his colleagues at Princeton Theological Seminary has professed equal puzzlement. Few family therapists or family-oriented pastoral counselors take exception to the preceding quotation; indeed, most of them would see their work as a practical application of the principle that Hiltner enunciated. Apparently, Hiltner was unable or unwilling to take his own principle seriously in terms of its meaning for therapeutic or pastoral practice.

Did Hiltner see in the active interventions of family systems counseling the threat of a return to the dominance and authoritarianism of the pastor against which he had fought so long? Or did he view family systems work as deceptive, manipulative? Most of the therapeutic theories which informed Hiltner's view of pastoral counseling hold that understanding and insight are prerequisites to change. For the most part, family-systems work believes that change precedes insight and is not dependent upon it. Was such an attitude toward the relationship between understanding and change more than Hiltner could accommodate? All of these possible objections have been voiced by insight-oriented psychotherapists, and they may have been true for Hiltner. In the end, though, our conclusions are speculative at best.

17. Hiltner, *The Christian Shepherd*, 57.

But given Hiltner's curiosity and wide reading, it is unlikely that he never developed some informed opinion about family therapy.

Conclusion

Those who have experienced the detailed dissection of a pastoral counseling interview at Seward Hiltner's hands know that it would be impossible to encompass his approach to pastoral counseling by simply reading his books. Similarly, no single chapter can do more than suggest to the reader what Hiltner was getting at in his writing and teaching. His grasp of theory was firm and wide-ranging. He evolved an approach to pastoral counseling that did indeed escape from an earlier pastoral authoritarianism or, to use one of his favorite words, imperialism. He took a method of counseling based on an anthropology with which he did not totally agree and adapted it for the practical use of the workaday pastor. He moved surefootedly from psychological theory to theological inquiry to the exigencies of a given real situation, and helped his students—through his books as well as his classroom teaching—to do the same.

Seward Hiltner brought pastoral counseling from pseudo-practical advice-giving to a place where it is a proper object of and contributor to theological inquiry. His vision of pastoral theology has no serious rival to this day. He achieved this monumental task because, among other things, he knew how to ask the right questions.

11

Pastoral Care and the Church

GENE T. FOWLER, JR.

When reading what Seward Hiltner wrote about pastoral care I have always appreciated his ability to place instances of care in their "real life" context, the church community. Yet, at the same time there is a certain frustration because the church usually seems to be no more than "background scenery" for the action taking place between pastor and parishioner. In one sense this is understandable given Hiltner's perspectival approach in which a certain point of view is in focus while others recede to the "background." On the other hand, that "background scenery" is often a very real and important factor in care. This situation gives rise to two questions. What exactly did Hiltner write about the church, and how is the church related to pastoral care in his writings?

This issue, the relation between the church and pastoral care, is a concern of several contemporary pastoral theologians. According to Don S. Browning, in *The Moral Context of Pastoral Care*, "recent theory and practice of pastoral care has been without an ecclesiology. . . ."[1] Donald Capps also has addressed this issue in *Life Cycle Theory and Pastoral Care*. According to Capps, "There is widespread agreement

1. Don S. Browning, *The Moral Context of Pastoral Care* (Philadelphia: Westminster, 1976), 21.

among pastors today that pastoral care is not limited to pastoral counseling or, for that matter, to the care of individuals. We agree that it has something to do with the care of the 'church,' here understood as the parish or congregation. Yet, we have had considerable difficulty over the years in conceptualizing this aspect of pastoral care."[2] Very recently, Alastair V. Campbell entered this discussion in *Professionalism and Pastoral Care*. He states the issue in terms of a question: "Will it be from increased professionalization [of the clergy] or from the use of the variety of gifts within the membership [of the church] as a whole that an innovative and responsive pastoral care will come?"[3]

In light of this contemporary concern in pastoral theology, I propose the thesis that the church may be placed in dialogue with care, using the Hiltnerian corpus, in such a way that the dialogue may be of some use to contemporary pastoral theology as it attempts to shed new light on the church-care relation. Such a dialogue may be helpful by illustrating many of the various factors that must be dealt with when exploring that relation.

I will first review the relevant works on the church. This will be followed by a discussion of one particular form of pastoral care, which Hiltner called precounseling. I will then explore the issues that emerge when the Hiltnerian view, or views, of the church come into contact with precounseling.

The Church in the Hiltnerian Corpus

Hiltner discussed the church in at least four distinct ways: as the object of the proposed discipline of organizing; as a doctrine or a church metaphor interpreted dynamically; as a community in relation to a community; and as the context for pastoral counseling. Each particular way of discussing the church is connected with an equally particular way of discussing psychology or another social science.

The Church and Organizing

Organizing is one of the three disciplines that Hiltner proposed in *Preface to Pastoral Theology*. Like communicating, organizing was to be a cognate discipline of shepherding, or pastoral theology. Hiltner defined organizing as that perspective "upon the operations of pastor and church that makes the fellowship cohere and that determines its

---

2. Donald Capps, *Life Cycle Theory and Pastoral Care* (Philadelphia: Fortress, 1983), 56.

3. Alastair V. Campbell, *Professionalism and Pastoral Care* (Philadelphia: Fortress, 1985), 23.

relationships as a fellowship with everything that is not of the fellowship."[4] Fellowship has to do with the processes by which an association becomes a "body" and acts like a "body." Organizing also has to do with the processes by which the interconnected parts of a "body" are formed, maintained, and act. The main object of the organizing point of view is the church, which Hiltner defined as the "body of Christ." Thus, organizing, as Hiltner used it, refers to the production and function of a "body," all of whose organs function in such a way that they mutually support that "body of which Christ is head."

The church as the "body of Christ" is a biological metaphor of the church. Hiltner supported this type of metaphor, stating that every new advance in biology brings new potential for understanding the body metaphor in greater depth. However, he also acknowledged that there are occasions when this particular metaphor is inadequate for discussing the church.

Drawing on biology as it had progressed in the first half of this century, Hiltner interpreted the "body of Christ" metaphor. For example, one biological principle is that an "organ never grows by mere accretion, but according to a pattern determined by its function within the total body." Such a pattern is developmental, proceeding from an "original diffuse unity toward finer and finer differentiations, all of which, however, are to result in a new and more intricate order of functional unity." This principle is then applied to the function of organizing the church, or to the actual processes that take place to produce the church as "body." For instance, in light of the biological principle just mentioned, organizing is not to be seen as mere accretion. Rather, the patterns of organizing must be appropriate for functioning within the total church body.[5]

Hiltner goes on to add several more layers of concepts to the basic biological metaphor, focusing on its organic processes. The initial layer that is added to the organizing process of the church has three aspects: nourishing or aiding its development; purifying or protecting it from internal or external threats; and relating it, either positively or negatively, to bodies other than the church, that is, other institutions. Depending on the church event taking place, one of these aspects will tend to come into sharp focus. For example, according to Hiltner, relating tends to be "dominant" when the event has to do with social ethics.[6]

The next layer has to with "how" the church is organized in each of the three aspects just mentioned. How do we actually carry out

4. Seward Hiltner, *Preface to Pastoral Theology* (Nashville: Abingdon, 1958), 61.
5. Ibid., 199–200.
6. Ibid., 201.

nourishing, protecting, and relating? In order to answer this question, Hiltner draws on a distinction made by Ernst Troeltsch between the "church type" of church and the "sect type" of church. An actual church includes both types, though that church will tend to act predominately within one type or the other. For example, the "church type" nourishes primarily through rituals and rites. The "sect type" nourishes primarily by means of "the Word." The "church type" protects primarily through guaranteeing something about its priesthood, such as apostolic succession, while the "sect type" protects through entrance requirements for members and clergy alike (mainly having a certain type of religious experience and bearing witness to that experience before the group). The "church type" relates by moving toward control of other institutions and culture. In contrast, the "sect type" tends to move toward withdrawal. Since no church fits either ideal exactly, both types of nourishing, protecting, and relating can be observed in actual churches, though one type will predominate. Hiltner provides a fairly detailed verbatim analysis which illustrates how he sees all of this working out in actual practice.[7]

The final layer has to do with group dynamics. At the time of writing the *Preface*, Hiltner noted that little basic research had been done on understanding the church with the help of the modern study of small groups. He went on to illustrate the type of use that could be made of group dynamics for study of the church. Two important principles of a group are that it has a task, or goal, and a process, which produce the quality of interaction among its members, including its leader. Hiltner discusses various ways that these two factors are related and what types of groups emerge depending on how the relationship between the two factors develops. Then he makes application to the church, concluding that "in the church as nowhere else organizing must show an integrity between task and process."[8]

This last suggestive layer provides a natural bridge to the next church discussion. In 1972, Hiltner once again brought psychological dynamics, not specifically group dynamics, into an encounter with metaphors of the church.

The Church and Psychological Dynamics

In *Theological Dynamics*, Hiltner attempted to delineate how theology, understood dynamically, is both enriched by dynamic psychology and illuminates psychology. Dynamics is defined by Hiltner as "a study of the energy components: the conflicts among energy dimen-

7. Ibid., 201–4.
8. Ibid., 214–15.

sions, the tensions and counterbalances among forces, and the variety of equilibriums."[9] Hiltner reached his position on dynamics through his study of dynamic psychologies, beginning with Freud, and with some references to dynamics in sociology.

One lesson that Hiltner learned from the study of dynamics is that close attention to the "specifics" of a situation is required if dynamic forces are to be perceived in their various levels and complexity. Thus, in bringing dynamics to theology Hiltner remained "as close to specifics as possible."[10] This is also true of Hiltner's discussion of the church in *Theological Dynamics*. It is designed to reveal "dynamic forces" at work in the church.

The main religious resource that Hiltner draws on in his church discussion is the Bible. Specifically, he cites several biblical metaphors of the church, interpreting each of them dynamically. To his credit, Hiltner does not attempt to abstract a single doctrine of the church from the various metaphors. Rather, he allows a plurality of positions on the church to exist simultaneously in accord with the particular vision of the church connected with each metaphor.

According to Hiltner, there have been three biblical church metaphors of major importance during the history of Christianity: the Pauline "body of Christ"; the church as "covenant community"; and the "household of God." In order to provide continuity with the discussion of organizing, I will continue with the "body of Christ" metaphor. The three principal features of this metaphor, says Hiltner, are that Jesus Christ is related to us in the same way that a head is related to a body, that we are organically members one of another, and each church participant is needed in the same way that every part is needed to make an organism function.[11]

Dynamic analysis of this church metaphor helps to reveal both its strengths and its temptations, according to Hiltner. From the dynamic point of view, the "headship" (at the human level of leadership) and "body" relation, for example, is most centrally about our "human interrelatedness" and not about "who" is to control it. One strength that dynamics helps to reveal is that the head-body relationship needs to be in accord with the focus on "human interrelatedness." If headship at the human leadership level "becomes more responsibility than privilege, then the great merit of the body metaphor is our realization that we work in organic interrelationship, and that is our strength."[12]

---

9. Seward Hiltner, *Theological Dynamics* (Nashville: Abingdon, 1972), 14.
10. Ibid., 182–83.
11. Ibid., 110.
12. Ibid., 112.

Of course, dynamics helps to reveal the forces at work in such interrelationships.

The other side of the head (leadership)-body relationship is its temptations to distortion. One possible distortion is coerciveness on the part of leadership. Just as the headship of Christ is not to be seen as a dictatorship, so church leadership "must be carried out with the best possible checks on arbitrary powers."[13] Coercion tends to produce a body whose parts are "frozen" and which finds itself in a "defensive" stance attempting to protect itself against society. The undesirable results of such distortion highlight the necessity of reflecting on the relationship of the church to local and worldwide communities.

The Church and Community

Hiltner concludes his church discussion in *Theological Dynamics* by considering two fundamental and interrelated aspects of the church's relationship to the community. One is about how the church deals with its power in relation to the power of other social institutions. The other is about how the church is to interpret its service to the world.

Hiltner draws on the Tillichian principle that the use of power is "always to be for the ends of justice, and to the extent that this is done, love in the theological sense is at work."[14] Thus, he concludes that the church cannot bypass power issues and has the obligation to use its power toward increasing justice, however justice and power may be defined. To this end "sociodynamics" can help the church to understand complex social issues having to do with "love, power, and justice."

The church's service to the worldwide community is discussed as mission. He acknowledges the crucial importance of evangelism. Yet this alone does not fulfill the mission of the church. Without apology, the church ministers directly to the needs of disadvantaged peoples. This position is taken with the knowledge that some disagree with "direct service" because it may help to mask the enormity of need.

Particular church metaphors are not alluded to in this discussion. However, Hiltner does note that none of the church metaphors that he examined support the "atomistic view" that the church keep silent about issues of power and service in relation to community. In this light, perhaps something can be said about the "body of Christ" metaphor. Just as an organic body interacts with an environment, so the church as the "body of Christ" interacts with communities. As a "body" the church creatively interacts with communities to increase justice and to satisfy the needs of the disadvantaged.

13. Ibid., 112.
14. Ibid., 122.

So far we have seen that Hiltner has much to say about the church. Its members and actions are related and organized in certain ways; dynamics can be used to reveal its strengths and shortcomings; and it is related to community in important ways. We can now consider one final way that Hiltner addressed the church.

The Church as Context of Pastoral Counseling

The resource for this section is *The Context of Pastoral Counseling*, co-authored by Hiltner and Colston. To set the stage for the ensuing discussion of the church, it will be necessary to say something about the book.

Hiltner and Colston did an empirical study in order to discover some things about pastoral counseling. The book is their report on that study. Colston served as the pastoral counselor (independent variable) who was to do counseling at Byrn Mawr Community Church in Chicago and at the University of Chicago Counseling Center (dependent variables). Individuals who sought counseling, some at the church and some at the counseling center, were asked if they would participate in the study. Those who agreed were given psychological tests before counseling started, immediately after it was terminated, and six months following termination. The tests were administered and interpreted by clinical psychologists at the counseling center. The co-authors compared and contrasted the test results of the counseling done in the two settings.

Where do we encounter the church in this study? According to the co-authors, the uniqueness of pastoral counseling, and, consequently, its difference from other counseling, is its context. The church, treated as "setting," is one of the four contextual dimensions posited. The other three dimensions of context are "expectation," "shift in relationship," and "aims and limitations." The basic similarity between pastoral and other counseling is that "the processes involved in counseling, at the level of interpersonal relationships, are the same."[15]

The church as setting involves not only the physical place but all that people find to be symbolic about the church, from the pulpit and Bible to liturgical music and prayer. For example, one counselee remarked that she used to "drive by this church on the way to work every morning. There was something reassuring about its dignity and beauty. I was going through a very hard time, and I tried to imagine what it would be like to belong to this church. I was looking for peace, and it looked calm and serene."[16]

---

15. Seward Hiltner and Lowell G. Colston, *The Context of Pastoral Counseling* (Nashville: Abingdon, 1961), 24.
16. Ibid., 31.

Whether the setting symbolizes something positive, negative, or ambiguous to the one seeking pastoral counseling, the pastor is inevitably associated with that setting in the mind and feelings of that person. Due to such an association, the church as setting is still a contextual factor even when the pastoral counseling happens in a home, business establishment, or some other place outside the church building.[17] Logically, this facet of the church as setting extends to the counseling center if the client knows that Colston is a pastor. One difference is that the client there is not seeking pastoral counseling. Another difference is that the client would necessarily associate Colston with the counseling center as physical setting and, therefore, with what the counseling center symbolizes to the client.

Hiltner and Colston contrast the church as setting with the setting of the counseling center, concluding that the latter tends to appear as "neutral ground" having the connotation of "objectivity" due to its connection with science. This observation raises an important question. Which setting best facilitates "successful" counseling? The co-authors learned that the most desirable setting is relative to the needs of individual clients. In an attempt to have the best of both worlds, Hiltner and Colston designed the pastoral counseling office in the church to be fairly barren so that it had a "neutral ground" feel to it. In this way pastoral counseling clients who reacted positively to church symbolism still had such symbolism since they were in a church building and were seeing a pastor, and clients who needed a more neutral environment did not find the office of the pastor to be as much of a negative influence.

The connection between setting and symbolism reveals the tremendous significance of viewing the church as setting for pastoral counseling. Hiltner and Colston expressed that significance in cautious, negative terms. A person who is attracted to a church setting cannot automatically be marked as "defensive and regressive in relation to any usual standards of progress in counseling."[18] They were rightly cautious in their claims because of the nature of their study.

If, however, we view the church as setting in relation to other aspects of church life we are reminded of the historical significance of that setting. The latest example that forces us to look anew at the significance of the church as setting is the movement in this country that is providing refuge to Salvadorans. In this case, the church as setting carries with it the symbolism of "sanctuary." Surely more study of the church as setting is in order, not only in relation to pastoral

17. Ibid., 32.
18. Ibid., 32–33.

counseling and other forms of care, but in relation to social action as well.

Precounseling

Having examined the four ways that Hiltner discussed the church, it is now necessary to examine pastoral care in the form of precounseling. *Pastoral Counseling* constitutes Hiltner's definitive treatise on pastoral counseling. It is here that he discusses precounseling.

What is now typically called "pastoral care and counseling," Hiltner called "pastoral work and counseling" in *Pastoral Counseling*. This "activity" flows from the "one role" of ministry. Though both "pastoral work" and "pastoral counseling" are part of the same ministerial activity, they are not exactly the same thing. Pastoral counseling is defined as "the attempt by a pastor to help people help themselves through the process of gaining understanding of their inner conflicts." For such counseling to take place the parishioner must recognize that something is wrong, at least to the extent that the difficulty is seen to be within. "Counseling deals with people who say, 'I want it. I must do something with myself . . . How can I proceed?' "[19]

Pastoral work is that caring activity which precedes, or is other than, pastoral counseling and which may or may not lead to pastoral counseling. Pastoral work is seen as "precounseling" in the sense that it may be engaged in for the purpose of leading to pastoral counseling, or it may unintentionally lead in that direction. Even pastoral counseling with one family member, for example, may serve as "precounseling" if it leads to another family member receiving pastoral counseling. In precounseling the parishioner has not yet reached awareness that the difficulty may be within. When the parishioner reaches such awareness, even minimally, and asks for counseling, precounseling then shifts to pastoral counseling.

Any attempt to discuss precounseling necessarily involves pastoral counseling because both share the same fundamental principles derived from pastoral counseling. Their difference hinges on "differences in translating these [principles] into action." For example, in pastoral counseling the pastor helps the parishioner to clarify elements of conflict associated with conflicted feelings when they emerge. This happens verbally in the context of the counseling relationship. In precounseling, this principle of clarifying conflict is translated into action somewhat differently. The pastor accepts the "conflicting pulls" a parishioner displays when trying to determine whether or not to get

19. Seward Hiltner, *Pastoral Counseling* (Nashville: Abingdon, 1949), 19–20, 147–48.

help. Hiltner emphasizes that the precounseling translation is not literal. However, a "free translation of the essential principle is sound."[20] While remaining aware of the precounseling-pastoral counseling relationship, we can now focus on certain precounseling principles without explicitly dealing with pastoral counseling.

Some Precounseling Principles

Taking the initiative. Hiltner tells the story of Mr. and Mrs. Bolton, a couple in early middle age, and Pastor Breen. Mrs. Bolton is active in church affairs and attends worship regularly. Mr. Bolton, a lawyer, attends worship usually once a month, which is the extent of his participation. For several weeks there has been a "whispered rumor" in the community that Mr. Bolton was seen with an attractive young woman on a weekend in a certain city. "The news comes to the ears of the pastor. Shall he do anything about it?"

In addition to weighing other factors, Pastor Breen reasons that "it is likely that the Bolton home life is not on the firmest of foundations. If it is not, now may be the last chance to save it by getting the Boltons to help themselves."[21] Pastor Breen decides that as pastor it is appropriate for him to involve himself in the situation in the form of precounseling. The only way that he can become involved, however, is by taking the initiative.

According to Hiltner, there are two types of initiative that the pastor can take and one type that must remain with the parishioner. The first type is "geographic" initiative, such as making a pastoral call. Pastor Breen put this type into practice beginning with a phone call to make an appointment with Mr. Bolton, and then by going to visit Bolton at his office. The next two types of initiative will be seen in relation to other precounseling principles.

Offering help. When Pastor Breen spoke with Mr. Bolton, he said, "Mr. Bolton, I'll put my cards on the table. I want to raise a question with you." He went on to tell Mr. Bolton about the rumor, clearly stating that he was not judging its truth or falsehood. If Mr. Bolton wanted to talk about it, then he, Pastor Breen, would be there. If not, then nothing else would be said, and the conversation would remain private.

This aspect of the conversation illustrates the principle that help is to be offered in such a way that it can be refused.[22] It occurs in conjunction with the second type of initiative taken by Pastor Breen, fac-

20. Ibid., 147, 132.
21. Ibid., 125–26.
22. Ibid., 126–28.

tual initiative. That is, he was willing to raise a certain question and discuss certain information.

Understanding any attitude. The initial response by Mr. Bolton was denial of the affair: "You don't believe there's any truth in this, do you?" Pastor Breen responded by reiterating his nonjudgmental stance. He avoided attaching any conditions to his understanding of the response given by Mr. Bolton. Had he subtly made innocence a condition of his understanding, for example, then Mr. Bolton would not have felt as free to take up the offer of help a few days later, since the rumor turned out to be true. A very similar principle is discussed by Hiltner in terms of being alert to evidence of wanting help, but not exploiting that evidence.[23]

Denying probable incorrect expectations. One valuable aspect of Pastor Breen stressing his nonjudgmental stance is that otherwise Mr. Bolton will most likely assume that the pastor is there to judge and condemn. Such an assumption or expectation may very well prevent offered help from being accepted. Whatever probable expectations are being addressed, explicitly denying them enables the parishioner to get a better picture of what the pastor can and cannot offer.[24]

Being willing to wait. Mr. Bolton did not want to talk about his situation so the pastor left. This is in accord with the type of initiative left to the parishioner, that is, psychological initiative. Two days after the pastoral visit Mr. Bolton called the pastor and said that he wanted to talk about his family situation. Such initiative marked the transition from precounseling to pastoral counseling.[25]

In concluding this section I would like to note that, according to Hiltner, he is the first to formulate a systematic comparison of precounseling pastoral work with pastoral counseling.[26] We can now ask if, in the Hiltnerian corpus, there is any room for a discussion between the church and pastoral work, or care, using precounseling as a kind of test case.

The Church and Pastoral Care

In this section I will bring each way that Hiltner discusses the church into dialogue with precounseling, beginning with the church as the object of organizing.

23. Ibid., 129–31.
24. Ibid., 130.
25. Ibid., 130–31, 127–28.
26. Ibid., 276, n. 1.

Precounseling and the Church
as the Object of Organizing

When Pastor Breen heard the "whispered rumor" about Mr. Bolton, why did he not think of it as a problem of the church fellowship rather than solely as that of individuals? If the rumor was widespread in the community, then undoubtedly church members were participating in the gossip. They may even have started it. Some of those church members may have been coming into contact often with Mrs. Bolton at church activities and were probably quite concerned about her. Perhaps some were becoming uncomfortable around her due to their own circumstances. Others may have taken a moralistic stance, condemning Mr. Bolton on the illegitimate basis of gossip. Finally, what about the gossip? With its power negatively to affect individuals and groups within the fellowship, is it not a moral concern? On the other hand, it seems appropriate for Pastor Breen to focus on the Boltons in terms of precounseling since they were the ones experiencing the marital difficulty.

Given the stance taken by Pastor Breen, one way to bring the church into the discussion within the Hiltnerian framework is in terms of "nurturing," or perhaps "protecting," the church. This now appears as an interdisciplinary dialogue between pastoral care (shepherding), focusing on the individual, and organizing, focusing on the church fellowship. There are several reasons why the church, in this instance, cannot be discussed from within pastoral care.

In *Preface to Pastoral Theology*, Hiltner touches on this issue by discussing the difference between shepherding, which focuses on pastoral care, and organizing, which focuses on the church fellowship. Historically, shepherding encompassed the church fellowship. One facet of this, for example, was called discipline. Originally, according to Hiltner, in discipline the welfare of both individual and church was sought, though that balance became distorted over the centuries. With the division of shepherding and organizing, Hiltner divides the two dimensions of discipline. "The first is of a shepherding character, part of what shall be called 'guiding,' in which what is dominantly intended is the welfare of the person involved. The other is of an organizing character. . . ." Such a division does not mean that Hiltner advocates no relation between them. Rather, "the most meaningful unity will emerge when each is seen rightly."[27]

Another reason that the church cannot be discussed from within pastoral care arises when we consider the Hiltnerian view of shepherding, apart from its relation with organizing. Continuing the dis-

27. Hiltner, *Preface to Pastoral Theology*, 68.

cussion of discipline, Hiltner articulates the way that he intends for shepherding to be understood. "What we seek above all to retain for the shepherding perspective is the quest for the good of the person or persons involved—temporarily, if need be, without thought of the larger good of larger groups or institutions." In several writings Hiltner explains shepherding by referring to the good Samaritan parable. For example, he explains the quote about shepherding just cited by saying that "it is simply the good-Samaritan principle in operation."[28] The "good-Samaritan principle" highlights a focus on the individual for certain purposes as opposed to a focus on the church.

The Hiltnerian position highlights the need for interdisciplinary dialogue. For example, I certainly support Pastor Breen's appropriate precounseling dialogue. However, it is possible that rather than temporarily setting aside the "larger good of larger groups or institutions" he could learn to carry on an interdisciplinary dialogue between shepherding and organizing, or whatever contemporary rubric is used to discuss the church fellowship, such as church and society. At the very least it would give him a basis for discerning the relation between communal dimensions of the precounseling situation and individual dimensions.

Precounseling and a Church Metaphor

Prior to geographic and factual initiative in precounseling, there is the need for evaluating the precounseling situation. How can a church metaphor, such as "the body of Christ," facilitate evaluation in precounseling?

Hiltner actually has Pastor Breen evaluating the precounseling situation toward the beginning of the story. First, he considers how he will "interpret his function." Will he wait until the Boltons come to him? Can he approach the woman who was supposedly seen with Mr. Bolton? Second, he considers his relation to the Boltons: "These are my people, the Boltons. They are members of that segment of the Christian fellowship of which I am shepherd."[29] On that basis, how should he act? Third, he considers the "whispered rumor" or gossip that is supposedly spreading through the community. What stance should he take toward the gossip? Fourth, he determines that he will take the geographic initiative. What strategy should be devised for approaching Mr. Bolton?

Obviously, this evaluation includes the communal dimension. If we include it as the initial moment of precounseling, then precounseling

28. Ibid., 68.
29. Hiltner, *Pastoral Counseling,*, 126.

necessarily includes this larger dimension. This is one point at which church metaphors may be especially helpful. The "body of Christ" metaphor, interpreted dynamically, may enable Pastor Breen initially to evaluate the precounseling situation effectively, for example. The way that it may do so is by enabling Pastor Breen to make judgments about all of the perceived factors in the situation from the standpoint of the strengths and weaknesses of the "body of Christ" as it manifests "human interrelatedness" in particular ways.

The first element in such an evaluation is to consider the "whispered rumor" or gossip about Mr. Bolton. This event sparks Pastor Breen's evaluation. He must respond in some way. He abstains from judging the truth or falsehood of the gossip, yet allows it to influence his actions. On what basis is such influenced pastoral action justifiable? Here is where the body of Christ metaphor first may be of use. It may enable the pastor to evaluate the source of the gossip so that action can be taken with the confidence that the pastor is not simply being manipulated.

One peculiarity of gossip is that individuals rarely can tell how widespread the gossip actually is. There are powerful individuals who can make gullible persons believe that the entire community is buzzing about some event when in reality hardly anyone has ever heard about it. In addition, the gossip is likely to be at least partially untrue, distorted, or completely false, yet there are persons who nearly always listen and get hurt repeatedly. In light of these realities the pastor can hardly afford to be one of those gullible persons. For example, Pastor Breen told Mr. Bolton the following: "There's a rumor which has spread very widely through the community that you are seeing a good deal of another woman. . . ."[30] If Pastor Breen's source is one of those powerful individuals then he has probably told Mr. Bolton a falsehood.

Let us suppose that a church member, who is also a member of the local community, told Pastor Breen the gossip about Mr. Bolton. On what basis does he evaluate what he is told? In light of the body of Christ metaphor the first point of evaluation is not Mr. Bolton, but rather the one telling the gossip. The head (leadership)-body relation is relevant here. As leader, Pastor Breen considers the interrelationship between himself and the one telling the gossip. For example, the person may be one of the powerful individuals, one of the gullible individuals, or perhaps an elder or deacon trying to be helpful. Depending on which one is speaking to Pastor Breen, he may decide to let the information go in one ear and out the other. If he does not have the capacity to do this, he may be drawn into a destructive rela-

30. Ibid., 127.

tion with persons who try to control him and the church. In this case his action would be the result of a manipulation that will probably have destructive results. Therefore, just because Pastor Breen refrains from judging the truth or falsehood of the gossip he is not automatically free to act. Instead, the one telling the gossip may be a better target for the precounseling initiative.

We have thus far considered one aspect of the leadership-member relation in the "body of Christ." In this relation, focusing on the example of gossip, there is the danger of coercion by the member (and by the pastor). Other facets of "human interrelatedness" include members with members, groups with members, and groups with groups. First, there is the danger that Pastor Breen will attempt to coerce Mr. Bolton. Second, what is the proper response of the "body of Christ" to Mrs. Bolton? Perhaps she is already aware of the affair. In that case, she may be receiving care from a group or an individual in the church in ways that Pastor Breen does not know about. Or, perhaps she is moving toward alienation from the church. Fourth, what is the proper response of the "body of Christ" to the Boltons if they decide to divorce? Even if precounseling is successful and the Boltons receive marriage counseling, the marriage is not necessarily going to be saved.

In all of these ways and more, the "body of Christ" manifests its "human interrelatedness" concretely. Such concrete manifestations reveal its strengths and weaknesses as the "body of Christ." Pastor Breen, drawing on this church metaphor for evaluation, can use this knowledge as a basis for taking the initiative in precounseling with Mr. Bolton, Mrs. Bolton, or even the church fellowship as a whole.

Precounseling and the Church in Community

What do precounseling and the church and community relation have to do with one another? One commonality is that they may be concerned with the same issue. Continuing the example of precounseling with Mr. Bolton, let us assume that "marriage and family" is an issue common both to precounseling and to the church and community relation. By focusing on this common issue it becomes possible to see at least one way that the two are related.

As mentioned earlier, the church uses its power to seek justice in community. In this age of "broken homes" the church remains a powerful force by setting forth values having to do with "marriage and family." The church has the opportunity to seek justice, whatever form that may take, on behalf of those who are strongly affected by divorce, spouse abuse, or child neglect.

Both Pastor Breen and Mr. Bolton are participants in the local church and in the local community, so both are necessarily affected by the powerful interactions of church and community regarding "marriage and family." Pastor Breen proceeded partly on the basis of his understanding of the church's implicit, if not explicit, position on "marriage and family," including an understanding of how that position affects his pastoral activity. Mr. Bolton had some expectations that Pastor Breen holds a certain position, in part because of his experience of local church and community.

Precounseling may also affect the church and community relation. It may do so by making those affected by the precounseling more aware of the issues involved. For example, as a result of his precounseling with Mr. Bolton, Pastor Breen may start a group for discussing "marriage and family issues," preach on that issue, or move his church toward explicitly developing its theological understanding of it.

Precounseling may affect individuals in the community. For example, suppose that Pastor Breen was successful in getting the Boltons into pastoral marriage counseling and that their marriage improved. Such precounseling and counseling may serve as precounseling for the woman involved in the affair. Noticing the change in Mr. Bolton, she may decide to seek counseling in order to discuss her own troubled marriage.

Finally, the community usually serves as the arena in which precounseling takes place. Consequently, precounseling is public insofar as it has a public context. For example, Pastor Breen went into the work place in order to speak with Mr. Bolton. Though he could keep the conversation private, Pastor Breen could not keep from being seen entering and leaving the office. Possibly, his visit became part of the community gossip about Mr. Bolton. In addition, Mrs. Bolton may have heard about the visit, presenting Pastor Breen with a potentially awkward situation. Publicness does not keep the pastor from doing precounseling. However, the public arena does present factors that help shape the precounseling situation. This issue of publicness shades into the next and final church and care dialogue having to do with context.

Precounseling and the Church as Setting

As we have seen, Hiltner and Colston wrote about the church as one contextual factor in pastoral counseling. As context the church was thought of as setting, which included religious symbolism. Can the church as setting also be part of the context of precounseling? The following shows that most of what is said about the church as setting in relation to pastoral counseling can be said about the church as setting in relation to precounseling.

Though precounseling may take place in the community, the church still counts as setting because, as in pastoral counseling, the pastor is inevitably associated with that setting by the parishioner. We see this in the initial part of the conversation between Pastor Breen and Mr. Bolton:

> **Bolton**: Hello, Dr. Breen. Sorry I haven't been able to get to church for the past few Sundays. Things have been at their peak here in the office, and I've been working part of the time over weekends.
> **Breen**: One look at me and you think of church, I take it.
> **Bolton**: (laughs) Well, you do remind me of it. When you telephoned, I supposed you wanted to talk with me about something like that.[31]

One symbolic element here is the worship service in relation to Mr. Bolton's pattern of attendance. If Pastor Breen is tempted to say something that might make Mr. Bolton feel guilty about his lack of weekly attendance then he may make it more difficult for Mr. Bolton to accept what he came to say and to take the psychological initiative later. This illustrates that the church as setting can be one significant factor in precounseling.

Church as setting may provide positive, ambiguous, or negative symbolism to the parishioner. To Mr. Bolton it seemed to be ambiguous. The next issue, which Hiltner and Colston did not pursue, is closely related to this point. The attitude of the parishioner toward the symbolism may change. It is interesting that Mr. Bolton called the pastor after the precounseling. This indicates that the church may mean more to him than he initially believed or revealed, or that he saw new possibilities in it.

Conclusion

I have explored Hiltner's writings about the church, and about precounseling. By bringing these two strands of Hiltnerian thought into dialogue, I have attempted to demonstrate some of the diverse directions which that dialogue takes. One reason for diversity is that there are a variety of ways to discuss the church. Also, the different forms that pastoral care may take add to the complexity of the dialogue. I focused on precounseling in order to highlight the issue of pastoral initiative, and as a vehicle for suggesting ways that the church may be related to care even when the focus is on the individual.

One implication of this dialogue for contemporary pastoral theology, as it pursues the church-care issue, is that the diverse ways of

31. Ibid., 126.

discussing the church need to be taken into account. Focusing only on one way of discussing the church, as context for example, in no way exhausts the issue. Another implication is that strict attention must be paid to ways that distinctions may be made between the various forms of pastoral care. Just as Hiltner creatively explored the notion of precounseling, today new ways of distinguishing between forms of care need to be explored. I believe that such exploration is part of what is needed if we are to discover new and creative ways of talking about the relationship between pastoral care and the church.

12

Caring for Society

> GENE T. FOWLER, JR.

Normally, the name of Anton T. Boisen is associated with the study of mental illness and hospital chaplaincy. He has been called the "father" of clinical pastoral education, and, more generally, he is referred to as one of the "fathers" of modern pastoral theology. References to Boisen usually focus on his study of the individual or ministry relating to the individual. It may be surprising to learn that he wrote a book on the church, *Religion in Crisis and Custom: A Sociological and Psychological Study,* and that he was at home with the sociology of religion as well as with the psychology of religion.[1]

I will explore what Boisen wrote about the church. I begin with the presupposition that understanding his church writings requires at least minimal knowledge of his views on the relationship between mental illness and religious experience. The reasons for this presupposition should become clear as the chapter unfolds. Thus, the starting point of this inquiry is a discussion of the mental illness that Boisen suffered and the conclusions that he drew after emerging from the darkness.

The church writings of Boisen are discussed in the second section of the article. Drawing on sociologists such as Max Weber, he explored

---

1. Anton T. Boisen, *Religion in Crisis and Custom: A Sociological and Psychological Study* (New York: Harper, 1955).

the notion that religious movements emerge in response to some forms of social crisis. In relation to this thesis he spoke of such things as the life cycle of the church, prophetic church leadership, and the relationship between the church and social change.

The final section contains what I believe to be the main implication of the Boisen church writings for pastoral care. My contention is that Boisen held a view of the church that facilitates exploration of pastoral care at the level of church and society. More specifically, the Boisen discussion is very suggestive for understanding how the church may care for society in times of crisis.

This is not a typical way of discussing pastoral care. Yet, theoretically and intuitively it seems proper to speak of the church caring for the world in some fundamental sense. Most importantly, this discussion is not disconnected from Boisen. It follows his work closely.

Boisen and Mental Illness

Born in 1876, Anton Boisen spent much of his childhood and adolescence in Bloomington, Indiana. After graduating from Indiana University in 1897, he did graduate work, taught high school, and became a French tutor at his alma mater. An ongoing struggle with sexuality and an overly strict conscience during this period of his life led to a decision to change careers and become a forester. Before leaving Bloomington to begin his new career in Maryland, and to attend Yale Forest School, he met Alice Batchelder and fell in love with her. This was in 1902. Alice did not reciprocate, and Boisen struggled with his inability to let her go for many years.[2]

In the fall of 1908 Boisen entered Union Theological Seminary in New York City as a Presbyterian ministerial candidate. Due to his interest in the psychology of religion, he studied with George Albert Coe, professor of education and psychology. After graduating in 1911 he was offered the opportunity to do sociological surveys of rural church communities in different areas of the country before settling into a pastorate. Following this experience he spent one year as a college chaplain and four years as a parish pastor serving two small churches, each for two years.[3]

World War I signaled the end of local parish work for Anton Boisen. He became a secretary with the Overseas Young Men's Christian Association and was among the first sent to France in September 1917.

2. Anton T. Boisen, *Out of the Depths: An Autobiographical Study of Mental Disorder and Religious Experience* (New York: Harper, 1960), 20–53.
3. Ibid., 60–71.

Upon his return to the United States, in July 1919, he worked for the Interchurch World Movement, directing its North Dakota Rural Survey, a sociological study. Following this assignment he intended to return to a pastorate. However, this was not to be. In October 1920, while visiting his sister in Massachusetts, he became psychotic and was committed to the Boston Psychopathic Hospital and within a week was transferred to Westboro State Hospital.[4]

Boisen had undergone several abnormal experiences in the past, one of which he called "near psychotic" in his autobiography, *Out of the Depths*. Yet, none had reached the extreme severity of his illness at this time. The illness was diagnosed as "catatonic dementia praecox" (now called schizophrenia). During the first three weeks of hospitalization, he was in a "violent delirium," being thrown into a world of terror, irrationality, and hallucinations.[5] For example, according to Boisen, one of his psychotic experiences involved the moon: "Then I found myself in the Moon. The idea of being in the Moon had been present almost from the beginning of the week. Now this became an outstanding feature. . . ."[6]

In the fourth week Boisen entered a period of remission. He wrote that much as one awakens from a bad dream, he "snapped out of it." However, he seems to have been alone in his opinion because the doctors refused to dismiss him from the hospital. For the next several months he remained at Westboro. Then on March 24, 1921, he suffered a relapse, once again becoming "acutely disturbed." The relapse lasted for ten weeks.[7]

It was not until January 1922 that Boisen left Westboro State Hospital. By this time he had decided to study mental illness, or schizophrenia, and become a psychiatric hospital chaplain. After preparing himself academically at Andover Newton Theological Seminary, Harvard Divinity School, and Boston Psychopathic Hospital, he began his pioneering work as a chaplain at Worcester State Hospital on July 1, 1924.[8]

Mental Illness and Religious Experience

Anton Boisen believed that the mental illness which he suffered was a religious experience. Examining some of the main features of this

4. Ibid., 72–87.
5. Anton T. Boisen, *The Exploration of the Inner World: A Study of Mental Disorder and Religious Experience* (New York: Harper, 1936), 3–4.
6. Boisen, *Out of the Depths*, 94.
7. Ibid., 95, 114–21.
8. Ibid., 140–50.

view will provide us with a basis for discussing his approach to the church.

Boisen distinguished between different types of mental illness. The distinction was between mental illness caused primarily by some organic or bodily difficulty and mental illness which results from certain kinds of psychological problems. He described this distinction, during his remission, in a letter to a friend: "As I look around me here and then try to analyze my own case, I would distinguish two main types of insanity. In the one there is some organic trouble, a defect in the brain or a disorder in the nervous system, or some disease of the blood. In the other there is no organic difficulty." He went on to explain that in the type of insanity not based on organic problems "the difficulty lies in the disorganization of the patient's world." The foundations upon which the "ordinary reasoning processes" are based become upset. Some situations such as death or disappointment compels the disorganized world to be reorganized "from the bottom up."[9]

In order to understand what Boisen meant when he referred to the patient's "world," it is helpful to recognize that he consistently used this word as a metaphor for the inner psychological life, usually as manifested in the schizophrenic. Apparently, it is based on an analogy drawn from his earlier forestry and sociological survey experiences in which he would travel to a new section of the country and, with the help of appropriate methods, survey a community or map a forest. His writings are filled with references to the "inner world." In addition, this metaphor is supplemented with similar metaphors such as "country" and "territory." In a letter to his friend, Fred Eastman, Boisen described his intention to study mental illness with such an image: ". . . I feel that the particular territory in which I lost my way is of greatest interest and importance. I want to explore and map that territory."[10]

Boisen did succeed in constructing such a map, and it is found in *The Exploration of the Inner World* (1936). The map begins at the point of his hypothesis that nonorganically-caused mental illness is to be explained "in terms of the disorganization of the patient's inner world consequent upon the upsetting of the foundations upon which the critical judgments are made and that, as such, it is closely related to certain types of religious experience."[11]

As the trail of the map is followed, the next part of the territory revealed is "causative factors" of mental illness. This included heredity,

9. Ibid., 97.
10. Ibid., 132.
11. Boisen, *Exploration of the Inner World*, 18.

early influences, intelligence, health, and life situation. The last factor, life situation, included social relations, sex adjustments, and vocational adjustments. Boisen determined that the category of social relations was the "primary evil" associated with the cause of mental illness. The individual accepts the judgments of groups in which he or she has been reared. Such persons stand condemned in relation to internalized standards provided by these "early guides." The result is a strong sense of personal failure.[12]

The next point on the map shows how individuals cope with the sense of personal failure. This is expressed in terms of three different "reaction patterns" exhibited by schizophrenics. The first one he called drifting, marked by apparent acceptance of defeat. There is listlessness and withdrawal into fantasy. The second one is delusional misinterpretation (paranoia), characterized by the refusal to admit defeat or error and an accompanying distortion of beliefs in order to avoid the sense of failure and guilt. The third type of reaction is panic, involving the awareness of danger which can result in an extreme emotional disturbance. In this type, the person does not give up the attempt to deal with problems or crises and has a much better chance of a positive outcome than those who exhibit the other two reaction patterns. Life-and-death issues are at stake, and the panic type tends either to "make or break" the person.

Boisen has three additional points on the map that must be mentioned. The first is "content of thought," including such things as hallucinations. Ideas of world catastrophe, death, rebirth, cosmic importance, and mission seem to predominate. The second is "religious concerns." Patients were categorized as having either marked religious concern, moderate religious concern, or no religious concern. The third, and final, point revealed is "the power of nature to heal." Boisen believed that functional, or nonorganically caused, schizophrenia was comparable to a fever or inflammation. It was nature's way of attempting to heal the mind.[13]

The map has not yet been interpreted in such a way as to facilitate disclosure of the relationship between religious experience and mental illness. The hypothesis quoted provides the first clue to this relation. Up to this point the focus has been on the disorganization of the patient's inner world. Now the focus shifts to the "upsetting of the foundations upon which the critical judgments are made," which is what brings about disorganization.

The word *foundations* refers to the individual's "philosophy of life."

12. Ibid., 21–28.
13. Ibid., 30–57.

Boisen defined this as "personality . . . viewed from the standpoint of meanings." It signifies the individual's orientation with reference to the external world, self conception, purpose in life, hierarchy of loyalties and values, and system of beliefs and attitudes. It is developed through language and is therefore a social process involving internalization of the "group organization and system of meanings." The concept of the philosophy of life was extremely important for Boisen because "it is the entire system of meanings which influences and determines all . . . reactions and all . . . thinking."[14]

What exactly is religious about one's philosophy of life? Boisen wrote, "This philosophy of life is to be termed religion in so far as it reaches the level of what for the individuals concerned are the supreme and enduring loyalties and values."[15] Several notions fundamental to Boisen's argument follow from this statement. First, the religion of the individual involves a connection or fellowship with what is believed to be highest in his or her hierarchy of values and loyalties. One of the deepest needs of the individual is to be a part of the group in which these values and loyalties reside.

Second, these highest values and loyalties get raised to the cosmic level and are "felt to be universal and abiding in human society." Third, the idea of God becomes the symbol of such values and loyalties and is a "composite impress" of those in the group with which the individual seeks identification.[16] Fourth, this fellowship with God, or what the idea of God represents, has a unifying effect on the personality.

Now it is possible to begin seeing what Boisen believed was the connection between mental illness and religious experience. Recall that the mentally ill person has a sense of personal failure, being condemned on the basis of values internalized from the group. The result is that the person becomes isolated from the group, the very location of those who provide what become the highest values and loyalties for the individual who can identify with the group. If mental illness involves the attempt to reorganize the inner world and its foundations, then it is inherently religious when the reorganization "reaches the level of what for the individuals concerned are the supreme and enduring loyalties and values."[17]

Not every mental illness reaches such a level. The litmus test for determining the types that do and those that do not is whether the outcome of the illness is positive or negative. This is based on a prin-

14. Ibid., 303.
15. Ibid., 212.
16. Ibid., 176, 196.
17. Ibid., 212.

ciple that Boisen borrowed from Coe. In the words of Boisen, "I hold with Prof[essor] Coe that the important consideration in any religious or mystical experience is the result attained and not 'how' it was attained."[18] Mental illness characterized by the panic reaction pattern is genuinely religious in that, due to the kind of reorganization mentioned, the result attained can be like the positive outcome of "religious or mystical experience." The types characterized by the drifting and delusional misinterpretation reaction patterns are not religious experiences, said Boisen, because they tend to result in negative outcomes.

In this section the focus has been on certain types of mental illness and religious experience. In the following section there is a shift to collective religion, or the church, in relation to society. How does the religious experience of the mentally ill person contribute to this larger perspective?

Boisen's View of the Church

The main resource for exploring the Boisen writings on the church is *Religion in Crisis and Custom: A Sociological and Psychological Study*. The book was begun in 1940 but for various reasons did not make its appearance until 1955, according to Boisen.[19] Its thesis, which comes directly from *The Exploration of the Inner World*, is that religious experience is rooted in the social nature of the human being and that such experience spontaneously arises under the pressure of crisis situations. The notion that the human being is social in nature focuses attention on the relationship between the individual and the group. Especially relevant in this regard is Boisen's idea, following George Herbert Mead, that "the personality is dependent upon language to provide the solid structure by which judgments are guided and action in large measure determined."[20] Language is the social means by which the group provides the values which become internalized.

The word *crisis* in the thesis can refer to the danger perceived by the schizophrenic who is characterized by the panic reaction pattern. In the last section it was seen that the attempt to reorganize the inner world in order to overcome the danger or crisis may reach the religious level and have a positive outcome. "Crisis" also can refer to dangers or problems happening at the societal level. Just as the individual may

18. Boisen, *Out of the Depths*, 127.
19. Ibid., 195.
20. Boisen, *Religion in Crisis and Custom*, 3–7.

respond to a crisis at the religious level, so the group may respond to social crisis at the religious level. Such group religion takes the form of a religious movement which may evolve into an organized church.

"Creativity" is also an important concept related to crisis. Boisen argued that in normal states of mind human beings tend to "think sluggishly in an accepted currency of ideas." In a time of crisis, when persons stand face to face with life and death issues, the intellectual and emotional processes accelerate. The "accepting currency of ideas" fails to provide the resources for expressing new ideas which "come surging in." In this way new insights are born in crisis and receive new expression. Thus, one reason why crisis is an important component in the development of new religious movements is that creativity, which fosters the new insights of the movement, arises during the crisis.

Boisen demonstrated this belief with his study of the growth of Holiness sects in this country during the economic depression of the 1930s. Following Ernst Troeltsch, he viewed a sect as a "voluntary organization made up of those who are morally and religiously qualified . . . [and which] . . . stands rigidly and uncompromisingly for what it conceives to be the enduring Christian principles."[21] The religious qualifications are rooted in a mystical experience preferably induced by the group.

Economic depression is one type of social crisis. Boisen noted that there was the expectation of an increased number of "mental breakdowns" following the crash of 1929. Yet this did not happen. Though the number of hospital patients did increase, explanations other than "mental breakdown" provided the explanations for that increase. Holiness sects, on the other hand, grew rapidly. According to Boisen, ". . . the Holiness sects of the more sedate variety increased 50 percent [in membership] and the more radical Pentecostal groups more than trebled."[22]

Boisen discussed various Holiness groups, explaining some of their teachings and the types of experiences they value. He also discussed the reasons for their phenomenal growth during the Depression. Though many factors contributed to their rapid growth, one of the most important, and the one of immediate concern, was economic distress. Focusing on the Pentecostal groups, he discovered that they drew primarily "from the underprivileged classes, upon whom the strains have fallen most heavily."[23]

21. Ibid., 3, 132, n. 15.
22. Ibid., 71.
23. Ibid., 71–85.

What, then, is the link between the economic distress of the "under-privileged classes" and increased membership of the Pentecostals? First, the crisis draws attention away from "intrapsychic tensions and problems," which are the main factors in nonorganic mental illness. Second, tensions may be lessened because the crisis provides satisfaction of the need for punishment. Third, attention is given to the suffering and needs of others. Since in the beginning stages of the Depression most relief came from friends and neighbors, the "strain was being shared and the sense of isolation thus tended to decrease." Recall Boisen's contention that one of the primary causes of nonorganic mental illness is acceptance of internalized social judgment, with the resulting sense of failure and isolation from the group. Therefore, he concluded that the Depression induced "a state of mind favorable to religious experience rather than to mental illness."[24]

Since people suffered together through no particular fault of their own, they were led to "think and feel together intensely about the things that matter most." Like the mental patient, they were "brought face to face with the ultimate issues of life; the great verities with which religion deals come alive." The kinds of intense mystical experiences characteristic of the Holiness sects were induced under group control. The importance of this is that the danger of "disturbance" was reduced to a minimum and constructive elements in them could be seen. Thus, with group support these experiences could "bring new life and hope and tap new sources of power."[25]

Boisen was not uncritical of the Holiness sects, but he did appreciate the positive elements in that movement. He also was keenly aware of one type of social crisis which rarely gives rise to spontaneous "religious quickening." It is the social crisis of war. Just as the attempt by the mentally ill individual to reorganize the inner world may fail, resulting in the drifting and delusional misinterpretation reaction patterns, so the group may react destructively to some kinds of social crisis, especially war.

War does produce effects which have religious value, wrote Boisen. It forces individuals and even nations out of old ways of thinking and acting. Also, it increases the sense of fellowship to the point where persons are willing to give their lives for the group. This approaches religion, and religion merges with patriotism. However, the increased fellowship does not carry over into a new religious movement because the characteristics of such fellowships are antithetical to religion.[26]

24. Ibid., 87.
25. Ibid., 87–89.
26. Ibid., 95–97.

The fellowship is restricted to the "in-group," to those who are on the same side in war. Simultaneously, the "out-group," the enemy, is hated. The "in-group" engages in faulty diagnosis and loss of perspective, blaming everything on the enemy rather than accounting for the "real evils, of the complex forces common to us all." Ethical standards are altered "through the ascendancy of the military way of life." There is the attempt to inflict the greatest possible damage on the enemy while maintaining the organization and strength of the in-group. Thus, free reign is given to "cruel and vengeful tendencies." For reasons such as these, "the social crisis which war represents increases the spirit of patriotism but does not give rise to vital religious movements."[27]

Boisen noted one major exception to this observation about war. The Hebrew-Christian religion developed in the midst of defeat in war. The Old Testament prophets struggled to answer questions about the misfortunes of their nation in war. One kind of answer was that the nation suffered because of its sins. This indicates self-blame rather than blaming the enemy. Such an answer sets the stage for religious development because when problems are addressed rather than avoided, there is a better chance of recovery both on a personal and a national scale. Another, deeper answer was that the Hebrew people were suffering for the "healing of the nations." This insight came to its climax in Jesus of Nazareth and was completed with Paul, wrote Boisen. The great achievement of this apostle was to "free the religion of Jesus from the ritualistic, racial fetters which would have kept it a small sect within the Hebrew religion."[28]

Religious Leadership

A social crisis may give rise to spontaneous "religious quickening," as seen in the Holiness sects during the Depression. This is not the whole story, however. According to Boisen, if the religious response to social crisis is to take the form of a social movement, the group experience must be "focalized" in some individual who voices the experience and becomes a religious leader.

The religious leader in question is the type which Weber called "charismatic." Boisen characterized such a person as one who has a religious, or mystical, experience that yields a sense of mission and who has the ability to attract a following. Such an experience, arising from a crisis, is favorable to the creative process which yields new insights. The social conditions under which the experience occurs is also important. An experience within the group context causes the

27. Ibid., 97–103.
28. Ibid., 103–6.

group to honor the person because the group may have helped to induce the experience and believes in it.[29]

In addition, the issue with which the future leader is grappling makes a difference in the resulting theology and in the type of movement that develops. If the problem is the need for personal salvation, then the theology most likely will be orthodox because religious ideas received from tradition now become meaningful. In this case the insight gained involves the conviction that the sources of spiritual power have been tapped anew. The message associated with the sense of mission is to others in crisis who can benefit from a similar solution. The development of certain Holiness groups in the 1930s is one example of the kind of movement which may develop around a leader whose crisis is personal. On the other hand, if the future religious leader is grappling with the "fate of one's people," as the Hebrew prophets did, then the new insight will involve the mission of those people and the meaning of their suffering.[30]

From Crisis to Custom

The charismatic religious leader gathers a following, and a religious movement is born. Normally, such a movement takes the form of a sect. Gradually, the sect develops into a church, which differs from a sect in that one can be born into it, and it is "not absolutist in its position but is ready to listen, to compromise, and to recognize other values."[31] Boisen provided a detailed example of this transition by tracing the development of the Methodist Church.

When a religious movement is in its original sect phase it exhibits a new vision and a missionary zeal. Boisen tended to call this phase of development the creative stage of religious movement. When the crisis passes and the organization develops, then assuming there is strong leadership, the next phase of development occurs. The sect becomes a church. The purpose of the church in terms of organized religion is to transform the "new vision and quickened purpose" which the church discovered in its creative stage into custom, or conventional practice, and habit. By this means the vision and purpose get transmitted from generation to generation.[32]

The Christian church is bound together through loyalty to that vision and purpose represented by the life and teachings of Jesus of Nazareth. There is commitment to that loyalty, and it is expressed

29. Ibid., 108, 110–12.
30. Ibid., 108–11, 113, 119.
31. ibid., 132, n. 15, 120–33.
32. Ibid., 38.

through regular assemblies for the purpose of worship and education, and sacrificial service. The transmission of vision and purpose into custom happens through the implantation of standards of conduct in communities. Boisen pointed to one of the chief means for accomplishing this when he observed that "the church is built upon the family unit." He contended that "it is chiefly through the family that its [the church's] ideals are made effective in human life."[33]

As generations pass, the children born into a church accept the vision and purpose transmitted to them, yet they allow the vision to fade to the point that the loyalty is maintained at the least possible cost. The result is that the distinctiveness and uniqueness which the church once had is lost, and it moves toward a "standardized pattern" in which it is hardly distinguishable from other churches.[34] Boisen suggested that when a church reaches this point it may be heading toward a terminal stage, which completes the life cycle of the church. It may unite with another church or continue to function, forming a "seedbed" for a new vision and new leadership at some future point.

The Church and Social Change

The church is closely related to society because it transmits its vision and purpose into custom. Its interaction with society may be conservative, inhibiting societal change, or creative, facilitating societal change. Boisen, with the aid of sociologists such as Weber, contrasted the Asiatic religions of India and China with the Hebrew-Christian religion. His purpose was to discover the main characteristics of religions which exhibit conservative tendencies and those which exhibit creative tendencies.[35]

The Asiatic religions, such as Buddhism and Hinduism, tend to be conservative regarding social change for several reasons, wrote Boisen. First, there is a magnification of the family. For example, "in China the authority of parents and ancestors has been supreme—even after they were dead. There has been no transcending it." The result has been an extreme traditionalism. Second, such religions have not practiced "religious assemblage" for the purpose of worship and education. The consequence is that there has been little opportunity "for the rethinking of religious beliefs in the light of changing conditions." Without such communal "rethinking," tradition and custom are given "full sway." Third, an additional factor is the conclusion of Weber that such religions have been associated with the special privilege of a

33. Ibid., 34–36.
34. Boisen, *Exploration of the Inner World*, 214.
35. Boisen, *Religion in Crisis and Custom*, 134–42.

dominant social class "and have served to keep the common people quiescent. . . ."[36]

According to Boisen, the Hebrew-Christian religion has been much more favorable to societal change. Unlike the Asiatic religions, Christianity has transcended the authority of the family. All finite loyalties are subordinated to the God "whose authority transcends that of the finite parents and of all earthly rulers."[37] Because of this emancipation from the traditional, Christianity fosters a more creative type of religious experience which can contribute to societal change.

In addition, Christianity provides the opportunity for rethinking beliefs in light of changing conditions through the "religious assemblage" of worship and education. According to Boisen, this has been an important factor enabling Christianity to adapt itself to "different social orders such as Roman imperialism, medieval feudalism, and modern industrial democracy." Finally, Boisen concluded that "religious assemblage" and emancipation from family domination in Christianity have facilitated resistance to "the encroachment of privileged classes and the dominance of tradition."

Narrowing his focus to the Christian tradition alone, Boisen concluded that when the church becomes involved in a struggle for power or for position, it enters a period of stagnation. In addition, the church may stagnate when it is dominated by a group which desires to "maintain its integrity against the onslaughts of a surrounding culture. . . ." When this happens, then conformity to custom and ritual becomes supremely important, and new insights and practices are "likely to be suppressed as evidences of disloyalty." On the other hand, creative manifestations of the church have been associated with social crisis. He cited the Protestant Reformation as one variant of this principle.[38]

Narrowing the focus still further, Boisen explored the conservative and creative manifestations of Protestantism in America. He set the stage for this through a sociological analysis of such things as the role of immigration in the development of religion in America. Next, he used a typological social-science method to identify the socially significant characteristics of the numerous Protestant churches in America. The characteristics, everything from interchurch relations to sources of religious authority, constituted categories for determining how the churches diverged from one another.[39]

Boisen's study of Protestantism in America focused less on social

36. Ibid., 134–36.
37. Ibid., 136.
38. Ibid., 136–39.
39. Ibid., 139–75.

change which the church could facilitate than on the religion which has evolved based on the principles of religious freedom. The structure of American society created a situation which maximized religious creativity, according to Boisen, as demonstrated by the diversity of Protestant churches. Though the diversity was emphasized, he also noted a core of characteristics common to all Protestant churches in America.

Boisen went on to assess what he determined to be the "central tenets" of American Protestantism, such as divine revelation. His evaluation was based on a set of criteria derived from his analysis of religious faith. Finally, he discussed religious practices, such as rituals, which churches use to perpetuate religious faith and by which the church is kept alive in an organized fashion.[40] Out of this grew a set of categories for assessing the "health" or "illness" of religious institutions.

Implications for Pastoral Care

The possibility of drawing implications for pastoral care from Boisen's writings on the church depends, in part, on affirming that there is value in his hypothesis about the relationship between social crisis and religion. Though there is much need for critical discussion in this regard, I will confine myself to one observation for the purposes of this article. Boisen argued for the use of scientific method in the study of religion. Though his scope may have stretched a little far in his church study, his serious attention to scientific method and his use of respected sociologists of religion resulted in scholarship which demands to be taken seriously.

Just as all scholarship is bound by time, so Boisen's work is confined by the psychiatric and sociological knowledge developed in the first half of this century. Therefore, a discussion in which implications for pastoral care are drawn must be suggestive. Contemporary theory in each of these fields may present new possibilities which Boisen could not have foreseen.

The main implication involves pastoral care at the level of the church and society. The church, the organized religion of the group or collective religion, cares for society in crisis. The most radical understanding of pastoral care in this context is that the *very emergence* of a religious movement in response to social crisis constitutes a form of caring for society. As a response to social crisis, the religious movement encourages the assumption of personal responsibility,

40. Ibid., 185–91, 212–45.

reflection on ultimate loyalties and values, and the attempt to get at and correct what Boisen called the real evils associated with societal complexities common to us all, rather than avoiding the real societal problems and blaming them on others.

This suggests that studying the emergence of religious movements in response to social crisis can provide clues for helping older churches of custom figure out how to care for society effectively in times of crisis. Boisen contended that if a church of custom did not have the resources to respond to social crises in new and creative ways that proved effective, it would tend to be replaced with a new church that could respond effectively. Sociology could be used by pastoral theologians for understanding both social crisis and the responses of churches that prove effective and ineffective.

Boisen provided an example, discussing what he believed would be the main social crisis facing the church in the latter half of this century.[41] The crisis evolves from problems associated with individualism and is carried to the level of the nuclear threat. He discussed these things under the rubric of "the world in the making" in the final chapter of his church study. Predicting that following World War II the world would undergo tremendous change, he spoke of a new world in the process of becoming and of a new social order being shaped. In accord with his study of the church and social change, he concluded that religious beliefs would be one causative factor helping to determine the character of society following World War II. Likewise, changing social and economic conditions would influence religious beliefs, as has been the case in the past.

The main characteristic of a changing world on which he focused was the "excessive individualism" fostered in the Western world in modern times. By individualism he meant the emphasis placed on the welfare of the individual with the accompanying assumption that "the free play of individual self-interest would bring about the welfare of all." One positive consequence of individualism, according to Boisen, has been the creation of a culture which stimulated creative capacities in "scientific discovery, in industrial development, and in commercial enterprise."

Individualism also resulted in some "great evils," he wrote. Using the image of the "law of the jungle," he argued that individualism fostered "cutthroat competition" which placed individual against individual, group against group, and nation against nation. Not enough emphasis was placed upon the "individual's responsibility for the common good." Following World War II, the "cutthroat competition" con-

41. Ibid., 251–60.

tinued, even among the victors, preventing recognition of the harmful side of individualism. The situation reached crisis proportions with the "ominous hydrogen bomb."[42]

Boisen observed that America began placing its trust in bigger bombs and more effective propaganda and that Russia and America became more hostile toward each other. He feared that the world would become an armed camp if this situation was not curtailed. His elaboration on this seems surprisingly contemporary if viewed from a global perspective: "There will be warring imperialisms, nations armed to the teeth, military chieftains in the saddle, the right of private judgment and free speech curtailed, private initiative reduced, and private ownership and management giving way to depersonalized corporations and cartels seeking to control the resources of the earth for their own profit." In this kind of situation, he argued, the role of religion becomes limited in favor of an "increased spirit of nationalism" and an "exalted" patriotism which encourages "unquestioning obedience to established authority."[43]

In contemporary terms the crisis of which Boisen spoke is captured under the rubric of the nuclear threat, in which every society lives with the possibility of annihilation. At the present time, this crisis may seem more like long-term stress than like a crisis. Either way there is a real sense of danger. Boisen attempted to connect the problem of "excessive individualism" and its resulting "cutthroat competition" with this crisis. This connection is helpful because it exemplifies the complex dynamics which result in the threat and keep it alive.

Also, the connection points to one difficulty which emerges with the notion that the church cares for society. On the one hand, the general concept of society is so large that it is necessary to narrow the focus to social crisis and, more specifically, to a particular kind of crisis. On the other hand, a particular social crisis, such as the nuclear threat, should not be oversimplified so that the complex forces which fuel it are overlooked. The difficulty is maintaining a balance between a manageable focus and allowing the complex forces associated with that focus to be seen. If they are not seen, then the church will be unable to care effectively.

Identifying a social crisis is only one half of the task. The other half is determining how the churches of custom can care effectively for societies living under the crisis. Unfortunately, Boisen did not speculate about possible strategies for addressing the nuclear threat or "ominous hydrogen bomb." In light of what he did write about the church, some initial, suggestive speculations are possible.

42. Ibid., 251–52.
43. Ibid., 252–53.

First, the churches of custom should reflect seriously on the type of church leadership needed in the situation of the nuclear threat. The image of leadership which emerges from Boisen's church study is that of the prophet. Some of the main characteristics of prophets, he wrote, are that they tap anew the sources of spiritual power and return anew to the central insights and motivations of religion. The example of the Hebrew prophets is especially illuminating since, as Boisen said, they grappled with the fate of their people, and their insight involved the mission and suffering of those people. The image of prophetic church leadership, with the characteristics just mentioned, will be related to the church's care of society in crisis in the next point.

Second, the churches of custom should use the process of transforming their central "vision and purpose" into custom, or conventional practice, for addressing the social crisis of the nuclear threat. This transformation, according to Boisen, happens through implanting standards of conduct in communities. Assume, for the sake of the example, that Boisen was correct in seeing "cutthroat competition" operating at the level of nation against nation in relation to the "ominous hydrogen bomb." In this case, churches logically should examine the customs which they are helping to create and the standards of conduct which they are implanting in communities. One goal of such examination would be to discover their role in contributing to "excessive individualism" and its negative effect of "cutthroat competition."

The next goal would be to implant new standards of conduct and create new customs designed to correct the "excessiveness" of individualism and to fight against "cutthroat competition." This is the point at which prophetic church leadership becomes important. Such leadership would have to articulate the content of the "vision and purpose" which gets transformed into custom. It becomes evident that this is a "grass roots" approach because it would be implemented at the congregational level as well as at larger levels of church organization.

There are three sense in which such a process constitutes caring for society. First, it encourages the church to engage in self-critique to determine how it may be contributing to the crisis. Second, it provides customs based on the "vision and purpose" of Christianity designed to counter forces associated with older customs which are contributing to the crisis. The example of "excessive individualism" has been used.

Third, the process provides an alternative to other, more negative, customs which may arise in response to the crisis. For example, Boisen says that in wartime the military provides standards of conduct which encourage those on one side to blame everything on the other side and to use violence against them. The military gains such power

because people are willing to obey an authority in exchange for protection. In a time of social crisis when entire nations are threatened,
then a militaristic atmosphere may develop, and such standards of
conduct are encouraged. How easy it is, for example, for some Americans to blame almost everything that is wrong with the world on
Russia while having difficulty engaging in self-scrutiny. It seems reasonable that the church would be caring for society when it facilitates
development of customs which encourage alternatives to blaming and
violence.

Using the example of the nuclear threat, I have attempted to show
that the Boisen church writings have implications for a discussion of
the church's pastoral care of society in crisis. There are three additional points which follow from this discussion, and I will mention
them briefly.

The first is about the way that the church implants standards of
conduct in communities. Boisen observed that Christian worship and
education have enabled Christianity to adapt itself to changing societal
conditions. Such regular assemblies have facilitated adaptation
because they provide the occasions in which Christians rethink their
beliefs in light of contemporary circumstances. Assuming that worship
and education are means for implanting standards of conduct which
generate customs, then it seems plausible that such assemblies can
contribute to the church's pastoral care of society in crisis. This is the
case insofar as they contribute to the creation of customs which have
a positive impact on the crisis and responses to the crisis.

The second point involves the earlier discussion of the church
engaging in self-critique in order to assess its role in the crisis. On
what basis does the church critique itself? The Boisen church study
suggests that criteria which form the basis of evaluation can be set
forth. Boisen proposed a set of criteria characterizing the church in
"institutional ill health" and in "institutional health."[44] The context of
the discussion was the perpetuation and recreation of religious faith.
He was concerned that problems within the institutional church could
inhibit the mission of the church in the world. When the church is
"ill," there is need for pastoral care of the church. Likewise, evaluation
of the church's institutional "illness" and "health" on the basis of developed criteria becomes the starting point for assessment of its role in
social crisis and of its ability to care for the society which suffers
because of the crisis.

The third and final point involves the potential impact that pastoral
care to society in crisis may have on individuals. In his study of the

44. Ibid., 230–44.

Holiness sects during the Depression, Boisen observed that the emergence of a religious movement enabled suffering persons who participated in that movement to cope positively with the social crisis. Some of those persons otherwise may have become mentally ill, and still others may have become violent. This suggests that pastoral care to society in crisis can affect the individual positively.

Furthermore, if, as Boisen argued, individuals are social in nature, then pastoral care of society in crisis could be seen as a form of preventive pastoral care where individuals are concerned. Caring at the larger levels of society and institutions should have a positive impact on persons, who internalize values of the group and who are loyal to the group. A good example of this may be found in the anxiety that many youth are experiencing because of the nuclear threat. The church caring for society in this crisis may have positive effects that will be seen only when the children of today become the adults of tomorrow.

Conclusion

I have attempted to present a picture of how Anton Boisen viewed the church as expressed in his writings. His view rests on the belief that there is a positive relationship between mental illness and religion. This belief, along with his use of the sociology of religion and the history of religions, results in a complex view of the church as it interacts with society.

I have argued that for pastoral care the main implication of Boisen's study is found in the realm of church and society in crisis. If the emergence of a religious movement constitutes a form of pastoral care to those who are suffering because of social crisis, then churches of custom can learn from such movements and from the crises to which they respond. They can learn how to care more effectively for a society in turmoil.

In this day when pastoral theologians must address such things as cultural pluralism and the nuclear threat in relation to the Christian tradition, it is helpful to look back to Anton Boisen for inspiration and guidance. In his preface to *Religion in Crisis and Custom*, Seward Hiltner wrote that ". . . the years but show how we are beginning to catch up to the depth of Boisen's original thought."[45] This statement holds true for us today because Boisen's understanding of the church has much to teach us about a society that is beset by crisis.

45. Ibid., xii.

13

Boisen as Autobiographer

> JAMES E. DITTES

N ear his eighth birthday, in the same year his father died, Anton T. Boisen lost the sight of one eye to another boy's toy gun, which he determined to face with unblinking stubbornness. Having just heard his grandfather describe the winking reflex as a "protective function," Boisen, characteristically, decided to face his attacker without this protection. "Half curiously, half defiantly, I resolved not to wink." The gun scored a direct hit on the pupil with an iron nail. "The eyelid was not touched," Boisen boasts, and he ends his account of the loss—never to be mentioned again in his autobiography—with a shrug: "I have not been aware of the difference."[1] But monocular vision does make a difference: it deprives the person of the principal capacity for depth perception. The author's not noticing the difference illustrates the point.

The unblinking facing of adversity, depth perception missing and unmissed—these are the paradoxically paired characteristics of *Out of the Depths,* that book in a lifetime of largely autobiographical writing which Boisen chose to subtitle "an autobiographical study. . . ."

"This is my own case record," the author announces in the opening

---

1. Anton T. Boisen, *Out of the Depths: An Autobiographical Study of Mental Disorder and Religious Experience* (New York: Harper, 1960), 31–32.

sentence, and indeed it is, no less and no more, "a simply, factual account,"[2] a thorough case record but only a case record. Boisen is unflinching in sharing with us the raw data of his distress (as in repeated disappointment and failure in work and in love and in relations with colleagues), of his obsessions (as in his lifelong infatuation with Alice Batchelder and his persistent struggle to control sexual imagery), of his psychoses (in episodes stretching between ages thirty and sixty). Unblinking, he labels himself at times, probably accurately, as "insane," a "failure," "weak." A case record it is, and a case record it remains, raw data reported honestly, left essentially uninterpreted in any recognizable depth, either psychologically or theologically, except in terms of the most general, abstract, and programmatic affirmations, not developed, that meaning and healing reside in the distress and the illness. "These five psychotic episodes . . . have left me not worse but better." "Our evil has been overcome for good."[3] This is about as deep or as explicit as the interpretation gets.

Boisen's most common, most satisfying, and most effective form of work was apparently what he called surveys, counting and classifying methods he learned at Yale Forest School. He conducted dozens of such surveys, resorting to them especially when the going got rough, as when his first ministry floundered or as therapy out of his psychosis.[4] He compiled naturalistic observations, inventories of recreation equipment, demographic counts by the score, topographic maps, charts of psychiatric symptoms and classifications of diagnoses, census counts of psychiatric illness and of Pentecostals, collections of case records, and more. His autobiography is one more careful compilation, unblinking but lacking depth perception.

The central theme of the book, the lifelong infatuation—obsession, really—with Alice Batchelder, cries out for probing analysis, surely as much in 1960 as in 1988, to anyone engaged in "exploration of the inner world"—an enterprise Boisen claimed for himself in those words as early as 1927, a decade before a book by that title. "It was a one-sided affair, a love that swept me off my feet,"[5] a passion heavily and obviously determined by Boisen's inner world, projected onto a figure he never had an opportunity to know well and who steadily discouraged his affection. He fell in love with her at first sight (while she was giving a public lecture) and pursued a relationship which was characterized by distance, geographical and emotional, and by periods of

2. Ibid., 198.
3. Ibid., 202, 209.
4. Ibid., 67, 122.
5. Ibid., 52.

up to several years without even any correspondence. The final distance was the death of the real Alice a quarter century before this book, a death barely noted—without a syllable of grief expressed. Yet the infatuation in Boisen lived on and remains central in his autobiography. As unblinking as the eight-year-old boy facing the toy nailgun, the eighty-five-year-old devotee insists on taking the love affair at face value, as experienced, unprobed. He fantasizes, even in his closing pages, that but for one momentary tactical blunder on his part, fifty years earlier, "Alice and I might have been married, and with her help I might have become a passably successful minister."[6]

He comes to the brink of the depth frequently, but backs away, unseeing. For example, after writing a letter to Alice, "I took the Bible again, and after a prayer I once more opened it at random. The verse I read was John 19:27: 'Then said he to the disciple, "Behold thy mother"!' " The very next sentence has all the naive candor of one unblinkingly honest about what he sees, because he is unburdened by seeing it in any depth: "I was deeply moved, for regardless of its origin, this 'message' pointed to what I was really seeking in Alice."[7] But the probing that his own words would seem to thrust on the story is denied as he moves on, apparently heedless of any psychological connection between Alice and the mother on whom he remained abundantly dependent, at least into his late forties, for emotional support, for sanction of career changes, for housing, and for financial support. So, too, with the fact, flatly recorded (in a letter to Alice, in fact) that some wildflowers he had picked for her found their way "to Mother instead—who will get them fresh in the morning."[8] Boisen tells us, but does not seem to notice, that his second hospitalization for schizophrenia followed closely his mother's death, even as his final hospitalization accompanied Alice's death. He does not seem to consider any pattern in these circumstances. He just reports them faithfully, his case record.

The writing of a religious (or any other) autobiography is an act at once public and private, but some are clearly more one than the other. Perhaps most autobiographies are written for others, to instruct them in what one has learned, or wants to have learned, perhaps to offer oneself as a model, or perhaps as an advance scout. Gandhi wrote his life story as daily serialized newspaper lessons on moral integrity. Malcolm X told his story as a political morality play. Jung used his autobiography as an excellent introduction to his psychological theo-

6. Ibid., 209.
7. Ibid., 55.
8. Ibid., 146.

ries. Augustine shaped his life account to become one of his powerful theological tracts. But such autobiography requires an interpretive theme; it requires a sense of crisis surmounted, a dramatic triumph that can lead others out of their crises; it requires a sense of identification or connection with the experience of others, some sense of writing about their experiences as well as one's own. These are not the characteristics of Boisen's book, and this is not the kind of autobiography he has written.

Alternatively, autobiography may be a more personal act, a form of therapy to get one's life arrayed, objectified. Teresa of Avila was commanded by her confessor to write, just for such therapy, and she found explosive catharsis in the telling, and probably also in what she found it possible to leave unsaid, and thereby to leave behind. Boisen's story feels more like that. It is not the therapy of interpretation, the discovery of patterns that give meaning, for that is not what this story does. It is the simple powerful therapy of unflinching telling, perhaps also with the hope of being heard. It is the therapy Boisen discovered, for example, on Easter morning of his twenty-second year. "It was a beautiful day, but there was no sunshine there for me, and no beauty—nothing but black despair. I came back to my room and threw myself on my knees with an agonized call for help. And help came! Something seemed to say to me almost in words, 'Don't be afraid to tell.' With this it seemed as though a great burden had been taken away. I felt very happy. That day I had a talk with Mother. What I said and what she said I do not remember. She understood. That was enough."[9] That is the kind of telling this book does. It is a mapping of the terrain, like the literal "rough topographical map of the grounds" or the inventory taking which Boisen found so therapeutic toward the end of the first hospital stay.[10] It is the therapy of telling which Boisen formulated when he wrote, "Sex education is not a matter of instruction, but of psychotherapy. It is dependent not so much upon what the teacher says to the boy as upon what the boy is able to say to the teacher."[11]

Out of the Depths compels comparison with Carl Gustav Jung's *Memories, Dreams, Reflections.* Born within a year of each other, both men were reflecting, in books published within a year of each other, on eight-and-a-half decades of turbulent inner history. Both find their lives shaped and energized, and also their telling of it focused, by a tumultuous psychological storm in midlife—Jung's more or less deliberate explorations of the unconscious, coming just before World

9. Ibid., 47.
10. Ibid., 126, 122.
11. Ibid., 200.

War I; Boisen's severe psychotic break coming just after. Intriguing parallels jump from the pages, perhaps accidental, perhaps meaningful. For example: Both were impressed by and bore the names of their grandfathers (for Boisen, Theophilus; for Jung, Carl Gustav), who were giants in their respective academic worlds. Both describe their fathers largely as failed men. Both feared the stigma of top grades in school.[12]

But such external similarities only sharpen the fundamental difference. Jung welcomes and trusts the unconscious imagination; Boisen fears it. Jung celebrates mystery; Boisen strives for control. Jung has transcended his psychic turbulence by immersing himself fully into it; Boisen is a man still sadly trapped in his pathology because he has stayed alien to it.

Both Jung and Boisen record excruciating struggles, early in their lives, with overwhelmingly intense unwanted imagery surging from within. Early in adolescence Jung wrestled for days to suppress the terrifying image of God defecating on the cathedral, a vision frightening because of its threat to undermine the conventialities by which this Swiss son of the manse had been taught to live. For years, Boisen strained in "a hard fight to keep wayward erotic ideation under control." For example, as he turned pages of a dictionary "obscene words would leap out of its pages and hit me in the eye." So urgent was the impulse driving against the stern suppression Boisen imposed on it that he found himself afflicted with an experience of "emission without erection. It occurred three times in rapid succession . . . it left me with a horrible sense of failure and guilt . . . it was the collapse of faith, which left me at the mercy of ideas of despair and self-pity."[13]

Both Jung and Boisen struggled against the threatening ideation, but the outcomes were as different as night and day. Jung dared to let the imagery become conscious, to let it "out of the depths," to integrate it, even to befriend it, and by so yielding to it, to rob it of its peril, its capacity for pathological mischief. Boisen was single-minded and apparently successful in his determination to quell these surges from "out of the depths." Unblinking, he would stubbornly face down the threat of external objects like a toy gun spitting nails, but when obscene words hit him in the eye, he turned away. Denied access to consciousness, Jung would have said, these insistent energies prevailed in their disruptive mischief-making, unconscious and therefore unintegrated and at odds with conscious life, pathological. Boisen

---

12. Ibid., 32; Carl Gustav Jung, *Memories, Dreams, Reflections* (New York: Random House, 1961), 43.

13. Boisen, *Out of the Depths*, 53, 46–47, 57; see also 63, 72, 74.

engaged in a battle for control and lost; the energies and images had their way with him.

Control was Boisen's prevailing strategy of life, and it had its limited success. His own brief evaluation of his "basic conflict" ("sexual hypersensitivity") is unremitting in the commitment of "self-discipline" at all costs.[14] He administered to himself a kind of management therapy, pulling himself out of illness and stress by planning schedules, mapping terrain, devising agendas. As noted, his most effective work professionally was in his precise descriptive surveys. His programmatic efforts in developing chaplaincy staff and opportunities for students were an effective extension of this "agenda-therapy," which, however, repeatedly ran into problems when his followers wanted to use these opportunities to explore psychological depths Boisen was unready to pursue. So, indeed, is the autobiography itself, a descriptive marvel, charting, one after another, each event—once over all lightly— but without shading or nuance or interpretation or thematic connection. *Out of the Depths* maps, very candidly, the surface of the experience.

The phrase *out of the depths* has many possible meanings as the title of an autobiography. The author does not tell us how many of them he had in mind or what was uppermost for him. Perhaps the unstated epigraph is Psalm 130, De Profundis: "Out of the depths have I called to thee, O LORD; Lord, hear my cry. . . ." Boisen is calling poignantly and fearlessly out of the depth of his own despair, frustration, and the confusion of his mental and emotional distress. To utter this cry, unblinking, in documented fullness, like the maps and surveys he loved to make of forests and church memberships, he charts the topography of his own pathology in up-close intimacy. This is the accomplishment of this autobiography and of the man. It was his dream that clergy and seminary students could come to learn how to listen to others who are ill as they call out of their depths. It was his unintended legacy that the clergy and students themselves learn to cry out of their own depths.

De profundis but not ex profundis. "Out of the depths" could mean to claim a movement, a progression, out of the depths of pathology into health. This is how the writer of the jacket copy for the first edition tended to interpret the book, the same writer who called the book a "case history"—a subtle but misleading revision of Boisen's own more accurate sense that this is a "case record." "History" implies movement, but it also implies a pattern of interpretation in the writing. To be sure, Boisen did find himself in effective and productive work, if

14. Ibid., 199.

not in satisfying relationships. But the point of view from which he writes never transcends his afflictions; the story is not understood other than in terms of the fear and fantasies which are part of his pathology. He does not speak from a standpoint out of the depths. He cries from out of the depths.

There are two kinds of "depths," experiential depths and interpretive depths, the depths of emotional distress and the depths of unconscious imagery and motivation. The psalmist and Boisen refer to depths in the first sense. "Depth psychology" (whether Freudian, Jungian, or other) refers to the second sense, and this is a depth with which Boisen was not familiar and which his autobiography does not explore. Boisen stays "out of the depths" in this sense, and the title is thus, certainly unintentionally, accurate. Boisen was not a man equipped with depth perception, but out of the depths he does cry with steady, unblinking gaze. A sturdy case record is enough to report the gaze—and the pain.

14

Hiltner's Contributions to Pastoral Care and Counseling

LISTON O. MILLS

I was a graduate student when I first met Seward Hiltner. He came to Louisville, to Southern Seminary, shortly after *Preface to Pastoral Theology* was published. He awed me then, and, though over the years we have become friends, there is a sense in which he still does.

This experience of awe will, I think, accompany any effort to comment on his contributions to pastoral care and counseling. Perhaps more than any single individual, his name has come to be identified with our common work. He has taught, written, consulted, interpreted, defined, and served as missionary over almost half a century. He called us to attention before the dilemmas and problems of all sorts and conditions of persons, including ourselves, and he led us as we sought a way to help.

I make no attempt here to say it all. It does seem, however, that four or five of his contributions to pastoral care and counseling may be singled out, and I shall do that, recognizing all the while that others might point to different ones. In the first instance, Seward has contributed and still does so by showing us the meaning of commitment and passion. His work in pastoral care does not hang in mid-air; it is connected to his person and to his sense of vocation as minister. He once described pastoral care as a "subject both broad and basic in the life of the church" and his task "to prepare men (and women) more adequately for the exacting ministry of Jesus Christ." Somewhat later he said:

> The focus of my concern remains where it has always been, with the people problem, and most especially with the problems of troubled people. Any expertness I have continues to come from my use of a theological perspective along with psychodynamic insights about people, how they got into their predicament and what we, especially we of church and ordained ministry, may do to help them.

Seward has never been accused of lukewarmness. But it is important to recall that his passion stems from his self-understanding as a minister of and in the church, called to understand and to serve its people. His point of entry and interest in pastoral care is reflected in these commitments.

This zeal in the tasks of ministry helps to account for a second contribution. His wish to serve fostered within him an initial disenchantment with the way pastoral care had been understood and provided. Later it fostered a readiness to acknowledge and to try a novel approach. Pastoral care was understood as kindness and concern; it was taught by anecdote or exhortation or by the hints and advice older ministers might offer the young. Hiltner at one point, while commending the faithfulness and concern which characterized much pastoral care, described it as disjointed and not systematic, as hortatory and not interpretative, as practical and not theoretical.

Whether fortuitous or providential, I will not say, but this disenchantment spurred a quest which led to Anton Boisen. Hiltner wanted to understand and to help. Boisen emerged from the "wilderness of the lost" with a tool that in the hands of Hiltner and others became the basis for both: the clinical case. Boisen focused on the person in trouble and utilized the case history to understand which forces and factors led to his/her plight and which were at work for healing. For us for whom the "living human document" has become a cliche to fully appreciate the significance of this approach, we must recall that it caused thinking about pastoral care to be reset.

Although many saw the significance of Boisen's efforts, it was Hiltner who, with the help of Russell Dicks' verbatim interview, attempted to refine the clinical approach and make it the gateway to a pastoral theology. It offered a starting point to discern clues to personal distress and potential avenues for help and made possible the utilization of psychodynamic insight. It provided a means to evaluate pastoral effectiveness and make a move toward pastoral competence. It was an opportunity to study theology and to generate the construction of theory in pastoral care. That it has become the cornerstone of the new pastoral care is in large measure because of Hiltner's attempts to articulate its importance and to refine it.

Another contribution seems to me to grow out of the commitment I mentioned earlier. In the midst of what must have been exhilarating times, he did not lose his moorings and insisted that definition must be a primary task in pastoral care. With the attraction of a new model, the temptation was strong, and succumbed to by many, to lay aside theology, to see the chasm between the old and the new as too wide to be bridged, to fall in with the times and grasp the revelations of human psychological complexity as negating ministry. But instead of stressing discontinuities with the past and tradition, Hiltner sought to reclaim biblical and historical images of ministry and to redefine pastoral care.

We have all benefited from his subsequent attempts to clean up a venerable image of pastoral care, that of the shepherd. Thus, by locating us squarely within the tradition, Hiltner insured continuity with the church and its history of ministry and that the wisdom of that tradition would not be lost. His redefinition has proven equally valuable. By defining shepherding as perspective he has made pastoral care potential in all ministry. By characterizing shepherding as tender and solicitous concern, he describes the motives necessary for any pastoral care act. And by specifying the acts themselves as those of healing, sustaining, and guiding he has provided boundaries for our tasks.

The image of shepherding as Hiltner has described it is both clinical and theological. It deals primarily with the motivation and attitude of the pastor, but it does not denigrate skills. At one and the same time it makes possible the utilization of psychological data in comprehending the needs of the sheep and the person of the pastor and yet insists that this understanding be theologically oriented as well. Thus pastoral care is no longer ringing door bells; it has intent and focus.

What has been said up to now made possible another contribution, that is, the move from pastoral psychology to pastoral theology and the emergence of a discipline. Attentiveness to cases and clear pastoral identity fostered images of technical competence and applied psychology. Seward called our attention to the necessity of placing the new findings of pastoral care under the theological criticism, seeing them in a theological context and insisting that they be permitted to contribute to theological understanding. He has not been content for our practice merely to profit from theological understanding. Instead he insists on a serious search for the theological dimensions of our healing, sustaining, and guiding. He insists that listening, accepting, and engaging in dialogue are themselves theological in character. He reminds us that the pastor's motivation, the church context in which care takes place, and the evaluation of the persons to be served are not simply psychological tasks; they are crucial to theologizing. In the process he calls us away from theological questions tacked on the end of case conferences about the use of "religious resources." He invites us to take part in the formation of a genuinely pastoral theology.

In this regard Seward was always careful to guard against excesses. When the field was heady and new, full of elan and romance, it was he who warned of the dangers of imperialism and faddishness. At the same time that he sought to elevate practice to an honorable place, he reminded us that it was possible to be so practical as to be meaningless. While insisting that we be both psychologically and theologically alert, he cautioned against the erection of either as an ideological barrier which would interfere with openness to cases and empirical/ clinical data. Always, he argued, pastoral care must be in tension: it is practical and theoretical, scientific and existential, psychological and theological, religious and secular, for clergy and for laypersons. To lose these tensions is to forsake and to distort the endeavor. Competence is to be prized and specialists are bound to emerge. But though skill in helping people is desirable, in itself it cannot maintain integrity in pastoral care. Pastoral care emerges from a concerned community which is explicit that its motive for such concern is the lordship of Christ.

I have spoken up to now primarily of Hiltner's formal contributions to pastoral care. Recognizing again that I cannot say it all, there is an incompleteness about these comments unless I go full circle, return to commitment, and suggest what to me is the vocational heart of his work. Seward was a minister. His writing, editing, consulting, and teaching all sought to enhance the work of ministry by insisting on the high place pastoral care should occupy in pastoral work. He sought to improve ministerial competence and to broaden their understanding. He introduced them to ideas, books, persons, and points of view. He attempted to enlarge their grasp of human distress and engender hope for human possibility. He was aware of their unique problems and served as their pastor. He insisted that they not be loners but work with other professionals; at the same time he served as spokesman and apologists to these same professionals. His was an independent voice, sometimes encouraging and sometimes criticizing, sometimes persuading and sometimes arguing, but always his goal was a more effective ministry that would claim and be proud of its heritage.

To speak of pastoral care is to speak personally. And personally I have had two concrete experiences of Seward's contributions to our field. The first is the aid he gave me as editor of *Pastoral Psychology*. The second occured to me when I recalled the close association I have had with ten of his Ph.D. graduates. In them I have seen the fruit of a rare gift that he often displayed, a capacity to affirm others and their strengths. Without sentimentality, he helped these men and women lay hold of their talents and deepened their confidence. He encouraged them to write and assured them that mortal books as well as great ones are needed. He made them aware of what he once described as the "discrepancy phenomenon"—the gulf between what is and what ought to be—and invited them to narrow the gap. In my judgment they have not failed him.

In reviewing editorials in *Pastoral Psychology* I found several he wrote on gratitude. We are asking him to accept ours. He has taught us that we should be trained practitioners, that we should attend to method and definition and theology, but also he has not let us lose sight of the fact that the calling is higher and the goal more distant than a simple technical competence and theological insight. This, in itself, is an act of care and a contribution that places us in his debt.

Conclusion
A New Theological Method

J. HAROLD ELLENS

When Seward Hiltner met Anton T. Boisen at the University of Chicago's Divinity School in 1932, Boisen was already seen as the father of clinical pastoral education. The encounter between the two ignited a flame that still burns broadly in the area of pastoral care and counseling. The light it has generated during the last half century made Hiltner the dean of pastoral theology,[1] though in a larger sense the work of these two giants is intricately and permanently intertwined.

The chapters of this book form a prism that helps us to see the variegated colors of thought and feeling that constitute the theological and pastoral tradition created by Boisen and Hiltner. That tradition is unique and crucial in the history of the church, because it is the only one that insists adequately upon two things: first, that human life and Christian ministry must be shaped by theological reflection, and second, that theology must be fashioned out of the concreteness of human experience and not out of the imagination of human speculation. Together both items imply that pastoral theology is primal in the encyclopedia of theological knowledge and that biblical and sys-

---

1. Kendig Brubaker Cully, "An Interview with Seward Hiltner: Dean of Pastoral Theologians," *The Review of Books and Religion* 10, no. 6 (Mid-March 1982): 5.

tematic theology are subsidiary to it in the sense that they must be rooted in the operational realities of sin and salvation and must answer to the authority claims of the "living human document."

The Boisen/Hiltner legacy provides an authentic foundation and model for the deconstruction and reconstruction of both theology and ministry. It illumines life from an empirical viewpoint and can serve as a touchstone for theological development into the twenty-first century. Its rich variegation and generative creativity provide an infinite number of nuances, modifications, and directions of development in terms of theological inquiry. For Hiltner, critical reflection on actual human experience is central to this new method. He reminds us that it was also a primary concern for Boisen:

> Boisen's purpose was only incidentally to offer education in pastoral care. He was primarily concerned to help the students learn theology itself by deepening their insights into what he called "the problem of sin and salvation" through the study of "living human documents" as well as through books and journals and sermons and reflective thought. He declared that he was not attempting to introduce a new theology in terms of content, but only a new method of theological study.[2]

In Boisen's case, the method emerged directly from personal experience.

> Both in the experience of his own mental illness, and then in his work with other mental patients, [Boisen] believed that he was seeing human life at a deep level where, especially in patients who were still visibly disturbed . . . a titanic battle was raging that would determine the entire future of the person. The battle might be lost, and then the patient would slide back into a life of withdrawal or blame or dependency or irresponsibility. But it might be won, and the person emerge with higher values, more deeply rooted convictions, and greater dedication than he had before. The latter outcome had, after all, been Boisen's own experience. He and his students, he argued, were not studying psychiatry and psychology as such, although he always acknowledged the help he had received from psychiatrists and psychologists. They were studying theology. . . .[3]

Rodney J. Hunter, in his chapter on "A Perspectival Pastoral Theology," crystallizes the point by saying that the Boisen/Hiltner perspective "challenges theology to consider the possibility that something

2. Seward Hiltner, "Fifty Years of CPE," *The Journal of Pastoral Care* 29 (1975): 90.
3. Ibid., 91.

of truly theological (and not merely psychological) significance can be learned by studying carefully the experience of ordinary people caught up in various forms of suffering, confusion, sinfulness, and despair." This approach is an exciting revolution in the history of Christian thought. It asks us to consider theology in terms of what we know from life's pilgrimage even as it directs us to reflect on life's pilgrimage as a theological odyssey. As a method, it seems congruent with the essential and existential claims of the incarnation.

Turning Points

Boisen and Hiltner are important turning points in the history of theological method. They became theological fulcrums, because they lived with unimaginable pain and insisted on facing it from a perspective of rigorous faith and keen theological analysis. They wanted to know the meaning of suffering in the light of God's providential care. They came to see that suffering is a potential resource for healing and redemption.

I am enthusiastic about their approach, because it rings true to, and illumines, my own personal pilgrimage.[4] I have ministered to people for thirty-five years, have taught two years for Seward Hiltner at Princeton Theological Seminary, and have provided psychotherapy for thousands of people during eighteen years of clinical work. I am convinced that every human being experiences suffering as a normal part of life's unfolding. No one gets away clean. The noteworthy fact is that some pain destroys while other pain heals and leads to dramatic surges of growth. The difference seems to be love. When we perceive that we are loved and cherished by God and others, our pain becomes an occasion for growth, but when we feel isolated and unloved pain seems to destroy and embitter us. The difference is no accident but a theological fact. Boisen and Hiltner perceived this truth, and the endeavor to understand it became a focal concern of their work.

The Boisen/Hiltner legacy gave me the eyes to see that our theological understanding and credal confessions must come out of our life experience and, in turn, they must address, and be an answer to, that experience. The significance of life is not exhausted until it is seen and experienced through the lens of genuine theological reflection. In that reflection, we see that God does not afflict us with pain or benignly permit it to come upon us. Instead he makes it his gracious business in history to enter into our pain and to employ it for our growth.

4. See J. Harold Ellens, *Psychotheology: Key Issues* (Pretoria: University of South Africa, 1987).

Boisen and Hiltner help us to see that life is a pilgrimage of responsibility in which we have the perpetual privilege of keeping an eye open to see how and where God is at work in our experience. Boisen discovered it in a surprising place. For him, mental illness, and not therapy, was God's resource to heal and to bring to spiritual maturation. To perceive suffering, even radical suffering, in this light is to turn an otherwise destructive experience into a redemptive and meaningful event.

An Evangelical Appraisal

There is much in what we have lifted out of the Boisen/Hiltner legacy that the evangelical faith can affirm. There are other points that it would want to add, some of which are implicit in the legacy itself.

Out of the Boisen/Hiltner legacy we have emphasized the role of critical reflection on human experience as a method of theological inquiry. The legacy itself sees that that is only part of the truth. It maintains that the gospel is given to us, primarily in and through the life and death of Christ, before we derive it from human experience or come to it by our own reason or strength. Both Boisen and Hiltner assume that God's truth must be revealed to us, but Hiltner is more explicit about it. He makes a distinction between the gospel and our understanding of it. On the one hand, he says that "the Christian revelation is unique, and it is the fact or event of Jesus Christ that makes it so. . . . Absolutely nothing can be regarded as of the same order as God's revelation of himself in Jesus Christ." On the other hand, he asserts with equal conviction that our understanding of the gospel is never complete, that in fact we must explore "the precise relevance of this revelation to every dimension of our own day and time."[5] He believes that the human sciences can help us in this understanding or, as he puts it in *Preface to Pastoral Theology*, "material of tremendous potential significance for the questions of theology is now available in the personality sciences."[6]

Hiltner's understanding of pastoral theology is a good illustration of his dialogic concern with both revealed truth and human knowledge. He defines pastoral theology as the branch of theological inquiry that brings the perspective of care to all the operations and functions of the church and that draws conclusions of a theological order from

---

5. Seward Hiltner, *The Christian Shepherd* (Nashville: Abingdon, 1959), 12–13. See also Anton T. Boisen, *The Exploration of the Inner World: A Study of Mental Disorder and Religious Experience* (New York: Harper, 1936), 191–92.

6. Seward Hiltner, *Preface to Pastoral Theology* (Nashville: Abingdon, 1958), 22.

reflection on these observations.[7] What is implicit and basic in this definition is that pastoral theology presupposes theology, that is, a revealed word about God. Questions of a theological nature that are brought to concrete acts of care come out of the gospel and lead back to it. Or, as Hiltner says, "pastoral theology . . . begins with theological questions and concludes with theological answers."[8]

Hiltner's final concern is not with revelation or psychological knowledge as isolated entities but with the potentially fruitful dialogue between them. The purpose of his *Theological Dynamics*, for example, is "to delineate the ways in which theology, understood dynamically, illuminates psychology, and is in turn enriched by dynamic psychology."[9] Where he achieves his purpose, he shows that the psychological sciences contribute richness to theological affirmations even as theological affirmations contribute an ultimate context to psychological findings. This is a limited but basic contribution, one that we can affirm and celebrate. It is an occasion of mutual enrichment where God's revelation in Christ is preserved as a unique event at the same time that our understanding of that event is given new and more concrete depth.

Other considerations follow from Hiltner's and Boisen's concern with revelation and human experience. An important one from an evangelical viewpoint is the recognition that theological analysis does not exhaust saving faith. To Boisen's and Hiltner's emphasis on critical reflection we must add the individual's own personal response in order to get a faith that heals. Neither Boisen nor Hiltner focuses on this issue in any extended way, but the issue is implicit in their positions, especially in Boisen's.

Boisen maintained that our basic problem is a feeling of guilt, a sense of personal failure that cuts us off from those who are most significant to us, from the "fellowship of the best." Our response to this problem is crucial. Boisen identified three major ways in which we can react to our situation, three different reactions patterns. First, we can deal with the situation by drifting, by making no attempt to face the difficulty but instead by following the line of least resistance, even to the point of withdrawing into a world of fantasy. Second, we can deceive ourselves, concealing the truth from ourselves through various means "in order to preserve [our] self-esteem and escape the sense of personal failure."[10] Finally, we can experience panic or anxi-

7. Paraphrased from ibid., 20.
8. Ibid., 24.
9. Seward Hiltner, *Theological Dynamics* (Nashville: Abingdon, 1972), 14.
10. Boisen, *Exploration of the Inner World*, 201.

ety, feeling the force of our dilemma and attempting to face it with some degree of honesty and responsibility. The three reactions often intermingle, but it is the last one that is central to both Boisen and our concern.

Against psychotherapists who tried to resolve a person's sense of guilt and inner disharmony by lowering the conscience threshold, Boisen maintained that the voice of conscience should be taken seriously, that in fact the conviction of sin is "the first step in the process of salvation."[11] This is true even if the sense of guilt takes clamorous and bizarre forms such as a preoccupation with death and world catastrophe. Boisen saw that the preoccupation was an externalization of an internal dissolution of the self. As he put it, "the idea of death and rebirth which recur so frequently in acute disturbances are by no means accidental. They represent the exact meaning of the experience."[12]

The individual has incurred "death and dissolution" because he or she has been disloyal to accepted group values and needs to be realigned with, and unified by, values considered to be more universal and abiding. Boisen knew that such drastic upheavals can end in permanent disintegration, but he also knew what others had overlooked— that the upheavals can be problem-solving experiences of a religious nature. The dividing line between destructive and reconstructive outcomes is the individual's reaction to his or her situation. People who feel the pangs of a stricken conscience and who deal with the sense of social isolation are the people who experience reorganization and greater unification, even to the point of centering their lives on "that which is supreme in [their] hierarchy of loyalties."[13]

Boisen seldom uses the term *repentance* for this process of transformation, and in fact he may intentionally avoid the term, but he makes a significant contribution to our understanding of it. First, he gives new credibility to religious concerns. Against the tendency to think of heightened religious interest as an escape from reality, Boisen shows that it is precisely the opposite, that it is a serious attempt to face trouble and to reorganize one's life around ultimate values. Religious concern, then, becomes an instrument of healing, and not a flight from the world. Second, Boisen directs us back to the Christian approach to healing even as he investigates its psychological dynamics. He makes conviction and confession of sin central to the whole

11. Anton T. Boisen, "The Therapeutic Significance of Anxiety," *The Journal of Pastoral Care* 5, no. 2 (Summer 1951): 2.
12. Boisen, *Exploration of the Inner World,* 204.
13. Ibid.

process of renewal. This shift focuses attention on "the sense of isolation and estrangement" as the real evil in mental disorder, so that "what is needed is forgiveness and restoration to the fellowship of that social something which we call God."[14] Third, Boisen reminds us that repentance is not necessarily a conscious, or even an intentional, act, one in which we say a quick "I'm sorry." Instead it is a wholistic response that is analogous to the healing thrust of fever in the body, and it can take the form of an acute disturbance that shakes us to our bootstraps. A simple "I'm sorry" turns into a supplicatory "O God be merciful!" Boisen usually elaborates this process in psychological terms, describing it as panic or anxiety, but theologically he is talking about a process that corresponds to repentance in a biblical sense. It refers to a realignment and renewal of the total person. We would make more explicit reference to Christ as the source and the object of that renewal, but Boisen's reminder that turning to God is not a self-generated work is a good correction to our legalistic demands.

Hiltner undergirded the evangelical perspective on pastoral care and counseling by his careful resistance to the psychological reductionism of pastoral theology. While he wished to glean the beneficial insights of scientific psychology, he insisted upon the supreme necessity of understanding the pastoral arts and sciences in terms of theological inquiry and pastoral models of applied ministry. Comparably, Boisen resisted the formulation of pastoral theology or the designing of pastoral work merely in terms of classical psychoanalytic models. He pressed for serious reflection on the actual spiritual formation of persons. Both men emphasized the importance of taking seriously the message of Scripture and the actual data of personal spiritual experience as a basis for our understanding of how pastoral theology and pastoral care and counseling should be shaped. In the process, they contributed significantly to how we should organize and carry out a ministry that cares for the spiritual and emotional life of God's people.

Boisen's and Hiltner's legacy helps to illumine our pilgrimage through ambiguity, brokenness, and grace. It offers a theological world view that is built out of the fire and feelings of real people trying to live before the God who has revealed himself to us. With a special sense of the divine providence of life and with a deep sense of gratitude to God for such giants of the church as Boisen and Hiltner, I join LeRoy Aden and our co-authors in offering this volume to the church and to our needy world. I believe that this volume is a work of great service and of permanent significance. Even more important, I believe that its practical theological usefulness honors the vision and memory

14. Ibid., 268.

of Anton T. Boisen and Seward Hiltner. If the church neglects or for-
gets these crucial turning points in its history, it will do so at great
peril to theological inquiry and pastoral ministry.

Bibliography

Aden, LeRoy. "Faith and the Developmental Cycle." *Pastoral Psychology* 24 (Spring 1976): 215–30.

Aden, LeRoy, and David G. Benner, eds. *Counseling and the Human Predicament: A Study of Sin, Guilt, and Forgiveness.* Grand Rapids: Baker, 1989.

Aden, Leroy, and J. Harold Ellens, eds. *The Church and Pastoral Care.* Grand Rapids: Baker, 1988.

Allen, Joseph L. *Love and Conflict: A Covenantal Mode of Christian Ethics.* Nashville: Abingdon, 1984.

Allport, Gordon W. *The Individual and His Religion.* New York: Macmillan, 1950.

Asquith, Glenn H., Jr. "The Case Study Method of Anton T. Boisen." *The Journal of Pastoral Care* 34 (1980): 84–94.

Batson, Daniel C., and W. Larry Ventis. *The Religious Experience: A Social-Psychological Perspective.* New York: Oxford University Press, 1982.

Becker, Ernest. *The Denial of Death.* New York: Free Press, 1973.

————. *Escape from Evil.* New York: Free Press, 1975.

Beers, Clifford. *The Mind That Found Itself.* New York: Longman Green, 1908.

Beit-Hallahmi, Benjamin. "Psychology of Religion, 1880–1930: The Rise and Fall of a Psychological Movement." In *Current Perspectives in the Psychology of Religion,* edited by H. Newton Malony, 17–26. Grand Rapids: Eerdmans, 1977.

Bellah, Robert N., et al. *Habits of the Heart: Individualism and Commitment in American Life.* Los Angeles: University of California Press, 1985.

Boisen, Anton T. "Cooperative Inquiry in Religion." *Religious Education* 40 (1954): 290–97.

_____. *The Exploration of the Inner World: A Study of Mental Disorder and Religious Experience*. New York: Harper, 1936. Reprint ed. Philadelphia: University of Pennsylvania Press, 1971.

_____. "In Defense of Mr. Bryan: A Personal Confession by a Liberal Clergyman." *American Review* 3 (1925): 323–28.

_____. Letter to Chester A. Raber, March 25, 1960. Boisen Files, Chicago Theological Seminary.

_____. *Out of the Depths: An Autobiographical Study of Mental Disorder and Religious Experience*. New York: Harper and Row, 1960.

_____. "Religious Experience and Psychological Conflict." *American Psychologist* 13 (1958): 568–70.

_____. *Religion in Crisis and Custom: A Sociological and Psychological Study*. New York: Harper, 1955.

_____. "Schizophrenia and Religious Experience." In *Collected and Contributed Papers*, vol. 1. Elgin, Ill.: Elgin State Hospital, 1932.

_____. "Theology in the Light of Psychiatric Experience." *Crozer Quarterly* 18, no. 1 (1941): 47–61.

_____. "Types of Mental Illness: A Beginning Course for Use in the Training Centers of the Council for the Clinical Training of Theological Students," vols. 1 and 2. Unpublished mimeographed booklets, 1946.

Boszormenyi-Nagy, Ivan, and Geraldine M. Spark. *Invisible Loyalties: Reciprocity in Intergenerational Therapy*. Hagerstown, Md.: Harper, 1973.

Brown, William Adams. *Christian Theology in Outline*. New York: Charles Scribner's Sons, 1906.

_____. *Modern Theology and the Preaching of the Gospel*. New York: Charles Scribner's Sons, 1914.

Browning, Don S. "A Doctrine of the Atonement Informed by the Psychotherapeutic Process." *The Journal of Pastoral Care* 17 (1963): 136–47.

_____. "The Influence of Psychology on Theology." In *The New Shape of Pastoral Theology: Essays in Honor of Seward Hiltner*, edited by William B. Oglesby, Jr., 121–35. Nashville: Abingdon, 1969.

_____. *The Moral Context of Pastoral Care*. Philadelphia: Westminster, 1976.

_____. *Religious Ethics and Pastoral Care*. Philadelphia: Fortress, 1983.

_____. *Religious Thought and the Modern Psychologies: A Critical Conversation in the Theology of Culture*. Philadelphia: Fortress, 1976.

_____, ed. *Practical Theology: The Emerging Field in Theology, Church, and World*. San Francisco: Harper and Row, 1982.

Campbell, Alastair V. "Is Practical Theology Possible?" *Scottish Journal of Theology* 25 (1972): 217–27.

_____. *Professionalism and Pastoral Care*. Philadelphia: Fortress, 1985.

_____. *Rediscovering Pastoral Care*. Philadelphia: Westminster, 1981.

Capps, Donald. "The Beatitudes and Erikson's Life Cycle Theory." *Pastoral Psychology* 33 (1985): 226–44.

————. *Deadly Sins and Saving Virtues.* Philadelphia: Fortress, 1987.

————. "Erikson's Life Cycle Theory: Religious Dimensions." *Religious Studies Review* 10 (1984): 120–27.

————. *Life Cycle Theory and Pastoral Care.* Philadelphia: Fortress, 1983.

————. *Pastoral Care: A Thematic Approach.* Philadelphia: Westminster, 1979.

————. *Pastoral Care and Hermeneutics.* Philadelphia: Fortress, 1984.

Cauthen, Kenneth. *The Impact of American Religious Liberalism.* New York: Harper, 1962.

Clark, Walter Houston. *The Psychology of Religion.* New York: Macmillan, 1958.

Clebsch, William A., and Charles R. Jaekle. *Pastoral Care in Historical Perspective.* Englewood Cliffs, N.J.: Prentice-Hall, 1964.

Clinebell, Howard J., Jr. *Basic Types of Pastoral Care and Counseling.* Rev. ed. Nashville: Abingdon, 1984.

Cobb, John B., Jr. *A Christian Natural Theology Based on the Thought of Alfred North Whitehead.* Philadelphia: Westminster, 1965.

Coe, George Albert. *The Psychology of Religion.* Chicago: University of Chicago Press, 1916.

Conn, Walter E. *Conscience: Development and Self-Transcendence.* Birmingham: Religious Education Press, 1981.

Cox, Harvey. *The Seduction of the Spirit: The Use and Misuse of People's Religion.* New York: Simon and Schuster, 1973.

Dean, William. *American Religious Empiricism.* Albany: State University of New York Press, 1986.

Ellens, J. Harold. "Biblical Themes in Psychological Theory and Practice." *The Bulletin* 6, no. 2 (1980): 2–6.

————. *God's Grace and Human Health.* Nashville: Abingdon, 1982.

————. *Psychotheology: Key Issues.* Pretoria: University of South Africa, 1987.

Emerson, James G. *Divorce, The Church, and Remarriage.* Philadelphia: Westminster, 1961.

————. *The Dynamics of Forgiveness.* Philadelphia: Westminster, 1964.

————. "Whither Pastoral Theology: A Look at Five Books." *Pastoral Psychology* 33 (1985): 217–20.

Erikson, Erik H. *Childhood and Society.* 2d rev. ed. New York: Norton, 1964.

————. *Identity and the Life Cycle.* International Universities Press, 1959.

————. *Insight and Responsibility.* New York: Norton, 1964.

Ezorsky, Gertrude. "Pragmatic Theory of Truth." In *The Encyclopedia of Philosophy*, vol. 6, edited by Paul Edwards. New York: Macmillan and The Free Press, 1967.

Farley, Margaret A. *Personal Commitments: Making, Keeping, Breaking*. San Francisco: Harper and Row, 1985.

Fishkin, James. *Beyond Subjective Morality*. New Haven: Yale University Press, 1984.

Foskett, John. *Meaning in Madness*. London: S.P.C.K., 1984.

Freud, Sigmund. *Civilization and Its Discontents*. Translated by Joan Riviere. London: Hogarth, 1969.

————. *The Ego and the Id*. Translated by Joan Riviere. London: Hogarth, 1927.

————. *New Introductory Lectures on Psychoanalysis*. Translated by W. J. H. Sprett. New York: Norton, 1933.

Fromm, Erich. *The Anatomy of Human Destructiveness*. New ed. New York: Holt, Rinehart, and Winston, 1973.

Gerkin, Charles V. *Crisis Experience in Modern Life: Theory and Theology in Pastoral Care*. Nashville: Abingdon, 1979.

————. *The Living Human Document: Re-Visioning Pastoral Counseling in a Hermeneutical Mode*. Nashville: Abingdon, 1984.

Gewirth, Alan. *Reason and Morality*. Chicago: University of Chicago Press, 1978.

Grant, Brian W. *Schizophrenia: A Source of Social Insight*. Philadelphia: Westminster, 1975.

Gustafson, James M. *Christ and the Moral Life*. Chicago: University of Chicago Press, 1979.

————. "Context versus Principles: A Misplaced Debate in Christian Ethics." *Harvard Theological Review* 58 (1965): 171–202.

Habermas, Jurgen. "The Theory of Communicative Action." In *The Theory of Communicative Action*, vol. 1, *Reason and the Rationalization of Society*. Translated by Thomas McCarthy. Boston: Beacon Press, 1985.

Hall, Charles E., Jr. "Some Contributions of Anton T. Boisen (1876–1965) to Understanding Psychiatry and Religion." *Pastoral Psychology* 19, no. 186 (September 1968): 40–48.

Hampshire, Stuart. *Morality and Conflict*. Cambridge: Harvard University Press, 1984.

Hartmann, Heinz. *Essays on Ego Psychology: Selected Problems in Psychoanalytic Theory*. New York: International Universities Press, 1965.

Hauerwas, Stanley. *The Peaceable Kingdom: A Primer in Christian Ethics*. South Bend, Ind.: University of Notre Dame Press, 1983.

Hiltner, Seward. *The Christian Shepherd*. Nashville: Abingdon, 1959.

————. "Clinical and Theological Notes on Responsibility." *Journal of Religion and Health* 2, no. 1 (1962): 7–20.

————. "Context: Yes—Abstractness: No." *Religion in Life* 35 (1966): 204–8.

————. *Ferment in the Ministry.* Nashville: Abingdon, 1969.

————. *Pastoral Counseling.* Nashville: Abingdon, 1949.

————. "Pastoral Psychology and Christian Ethics." *Pastoral Psychology* 4 (1953): 23–33.

————. *Preface to Pastoral Theology.* Nashville: Abingdon, 1958.

————. *Psychotherapy and Christian Ethics.* Unpublished doctoral dissertation, University of Chicago.

————. *Sex Ethics and the Kinsey Reports.* New York: Association, 1953.

————. *Theological Dynamics.* Nashville: Abingdon, 1972.

————. "Toward an Ethical Conscience." *Journal of Religion* 25 (1945): 1–9.

Hiltner, Seward, and Lowell G. Colston. *The Context of Pastoral Counseling.* Nashville: Abingdon, 1961.

Hiltner, Seward, and Karl Menninger. *Constructive Aspects of Anxiety.* Nashville: Abingdon, 1963.

Hirsch, E. D., Jr. "Old and New in Hermeneutics." In *The Aims of Interpretation.* Chicago: University of Chicago Press, 1976.

Hocking, William E. *Human Nature and Its Remaking.* New Haven: Yale University Press, 1929.

Hoffman, John C. *Ethical Confrontation in Counseling.* Chicago: University of Chicago Press, 1981.

Holifield, E. Brooks. *A History of Pastoral Care in America: From Salvation to Self-Realization.* Nashville: Abingdon, 1983.

Horney, Karen. *Neurosis and Human Growth: The Struggle Toward Self-Realization.* New York: Norton, 1950.

Hunter, Rodney J. "The Future of Pastoral Theology." *Pastoral Psychology* 29 (1980): 58–69.

————. "Law and Gospel in Pastoral Care." *The Journal of Pastoral Care* 30 (1976): 154.

————. "Moltmann's Theology of the Cross and the Dilemma of Contemporary Pastoral Care." In *Hope for the Church* by Jurgen Moltmann. Edited and translated by Theodore Runyon. Nashville: Abingdon, 1979.

Jacobson, Edith. *The Self and the Object World.* New York: International Universities Press, 1964.

James, William. *Principles of Psychology.* New York: Dover, 1950.

————. *Varieties of Religious Experience.* New York: Mentor, 1958.

Kegan, Robert. *The Evolving Self: Problem and Process in Human Development.* Cambridge: Harvard University Press, 1982.

Keller, Catherine. *From a Broken Web: Separation, Sexism, and Self.* Boston: Beacon, 1986.

Kohlberg, Lawrence. "Moral Stages and Moralization." In *Moral Development and Behavior,* edited by Thomas Lickona, 31–53. New York: Holt, Rinehart and Winston, 1976.

————. "The Claim to Moral Adequacy of a Highest Stage of Moral Development." *Journal of Philosophy* 70 (1973): 630–46.

Kohut, Heinz. *Self Psychology and the Humanities: Reflections on a New Psychoanalytic Approach.* Edited by Charles B. Strozier. New York: Norton, 1985.

Lapsley, James N. "Pastoral Theology Past and Present." In *The New Shape of Pastoral Theology: Essays in Honor of Seward Hiltner,* edited by William B. Oglesby, Jr., 31–48. Nashville: Abingdon, 1969.

————. "Practical Theology and Pastoral Care: An Essay in Pastoral Theology." In *Practical Theology: The Emerging Field in Theology, Church, and World,* edited by Don S. Browning. San Francisco: Harper and Row, 1982.

————. "Reconciliation, Forgiveness, Lost Contracts." *Theology Today* 23 (1966) 44–59.

Leuba, James H. *The Psychology of Mysticism.* New York: Harcourt, Brace and World, 1926.

Loder, James E. *The Transforming Moment.* New York: Harper, 1981.

MacDonald, Coval B. "Methods of Study in Pastoral Theology." In *The New Shape of Pastoral Theology: Essays in Honor of Seward Hiltner,* edited by William B. Oglesby, Jr., 164–78. Nashville: Abingdon, 1969.

McClendon, James W. Jr. *Biography as Theology.* Nashville: Abingdon, 1974.

McIntosh, Ian F. *Pastoral Care and Pastoral Theology.* Philadelphia: Westminster, 1972.

McKenzie, John G. *Guilt: Its Meaning and Significance.* Nashville: Abingdon, 1962.

McNeill, John T. *A History of the Cure of Souls.* New York: Harper and Row, 1951.

McPhee, John. *Coming Into the Country.* New York: Bantam, 1979.

May, Rollo. *Love and Will.* New York: Norton, 1969.

Meeks, M. Douglas. "Moltmann's Contribution to Practical Theology." In *Hope for the Church* by Jurgen Moltmann. Edited and translated by Theodore Runyon. Nashville: Abingdon, 1979.

Meland, Bernard E. "Introduction: The Empirical Tradition in Theology at Chicago." In *The Future of Empirical Theology,* edited by Bernard E. Meland, Chicago: University of Chicago Press, 1969.

Miller, Randolph Crump. *The American Spirit in Theology*. Philadelphia: Pilgrim, 1974.

Minear, Paul. *Images of the Church in the New Testament*. Philadelphia: Westminster, 1960.

Mitchell, Kenneth R. *Psychological and Theological Relationships in the Multiple Staff Ministry*. Philadelphia: Westminster, 1966.

Mowat, Farley. *Never Cry Wolf*. New York: Bantam, 1979.

Niebuhr, Reinhold. *The Nature and Destiny of Man*. New York: Charles Scribner's Sons, 1941.

Niebuhr, H. Richard. *The Responsible Self*. New York: Harper, 1963.

Nouwen, Henri. "Anton T. Boisen and Theology through Living Human Documents." *Pastoral Psychology* 19 (1968): 49–63.

Oates, Wayne E. *The Psychology of Religion*. Waco: Word, 1973.

_____. *Religious Factors in Mental Illness*. London: George Allen and Unwin, 1957.

Oden, Thomas C. *Care of Souls in the Classic Tradition*. Philadelphia: Fortress, 1984.

_____. *Contemporary Theology and Psychotherapy*. Philadelphia: Westminster, 1967.

_____. *Pastoral Theology: Essentials of Ministry*. San Francisco: Harper and Row, 1983.

_____. *The Structure of Awareness*. New York: Abingdon, 1969.

O'Donohoe, James. "Moral and Faith Development Theory." In *Toward Moral and Religious Maturity*, edited by Christiane Brusselman. Morristown, N.J.: Silver Burdett, 1980.

Oglesby, William B., Jr., ed. *The New Shape of Pastoral Theology: Essays in Honor of Seward Hiltner*. Nashville: Abingdon, 1969.

_____. *Biblical Themes for Pastoral Care*. Nashville: Abingdon, 1980.

Outka, Gene H. *Agape: An Ethical Analysis*. New Haven: Yale University Press, 1972.

Patton, John. *Is Human Forgiveness Possible? A Pastoral Care Perspective*. Nashville: Abingdon, 1985.

_____. "Harry Stack Sullivan's 'Expert in Interpersonal Relations.'" *Journal of Religion and Health* 9, no. 1 (1971): 162–70.

_____. *Pastoral Counseling: A Ministry of the Church*. Nashville: Abingdon, 1983.

_____. "There's Something about Lost Sheep." *Journal of Pastoral Care* 34, no. 4 (1980): 217–18.

Porter, E. H. *Introduction to Therapeutic Counseling*. Boston: Houghton Mifflin, 1950.

Pruyser, Paul W. *A Dynamic Psychology of Religion*. New York: Harper, 1968.

————. *The Minister as Diagnostician: Personal Problems in Pastoral Perspective*. Philadelphia: Westminster, 1976.

————. "Nathan and David: A Psychological Footnote." *Pastoral Psychology* 13 (1962): 14–18.

Richesin, L. Dale, and Larry D. Bouchard, eds. *Interpreting Disciples: Practical Theology in the Disciples of Christ*. Fort Worth: Texas Christian University Press, 1987.

Rieff, Philip. *Freud: The Mind of the Moralist*. 3d ed. Chicago: University of Chicago Press, 1979.

Rogers, Carl R. *Client-Centered Therapy*. Boston: Houghton Mifflin, 1951.

————. *Counseling and Psychotherapy*. Boston: Houghton Mifflin, 1947.

————. *On Becoming a Person*. Boston: Houghton Mifflin, 1961.

Sanborn, Hugh W. *Mental-Spiritual Health Models: An Analysis of the Models of Boisen, Hiltner, and Clinebell*. Lanham, Md.: University Press of America, 1979.

Schafer, Roy. *Language and Insight: The Sigmund Freud Lectures at University College, London*. New Haven: Yale University Press, 1978.

Smith, Archie, Jr. *The Relational Self*. Nashville: Abingdon, 1982.

Spilka, Bernard, Ralph W. Hood, and Richard L. Gorsuch. *The Psychology of Religion: An Empirical Approach*. Englewood Cliffs, N.J.: Prentice-Hall, 1985.

Starbuck, Edwin D. *Psychology of Religion*. New York: Charles Scribner's Sons, 1899.

Stokes, Allison. *Ministry after Freud*. New York: Pilgrim, 1985.

Strommen, Merton, ed. *Research on Religious Development: A Comprehensive Handbook*. New York: Hawthorn, 1971.

Taylor, Eugene, ed. *William James on Exceptional Mental States: The 1896 Lowell Lectures*. Amherst: University of Massachusetts Press, 1984.

Ter Linden, Nico. *In the Lord's Boarding House: Stories of Caring for Others*. Translated by Kenneth R. Mitchell. Nashville: Abingdon, 1985.

Thompson, Murray Stewart. *Grace and Forgiveness in Ministry*. Nashville: Abingdon, 1981.

Thornton, Edward E. *Professional Education for Ministry: A History of Clinical Pastoral Education*. Nashville: Abingdon, 1970.

————. *Theology and Pastoral Counseling*. Philadelphia: Fortress, 1964.

Thornton, M. *The Function of Theology*. London: Hodder and Stoughton, 1968.

Thurneysen, Eduard. *A Theology of Pastoral Care*. Translated by Jack A. Worthington and Thomas Wieser. Richmond: John Knox, 1962.

Tillich, Paul. *Courage to Be*. New Haven: Yale University Press, 1952.

————. *The Dynamics of Faith.* New York: Harper and Row, 1957.

————. "Estrangement and Reconciliation." *Review of Religion* 9 (November 1944): 6–19.

————. *The Eternal Now.* New York: Charles Scribner's Sons, 1963.

————. *Morality and Beyond.* New York: Harper and Row, 1963.

————. *Systematic Theology.* 3 vols. Chicago: University of Chicago, 1967.

Underwood, Ralph L. *Empathy and Confrontation in Pastoral Care.* Philadelphia: Fortress, 1986.

Williams, Daniel Day. *The Minister and the Care of Souls.* New York: Harper and Row, 1961.

Winter, Gibson. *Elements for a Social Ethic.* New York: Macmillan, 1966.

Wise, Carroll W. *Pastoral Counseling.* New York: Harper and Row, 1951.

Yinger, J. Milton. *The Scientific Study of Religion.* New York: Macmillan, 1970.

Index of Authors
and Subjects